Media Law in Finland

Media Law in Finland

Second Edition

Anette Alén-Savikko
Päivi Korpisaari

This book was originally published as a monograph in the International Encyclopaedia of Laws/Media Law.

Founding Editor: Roger Blanpain
General Editor: Frank Hendrickx
Volume Editors: Peggy Valcke & Eva Lievens

Wolters Kluwer

Published by:
Kluwer Law International B.V.
PO Box 316
2400 AH Alphen aan den Rijn
The Netherlands
E-mail: international-sales@wolterskluwer.com
Website: lrus.wolterskluwer.com

Sold and distributed by:
Wolters Kluwer Legal & Regulatory U.S.
7201 McKinney Circle
Frederick, MD 21704
United States of America
Email: customer.service@wolterskluwer.com

ISBN 978-94-035-3130-4

e-Book: ISBN 978-94-035-3131-1
web-PDF: ISBN 978-94-035-3132-8

The Authors

Anette Alén-Savikko is a University Lecturer at the Faculty of Law, University of Helsinki, Finland, focusing on information and communication technology (ICT) law. She defended her doctoral dissertation in 2014. Anette participates in an interdisciplinary research project called *Communication Rights in the Age of Digital Disruption* (CORDI) (https://cordi.blog/). She has previously been involved in various research projects under the umbrella of free speech and participated in the interdisciplinary research project *Facing the Coordination Challenge: Problems, Policies, and Politics in Media and Communications Regulation* (http://blogs.helsinki.fi/face-project/). In addition, Anette has also been a national expert in studies in the field of media and communications, including the *Study on Investigative Journalism* (European Centre for Press and Media Freedom (https://ec.europa.eu/digital-agenda/en/media-freedom-pilot-projects) and the *Study on Sport Organizers' Rights in the EU,* which focused on copyright and media rights (together with Prof. Taina Pihlajarinne; *T.M.C. Asser Instituut* in cooperation with *Instituut voor Informatierecht*, University of Amsterdam).

Anette is particularly interested in the legal dimensions of digitalization in the media sector. Among her areas of interest are copyright in the digital environment as well as protection of personal data. Currently, Anette explores news automation and demands for accountability and transparency.

Anette lectures and teaches courses on intellectual property (IP) law, among others. She also publishes regularly on various topics related to IP law and ICT law. Moreover, Anette is extremely interested in university pedagogy and educates herself with regard to teaching and learning.

For more information, *see* https://researchportal.helsinki.fi/en/persons/anette-alen-savikko.

The Authors

Päivi Korpisaari is Professor of Communication Law at the Faculty of Law, University of Helsinki. She became Master of Laws in 1993, Licentiate of Laws in 2000, Doctor of Laws in 2007 and Docent of Communication Law in 2011. She worked as a lawyer from 1992 to 1993 in a law firm and as a younger judge in 2004–2005 at the District Court of Riihimäki. She then worked as a presenting officer at the Court of Appeal of Helsinki between 1995 and 1998. Before her research work she also worked as a legal counsel at the Finnish Soil Mechanics Association from 1998 to 2003.

Korpisaari has worked as a researcher – and later as a professor – at the University of Helsinki since November 2003. She has published many books and articles in the field of media and communication law, information law, tort law, criminal law and constitutional law. Her main fields of research are media and communication law, tort law, data protection law, constitutional law, human rights law, and criminal law in respect to 'freedom of expression offences'. She has been a member of law preparation groups and written legal reports to aid legislative work for the Ministries of Justice, Environment, Internal Affairs and Transport and Communications.

She has been a national expert in studies in the field of media and communications. She has also been a Finnish writer of the *Yearbook of European Tort Law* for many years.

Professor Korpisaari has led three research projects relating to personal data protection, namely *Henkilötietojen suoja digitalisoituvassa yhteiskunnassa* ('Personal Data Protection in Digitalising Society'), *Information Security of Location Estimation and Navigation Applications,* and *MyGeoTrust* (concerning the legal team, *see* http://mygeotrust.o rg), which was a project striving to create an alternative mobile platform for location-based services that would ensure excellent privacy protection for its users. Currently she is leading two research projects. One is *Viha ja julkisuus: päätöksentekoon vaikuttamaan pyrkivä vihapuhe yhteiskunnallisesta ja oikeudellisesta näkökulmasta* ('Hate and Publicity: Hate Speech That Aims to Influence Societal Decision-Making': A Social and Legal Perspective), which focuses on the hate speech targeted at the individuals. The other, *Neutral Host Pilot,* will demonstrate and utilize fast 5G-network-based connectivity and data platforms optimized especially for local needs of smart cities. Legal research is conducted on 5G ecosystems and AI focusing on data protection and communications and spectrum sharing regulation as well as competition law. She also supervises several doctoral candidates and has completed a teacher's degree in University pedagogy.

For more information, *see* https://tuhat.halvi.helsinki.fi/portal/fi/persons/paivi-ko rpisaari-ex(8faaa596-233c-4139-9c34-24fe3388900a).html and https://helsinki.acad emia.edu/PäiviTiilikka.

Table of Contents

Table of Contents

List of Abbreviations

AVMSD	Directive (EU) 2018/1808 of the European Parliament and of the Council of 14 November 2018 amending Directive 2010/13/EU on the coordination of certain provisions laid down by law, regulation or administrative action in Member States concerning the provision of audiovisual media services (Audiovisual Media Services Directive) in view of changing market realities
CJEU	Court of Justice of the European Union
CMM	Council for Mass Media; Julkisen sanan neuvosto
ECHR	European Convention on Human Rights
ECSA	Act on Electronic Communications Services
ECtHR	European Court of Human Rights
EECC	European Electronic Communications Code
FCCA	Finnish Competition and Consumer Authority; Kilpailu- ja kuluttajavirasto (from 1 January 2013; formerly the Finnish Competition Authority; FCA; Kilpailuvirasto)
FEA	Freedom of Expression Act; the Act on the Exercise of Freedom of Expression in Mass Media (460/2003); sananvapauslaki; laki sananvapauden käyttämisestä joukkoviestinnässä
FICORA (TRAFICOM)	Finnish Communications Regulatory Authority; Viestintävirasto; Vivi. As of 2019 FICORA is called TRAFICOM (Finnish Transport and Communications Agency)
HE	Hallituksen esitys; Government bill
KM	Komiteamietintö; Committee report
LaV	Eduskunnan lakivaliokunta; Legal Affairs Committee
LiV	Eduskunnan liikenne- ja viestintävaliokunta; Transport and Communications Committee
OA	Openness Act (621/1999); Laki viranomaisten toiminnan julkisuudesta (julkisuuslaki)
PeV	Eduskunnan perustuslakivaliokunta; Constitutional Law Committee

List of Abbreviations

PeVL	Perustuslakivaliokunnan lausunto; Statement of the Constitutional Law Committee
SiV	Eduskunnan sivistysvaliokunta; Education and Culture Committee
TLA	Tort Liability Act (412/1974); Vahingonkorvauslaki
TRAFICOM	Finnish Transport and Communications Agency
Yle	Yleisradio; Finnish public service broadcasting company

Acknowledgements

The authors would like to express their warmest thanks to research assistants, law students Floora Kukorelli and Helmi Yli-Äyhö as well as Annika Antikainen and Oona Ojajärvi, who have helped to update this work.

Acknowledgements

General Introduction

§1. General Background of the Country

I. Political and Legal System of the Country

A. State

1. Finland is a sovereign republic which became independent by force of the Declaration of Independence on 6 December 1917. Prior to independence Finland was an autonomous Grand Duchy in the Russian Empire (1809–1917), before which it was under Swedish rule from the twelfth century.

Setting aside constitutional acts before independence, Finland's first constitutional act came into force in 1919. The delay was caused by the 1918 Finnish civil war. The core act was the Constitution Act (*Hallitusmuoto* 94/1919), which was later accompanied by three other constitutional acts. Constitutional reform has been carried out in phases. In the 1990s only the provisions containing fundamental rights were amended. This was followed by a full constitutional reform at the turn of the millennium, whereby the constitutional acts were codified in one single act. Moreover, fundamental rights were incorporated in the act largely as amended in 1995. Currently, the Finnish constitution is established in the Constitution of Finland (*Suomen Perustuslaki* 731/1999) (§ 1(2)).[1] The act rests on democracy and the rule of law as well as the separation of powers (Chapter 1). Legislative powers are exercised by the Parliament, governmental powers by the President of the Republic and the Government, whereas judicial powers are vested in courts of law (§ 3). Fundamental rights are included in Chapter 2.

2. The President of the Republic leads foreign policy in cooperation with the Government and acts as the Supreme Commander of the Defence Forces. Election of the President takes place every six years by means of direct vote.[2] The Finnish Parliament is unicameral, and its two-hundred members are elected every four years. The Parliament's duties include legislating, ratifying treaties, and deciding on the State budget. It also supervises State finances and oversees the Government

1. Unofficial translation by the Ministry of Justice; amendments up to 1112/2011 included: http://www.finlex.fi/en/laki/kaannokset/1999/en19990731.pdf (28.8.2019).
2. *See* https://www.presidentti.fi/en/ (28.8.2019).

(Chapters 3–4 of the Constitution).[3] Finland has a multiparty political system, which means coalition Governments are typical. The term 'government' is used both for the governing and decision-making bodies. The activities of the Government are directed by the Prime Minister, who is usually the leader of the party with the most parliamentary seats (Chapters 5–6, 8 of the Constitution).[4]

The most popular parties have traditionally been the National Coalition Party (*Kansallinen kokoomus*), the Social Democratic Party (*Sosiaalidemokraattinen puolue*), and the Centre Party (*Suomen Keskusta*). However, in 2011 the True Finns (*Perussuomalaiset*) received an unusual increase in the number of votes.[5] Despite the number of votes, the True Finns declined to cooperate with the other political parties and remained in opposition.[6] In the 2015 elections, the True Finns were among the largest parties and gained their place within government. The True Finns maintained their popularity in the 2019 elections, but they remained in opposition.

B. Provincial, Municipal and Regional Self-Government

3. Section 121 of the Constitution guarantees self-government for municipalities and other administrative areas as well as for the Sámi people in their native region.

1. Municipalities

4. Finland is divided into municipalities. Their administration rests on the self-government of their residents as enshrined in section 121(1) of the Constitution. According to section 1 of the Local Government Act (410/2015) the purpose of the Act is to establish the conditions in which, in municipal activities, the self-government of the residents in a municipality can take place and opportunities can occur for the residents to participate and exert an influence. A further purpose of the Act is to advance and facilitate the systematic nature and financial sustainability of municipal activities.[7]

---

3. *See also* 'Eduskunta – Riksdagen. The Parliament of Finland': https://www.eduskunta.fi/EN/Pages/default.aspx (28.8.2019).
4. *See also* 'Finnish Government': http://valtioneuvosto.fi/en/government (28.8.2019).
5. *See* 'True Finns the biggest winner in elections. Coalition Party the largest party in the parliamentary elections 2011.' Statistics Finland: http://tilastokeskus.fi/til/evaa/2011/evaa_2011_2011-04-18_tie_001_en.html (28.8.2019).
6. Interestingly, in Finland a complaint was filed before the Council for Mass Media (CMM) concerning compliance with the Guidelines for Journalists when using a nickname for the True Finns in the mass media, 'Trushies' (implying tushies), in Finnish '*Persut*'. The Council found no offence in this usage and no need for a prohibition on individual words (4592B-G/YLE+SL+TV/11, 21.9.2011). However, the attached statement from Kotus, the Institute for the Languages in Finland (at the time known as the Research Institute for the Languages in Finland), recommended the use of official party names in formal contexts.
7. Unofficial translation by the Ministry of Finance: https://www.finlex.fi/fi/laki/kaannokset/2015/en20150410.pdf (28.8.2019).

While the number of municipalities is currently over three hundred, municipal reform has been made: the current Local Government Act replaced the previous one (365/1995) in May 2015. The reform leaves the relationship between municipalities and the state largely untouched, while the most significant changes relate to EU-level requirements for economic policy coordination. Provisions on cooperation between municipalities and joint municipal authorities will be clarified. The trend is nevertheless towards the formation of bigger and stronger municipalities, and changes in municipal boundaries are to be expected. However the so-called forced merger of municipalities (at the behest of a liquidator) is limited to cases of severe economic difficulty that endanger the provision of services to habitants in the municipality.

In recent years, mergers of several municipalities into one larger entity have taken place, which has reduced the number of municipalities. Plans for a merger in the capital region have also been presented. All in all, the number of municipalities has been declining for decades.[8] However, the pace of mergers has declined, and no mergers have been executed since 2017.[9] This may partly stem from complexities regarding the regional government, health, and social services reform.

2. The Åland Islands

5. The Åland Islands form an autonomous Swedish speaking part of Finland. Their special status and right to self-government are confirmed in section 120 of the Constitution. The self-government and competences of the Province of Åland are regulated in the Act on the Autonomy of Åland (*Självstyrelselag för Åland* 1144/1991),[10] whereby the Swedish language and culture of Åland are respected.

The original Act 124/1920 confirming Åland's autonomy dates back to the 1920s. The position of Åland as a part of Finland and its autonomous status were decided and recognized by the League of Nations in 1921. Thus, despite the wishes of Ålanders, the islands were not united with Sweden. The neutrality of the Islands was also established. In turn, demilitarization had already occurred in 1856 through the Convention on the Demilitarisation of the Åland Islands.[11] The so-called Åland Protocol accompanied the accession of Finland to the European Community (EC). Thereby, the area's somewhat special status is also acknowledged at the EU level. Indeed, with regard to indirect taxation, Åland is a tax-free area.[12]

---

8. *See* https://www.kuntaliitto.fi/asiantuntijapalvelut/kuntanumerot-ja-kuntapohjaiset-aluejaot (28.8.2019); appendix; source: Tilastokeskus (Statistics Finland).
9. *See* 'Kaupunkien ja kuntien lukumäärät ja väestötiedot' (Number and Demographics of Cities and Municipalities) 3.4.2019: https://www.kuntaliitto.fi/tilastot-ja-julkaisut/kaupunkien-ja-kuntien-lukumaarat-ja-vaestotiedot (28.8.2019).
10. Unofficial translation by the Ministry of Justice; amendments up to 68/2004 included: http://www.finlex.fi/fi/laki/kaannokset/1991/en19911144.pdf (28.8.2019).
11. *See* the unofficial translation by the Ministry of Justice; amendments up to 68/2004 included: https://www.finlex.fi/fi/laki/kaannokset/1991/en19911144.pdf (28.8.2019) prologue; *see also* Silverström 2013.
12. *See* http://www.aland.ax/en/facts-about-aland/aland-the-nordic-council-and-the-eu/ (28.8.2019).

Åland consists of over 6,500 islands,[13] with a population of around 29,500 (2017).[14] Right of domicile is regulated in Chapter 2 of the Act on the Autonomy of Åland. Section 10 refers to the Act on the Acquisition of Real Property in Åland (3/1975), according to which restrictions apply to people without the right of domicile as well as to corporations. According to section 11, the right of a person to conduct business without the right of domicile may also be restricted by provincial law.

6. Swedish is the official language of Åland (§ 36 Act on the Autonomy of Åland). Finnish citizens may, however, use Finnish in court and before officials in matters concerning themselves (§ 37). Åland also has its own flag.

In issues related to autonomy, the Åland Parliament represents the people of the Islands while the Government of Åland together with officials under its umbrella handle the administration (§ 3 Act on the Autonomy of Åland); the Finnish State Government is represented by a Governor (§ 4). The Åland Parliament and the Government of Åland are further regulated in Chapter 3 of the Act on the Autonomy of Åland whereas Chapter 4 contains provisions on the provincial authority and competences. The Parliament enacts provincial laws and confirms the budget for Åland (§§ 17, 44). Decrees may be issued if authorized by provincial laws (§ 21). The legislative competences for explicit areas are listed in section 18 of the Act on Autonomy. These areas include decisions on municipal boundaries, the provincial flag as well as the postal service and the right to conduct broadcast and cable transmission activities with some exceptions (*see* esp. § 27). Moreover, Åland officials operate where administration of matters within the legislative competence of the Province is concerned (§ 23).

Similarly, the competence of the State is regulated in Chapter 5 of the Act. This includes (§ 27) areas such as the Constitution, foreign relations and trade, surnames and forenames, as well as marriage, inheritance, and other family relations. It also covers copyright, patent, unfair business practices, promotion of competition, and consumer protection (§ 27, point 10) while telecommunication is also covered but permission for general telecommunications activities by the State official requires consent of the provincial Government (§ 27, point 40). Taxes belong to the realm of State competence, with the exception of municipal tax and additional tax on income for Åland, among others (§ 27, point 36; § 18, point 5).

Chapter 9a of the Act on Autonomy contains detailed provisions on EU matters, such as the preparation of national positions and the national liability of Åland in cases of Member State liability.

---

13. *See* 'Fakta om Åland – Statistik ock fakta' (facts about Åland Islands – statistics and facts): http://www.aland.ax/fakta/statistik/ (28.8.2019).
14. *See* the population statistics of Tilastokeskus (Statistics Finland) at http://www.tilastokeskus.fi/tup/suoluk/suoluk_vaesto.html (28.8.2019).

3. The Sámi People

7. The Act on the Sámi Parliament (974/1995)[15] regulates the linguistic and cultural autonomy of the Sámi people. The Sámi people are recognized as indigenous people, and the Sámi Parliament (*Sámediggi*) is the body responsible for planning and implementing Sámi cultural self-government. It continues the work of its predecessor, the Sámi Delegation (*Sámi Parlamenta*), which operated from 1973 to 1995. Members of the Parliament are elected every four years from among the Sámi people (§ 10; for a definition of a Sámi, *see* § 3). In administrative terms, the Sámi Parliament operates under the Ministry of Justice (§ 1(2)), but it is an independent body.[16]

There are around 10,000 Sámi people in Finland, and three different Sámi languages are spoken in the country.[17] The preservation and development of the Sámi language is protected by the Sámi Language Act (*saamen kielilaki* 1086/2003).[18] The Sámi native region has also been taken into account in relevant legislation (e.g., land use, mining activity). Moreover, the Skolt region and Skolt culture are secured and developed pursuant to the Skolt Act (253/1995). The region is defined in section 2 of the act while provisions related to land, water, and livelihood are included as well.

Both recent and long-term developments regarding the Sámi self-government have been linked to amending the Act on the Sámi Parliament as well as to the ratification of ILO Convention No. 169 on the rights of indigenous and tribal peoples. To this end, the aim has been to renew the regulation concerning parliamentary bodies and the electoral system as well as to modernize legislation and meet the needs of international standards (e.g., the definition of a Sámi; cf. § 3 the Act on the Sámi Parliament).[19]

II. Geography, Population, and Culture

8. Finland is a relatively large but sparsely populated country, spanning 304,000 km^2 of land but with a population amounting to just 5.52 million (2019).[20] Finland

15. Unofficial translation by the Ministry of Justice; amendments up to 1026/2003 included: http://www.finlex.fi/fi/laki/kaannokset/1995/en19950974.pdf (28.8.2019).
16. *See* 'The Sámi Parliament – The represantative self-government body of the Sámi': https://www.samediggi.fi/task/?lang=en (28.8.2019).
17. *See* 'Sámi in Finland': https://www.samediggi.fi/sami-info/?lang=en (28.8.2019).
18. Unofficial translation by the Ministry of Justice: http://www.finlex.fi/en/laki/kaannokset/2003/en20031086.pdf (28.8.2019).
19. *See* Government bill (HE 167/2014 vp); the bill did not proceed to a second handling. *See also*: 'Proposal reforming the Act on the Sámi Parliament is not taken forward': https://oikeusministerio.fi/-/saamelaiskarajalain-uudistamisesityksella-ei-edellytyksia-edeta?languageId=en_US (28.8.2019).
20. *See* Maanmittauslaitos: 'Maanmittaus 2013. Maanmittauslaitoksen vuositilastoja' (National Land Survey of Finland: Land survey 2013. Annual statistics of National Land Survey of Finland): http://www.maanmittauslaitos.fi/sites/default/files/mml_vuositilasto_2013.pdf and preliminary population statistics at http://www.stat.fi/til/vamuu/2019/07/ (28.8.2019).

is geographically and culturally a part of Scandinavia and is listed among the Nordic countries, together with Sweden, Norway, Denmark, and Iceland. However, Finland's position is also peculiar in many regards.

Finland shares both a long history and a long border with Russia. Moreover, linguistically, Finland's roots lie outside the Nordic countries. The Finnish language is unrelated to Germanic languages (e.g., Swedish, Norwegian and Danish); rather, it is a member of the Finno-Ugric family, together with Hungarian and Estonian. This, of course, has major implications for the media landscape: Finland represents a *small linguistic area* with about 5 million native speakers. Swedish is the second official language, and the Swedish speaking minority in Finland accounts for 5% of the population (2018).[21] The main areas where Swedish is spoken include Åland, the western coastline, and the archipelago outside Turku.[22]

Depending on the method of statistics, the share of foreigners in the total population is between 4.7% and 7% (260,000 to 380,000 persons). The largest group of foreigners is by far Estonians, the second largest Russians, followed by various other nationalities (2018).[23] Finland has thus a small immigrant population compared to many other EU-countries, and foreigners mostly live in large cities or urban areas, such as the capital region.

§2. The Media Landscape

9. Some characteristic conditions have arguably played a major role in the development of the Finnish media industry and in the forming of guiding principles in the area. Alongside the above-mentioned small population and unusual language, these conditions include Finland's large geographical area, agrarian background, economic growth and market size, socio-political structure, tradition of political coalitions, cultural and linguistic characteristics, as well as a somewhat original style of policy.[24] Sparse population, long distances, and two official languages represent peculiarities of the Finnish media market and landscape.[25]

I. Historical Background

A. *The Press*

10. Finland has traditionally been a country of (large) newspapers. The historical background of the Finnish press is tightly linked to Finland's time under Swedish rule. In comparison to Central Europe, the Finnish press has a relatively short

21. *See* http://www.tilastokeskus.fi/til/vaerak/2018/vaerak_2018_2019-03-29_tau_001_fi.html (28.8.2019).
22. *See also* Bruun 2001, 15.
23. *See* https://www.tilastokeskus.fi/tup/maahanmuutto/maahanmuuttajat-vaestossa/ulkomaan-kansalaiset.html, and http://www.tilastokeskus.fi/til/vaerak/2018/vaerak_2018_2019-03-29_tau_001_fi.html (28.8.2019).
24. Sumiala-Seppänen 1999, Ch. 1; Hellman 1999, 58, 431.
25. *See*, e.g., Lehtisaari 2015, 142.

history, dating back to the late eighteenth century, although Swedish media developments, of which Finland was a part, date back to the mid-seventeenth century. The language of the first publications was mainly Swedish, although a first newspaper in Finnish language was published for one year as early as 1776. Nevertheless, it was only from the mid-nineteenth century that Finnish language publications managed to gain more ground, and a drastic increase occurred at the turn of the century.[26]

Freedom of the press had been established in 1766, accompanied by a ban on preventive censorship. However, there were various periods of more or less extensive control over publishing, and freedom of the press was also later abolished for a period. Moreover, the time during which Finland was an autonomous Grand Duchy in the Russian Empire (1809–1917) witnessed strict control over publishing. Indeed, a Censorship Decree was issued in 1829 and accompanied by the so-called Language Decree of 1850, banning all publishing in Finnish. The two specific periods of oppression (1899–1905; 1908–17) were also characterized by various forms and degrees of censorship. Furthermore, in the early and mid-twentieth century, military propaganda and censorship reigned, even though Finland was already independent, and this was followed by Finlandization in the Cold War era.[27] The first constitutional act of independent Finland (94/1919) was complemented by the Freedom of the Press Act (1/1919). Later, alongside general amendments to basic rights, press freedom was included in section 10 of the Constitutional Act (*see* Act 969/1995), and, following the latest phase of constitutional reform, it is now enshrined in section 12 of the Constitution of Finland (731/1999).

The Finnish press continued to grow from the turn of the twentieth century onwards, fuelled by major socio-cultural, economic, and political factors, such as population growth, increased literacy due to school and library networks, politicization, as well as the development of press activity and transportation. Along the way, newspapers and periodicals began to separate.[28]

11. Alongside universal (daily) newspapers, the landscape of the Finnish press has been characterized by an array of local and regional papers with strong political flavours, especially until the Second World War. Indeed, much like other Nordic countries, the Finnish press from 1900 to the 1930s has been characterized as a 'party press system'. Towards the mid-1900s, economic considerations gained ground in publishing and there were tensions between ideological and economic views, whereas the war years entailed regulation instead of a focus on the rules of competition.[29]

26. *See*, *e.g.*, Tommila – Salokangas 1998, 11–13, 18–19, 23–30, 77.
27. For the history, *see*, *e.g.*, Ståhlberg 1913; Tommila – Salokangas 1998, 14–22, 38–42, 72–76, 231 et seq., 278–280 and a book which is published by the Swedish parliament in 2016: Fritt ord 250 år. Tryckfrihet och offentlighet i Sverige och Finland – ett levande arv från 1766 (Press Freedom 250 Years. Freedom of the Press and Public Access to Official Documents in Sweden and Finland – a living heritage from 1766): https://www.riksdagen.se/globalassets/15.-bestall-och-ladda-ned/andra-sprak/tf-250-ar-eng-2018.pdf (26.7.2020).
28. Tommila – Salokangas 1998, 78–90.
29. Tommila – Salokangas 1998, 182, 209–243.

In subsequent years, leading newspapers began to dominate the rivals of their respective regions. However, in Finland, local papers also increased in amount. Nevertheless, as a response to the erosion of the party press system and other developments, demands for press subsidies increased in 1960–1970s. The press, newspapers in particular, was granted various forms of direct or indirect aid, including party subsidies and a VAT exemption. Newspaper delivery rates had been tackled already in the 1950s. The state-aid scheme was later amended.[30]

The number of newspapers increased until the end of 1980s, largely in the form of local papers. Then again, the circulation and coverage of major newspapers was superior. However, the economic depression of the 1990s meant decreases both in the number of newspapers as well as in circulation. Compared to newspapers, periodicals survived somewhat better. Major changes in the 1980–1990s included concentration of ownership, the abandoning of party affiliations by the mainstream press, and an increase in cooperation over content (e.g., shared news bureaus).[31] The newspaper industry has been facing severe challenges in the new digital environment due to negative changes in readership and circulation, while advertising revenue has also been diminishing.[32] The national public service broadcaster has also faced criticism in this context on its role in the media market and in the online environment.

B. Broadcasting

12. In Finland, the national public broadcaster, Yleisradio, was established in 1926, and a few decades later, after a few twists and turns, television broadcasts formed an extension to radio activities.[33] These ‘twists and turns’ refer to the fact that Yleisradio was initially unenthusiastic about television activities, and the first television broadcasts in Finland were actually pioneered by a group of radio engineers, who later formed TES-TV and Tesvisio. Yleisradio followed with regular television broadcasts a few years later in 1958.[34]

From the start, Yleisradio had a de facto monopoly organized via a protectionist licensing policy; thus, its position rested on governmental practice regarding licensing and not on law. Initially the State did not own the company; instead, it provided the legal framework for the collection of licence fees, dictated the company’s operating licence, and exercised supervision.[35]

13. In 1934, however, Yleisradio was nationalized: the Act 216/1934 concerned the right of the Council of State to transfer state property acquired for purposes of

30. Tommila – Salokangas 1998, 244–267. *See also* Nieminen – Nordenstreng – Harjuniemi 2013, 184–188.
31. Tommila – Salokangas 1998, 101 et seq., 283–287, 296–320.
32. Lehtisaari et al. 2012, 7; for Finnish daily newspapers in the converged media landscape, *see* ibid. in toto.
33. Sumiala-Seppänen 1999, Ch. 1 and Ch. 2; Hellman 1999, 58 referring e.g., to airwaves being a ‘scarce public utility’.
34. Sumiala-Seppänen 1999, Ch. 2.
35. Sumiala-Seppänen 1999, Ch. 1.

broadcasting activity to a joint-stock company.[36] A decade later, a legislative amendment, the so-called Lex Jahvetti (774/1948), was enacted, whereby the Parliament became the appointer of Yleisradio's Administrative Council.[37] The early period has generally been characterized by 'distance' in relation to society. Later, starting from 1965, Yleisradio executives were appointed for five years under political mandates, with the composition of the company's management largely reflecting political representation in Parliament. Until the 1980s, management efficiency remained secondary to political considerations. However, Yleisradio also made a strong contribution to social change during the period. Finally, as the 1990s approached, the company began to adapt to changes in the market, including European developments and globalization.[38] As a result, 'Lex Jahvetti' was set aside by the Act on Yleisradio Oy (Finnish Broadcasting Company) (*laki Yleisradio Oy:stä* 1380/1993).[39]

From the beginning, Yleisradio has taken a negative stance towards advertising as a part of its financing.[40] Nevertheless, in the 1950s, Yleisradio agreed to lease programming time to a commercial entity, leading to the formation of Finland's first commercial television broadcasting company in 1957. This situation has been deemed a compromise where Yleisradio shared its operating licence with the new company, called Oy Mainos-TV-Reklam Ab (later MTV). The latter operated as an auxiliary to Yleisradio. In comparison to television in other Nordic countries, the Finnish model arguably featured a commercial and entertainment orientation from an early stage.[41]

14. In the early 1960s, developments in the field of television placed Yleisradio in the position to buy the shares of its competitor, Tesvisio. Nonetheless, the option of another channel prevailed in the negotiations. In the middle of the 1960s, the channels operating under Yleisradio were renamed Channel 1 and Channel 2. In the early 1980s, Yleisradio's news monopoly came to an end when MTV began featuring television news. Finally, in 1993, MTV began operating its own channel with its own licence.[42]

After Tesvisio was subsumed into Yleisradio's umbrella, MTV had a monopoly on the time and money allotted to television commercials. In turn, Yleisradio relied

---

36. *See* § 2 of the Act on Yleisradio (1380/1993), which notes that '[t]he State shall own and control the share capital of the company to an extent which corresponds to at least 70% of all the shares in the company and of the votes generated by all the shares in the company.'
37. *See* § 5(2) of the Act on Yleisradio (1380/1993), which states that the twenty-one members of the Council shall be elected by Parliament in its first session of the parliamentary term.
38. Sumiala-Seppänen 1999, Ch. 1 with references.
39. Unofficial translation by the Ministry of Transport and Communications; amendments up to 436/2017 included: http://www.finlex.fi/fi/laki/kaannokset/1993/en19931380.pdf (28.8.2019).
40. Sumiala-Seppänen 1999, Ch. 2 and Ch. 3; *see also* Ch. 5 of the original Act on Yleisradio (1380/1993) where a ban on advertising was included (currently § 12 in Ch. 5).
41. Sumiala-Seppänen 1999, Ch. 3 with references; Hellman 1988, 64 et seq. *See also* Hellman 2012, and about YLE's history Martti Soramäki: Yleisradion hallinnon ja ohjauksen kehitys 1926–2017. Kehityskaari eduskunnan alaiseksi yhtiöksi. Liikenne- ja viestintäministeriön julkaisuja 17/2017: https://julkaisut.valtioneuvosto.fi/handle/10024/160414 (13.8.2020).
42. Sumiala-Seppänen 1999, Ch. 3 with references.

principally on licence fees imposed on viewers (i.e., owners of TV sets) for its funding.[43] Chapter 4 of the original Act on Yleisradio (1380/1993) contained provisions concerning the company's financing. Although the chapter was repealed by Act 746/1998 implementing the Television without Frontiers Directive as amended by Directive 97/36/EC payments collected from the viewing public still remained the main source of funding.[44]

Previously, other corporations, such as MTV, had also contributed to Yleisradio's financing via so-called public service payments. After investigation by the Finnish Competition Authority (1.1.2013 onwards the Finnish Competition and Consumer Authority, FCCA), the payments were abolished. In its decision (806/61/96, 21.11.1996), the FCA stated that an initiative on the matter had been submitted to the Ministry of Transport. With the amendments enacted in 1998, the payment system was replaced by licence fees imposed on other parties in the field of television and radio.[45]

The financing scheme for Yleisradio was debated for several years before an agreement on a new system was finally reached in 2011, by which a so-called public broadcasting tax replaced licence fees in 2013, signifying direct funding from the state budget.[46] The tax is regulated in the Act on Public Broadcasting Tax (484/2012).[47]

In Finland, FM radio emerged in the 1950s. Networks expanded together with infrastructure constructed for television, and commercial radio activity commenced in the 1980s. Fixed-term licences were granted to local radio, which led to a strong emphasis on local content. However, a radical process of reconstruction in the sector, beginning with the depression of the 1990s, has meant that today less local content is available. The trend is towards national consolidation and the proliferation of syndicated channels, and cooperation has also increased between local radio stations. Moreover, the structure and operation of Yleisradio's public service radio partly resembles a syndicate.[48]

Alongside the radio channels provided by Yleisradio, there are dozens of licensed commercial radio channels. However, Yleisradio has been the biggest player in terms of radio activity.

As a consequence of the EEA Agreement, in 1994, the TVwF Directive became legally binding in Finland. Moreover, Finnish regulation of television and radio broadcasting activity was amended in 1998 (in force 1999), both in order to comply with the developing Community legislation, including Directive 97/36/EC, and to

43. Sumiala-Seppänen 1999, Ch. 3.
44. *See* the Government bill (HE 34/1998 vp).
45. *See* Government bill (HE 34/1998 vp); Neuvonen 2012, 276.
46. *See also* Lehtisaari et al. 2012, 9.
47. More on Yle's funding, *see* Om Vox Publica: 'Skatt istedenfor TV-lisens: Erfaringer fra Finland' (Tax instead of the TV license: Experiences from Finland): http://voxpublica.no/2016/06/skatt-istedenfor-tv-lisens-erfaringer-fra-finland/ (28.8.2019).
48. *See* Lehtisaari et al. 2012, 8; Neuvonen 2012, 277–278; Radion tulevaisuus. Liikenne- ja viestintäministeriön julkaisuja 8/2014 (The Future of Radio. Publications of the Ministry of Transport and Communications 8/2014), 9, 12, 16–17, 20, 40–42: http://www.lvm.fi/documents/20181/797516/Julkaisuja+8-2014/89d86ddc-8d3e-4bf6-bd9e-7e3010598d52?version=1.0 (28.8.2019).

respond to changes in communications technology and the market.[49] Later, amendments were made in accordance with the AVMS Directive (2007/65/EC). Currently, the legal landscape is being transformed due to the European Electronic Communications Code (EU) 2018/1972 (EECC) and the reformed AVMS Directive (EU) 2018/1808 (AVMSD) which are being implemented in national legislation during the end of 2020.[50] Key points in AVMS include, for example, that it extends the scope of the directive to cover video-sharing platform services beyond video broadcasting and video-on-demand. It also increases obligations aimed at protecting minors, and also the public. The directive also introduces an obligation for on-demand audiovisual media services, who must ensure that 30% of the works in their catalogues are European. Some other key elements of the directive include that television advertising time will be limited to 20% of broadcasting time in each hour of the day. EECC aims on the one hand to protect end users, by for example, obligating the Member States to ensure availability of affordable and adequate broadband and voice communications services. The end users are also protected by, for example, setting the time of subscriber contracts up to a maximum of 24 months, and stating that the end user must be informed if the contract is prolonged automatically. The end user's right to terminate the contract is also regulated in the directive, for example, when the telecommunications operator changes the terms of the contract also have a right. On the other hand, the directive also aims to promote the availability of high-speed wireless broadband connections as well as data security, and is said to facilitate 5G network deployment.

Furthermore, the Act on the Exercise of Freedom of Expression in Mass Media (*laki sananvapauden käyttämisestä joukkoviestinnässä* 460/2003)[51] was enacted in the new millennium in order to modernize the provisions concerning publishing and broadcasting (e.g., responsibilities) previously included in the Act on the Freedom of the Press (1/1919) and the Act on Radio Liability (219/1971). However, the Act covers new forms of mass media, such as on-demand media services, as well.

15. Finnish television began digitalization at the turn of the millennium. Subsequently, a transition to high definition television has been planned, with a possible switch-off of standard definition broadcasts in 2026. Moreover, with relaxation related to licensing and resisting foreign entry, new players have entered the Finnish television industry: for instance, Fox International launched a free-to-air channel in Finland in 2012.[52] In contrast, analogue distribution of radio transmissions continues, and commercial digital radio services are gaining little ground. This is because there are no clear benefits to be gained from digitalization, since the spectrum is used efficiently, the quality of broadcasts is high, and FM receivers are ubiquitous (homes, cars).

---

49. *See* Government bill (HE 34/1998 vp).
50. *See* Government bill (HE 98/2020 vp). The progress of the process can be tracked at https://valtioneuvosto.fi/hanke?tunnus=LVM004:00/2019 (26.7.2020).
51. *See* unofficial translation of the Ministry of Justice; available at http://www.finlex.fi/fi/laki/kaannokset/2003/en20030460.pdf (28.8.2019).
52. *See, e.g.*, Lehtisaari 2015, 140; Lehtisaari et al. 2012, 8.

II. Overview of Media Markets and Main Actors

16. The Finnish media market is relatively small, well-developed and in some respects characterized by competition, and the mass media market accounts for some EUR 3.8 billion (2018). The market value increased by 0.9%, or EUR 33 million, in the previous year.[53] The biggest companies in the field of television include Digita Oy, Sanoma Entertainment Finland Oy, Yleisradio Oy, and MTV Media Oy, whereas the field of telecommunications and broadband includes major actors such as Telia Finland Oyj, Elisa Oyj, and DNA Oyj. Also The Finnish News Agency STT (Suomen Tietotoimisto), that was founded in 1887, plays a major role at the Finnish media market. It sells news and photos to media companies. It is owned by more than thirty stakeholders. Sanoma Media Finland Oy is the biggest owner with its 75.42% ownership.

17. The Finnish mass media market is rather concentrated: actors with the largest turnover in electronic mass communication include Sanoma Oyj, Yleisradio Oy and Bonnier Ab.[54] Concentration also characterizes the Finnish newspaper industry, where over a half the market is in the hands of a few major companies. Sanoma holds a powerful position. Among Finnish newspapers, *Helsingin Sanomat* is the only publication with major national potential, whereas major regional newspapers often dominate in their respective areas. The market structure in the newspaper industry has three levels: national, regional, and local.[55]

Moreover, the market contains cross-ownership and cooperation with regard to marketing (e.g., newspapers)[56] and news gathering and publication. Major media companies also cover multiple channels and various sectors of the field. For example, Sanoma Media Finland offers news and entertainment in print, audiovisual, and radio media, and it also operates online and offers mobile services. Nelonen Media, as a Sanoma company, covers a handful of television channels and radio channels. Another large player in the market, Alma Media Oyj, offers a wide range of local, regional, and national print media, as well as various online services. The merger leading to SanomaWSOY in the late 1990s was deemed to be establishing an important division between the Sanoma Media group and the Alma Media group in the Finnish media market.[57]

Digita Oy offers nationwide communications infrastructure in Finland. Its terrestrial television networks cover basically all Finns. Digita is responsible for the planning, construction, and maintenance of Finnish broadcasting networks, mobile telecommunications networks, and transmission stations. Digita offers and sells

53. *See* Tilastokeskus: Joukkoviestinnän markkinatrendit ennallan vuonna 2018 (Statistics Finland: Mass media market trends remain unchanged in 2018) https://www.tilastokeskus.fi/til/jvie/2018/jvie_2018_2019-11-22_tie_001_fi.html (published 22.11.2019, 13.8.2020). *See also* Lehtisaari 2015, 130–131, 142–143, 145–146. Lehtisaari (2015, 142) notes that the small Finnish media market has accommodated relatively numerous media companies while the state has also been supporting this.
54. *See* the information provided in the Government bill (HE 221/2013 vp), 8–9. *See also* Lehtisaari 2015, 145.
55. Nieminen – Nordenstreng – Harjuniemi 2013, 180–181. *See also* Lehtisaari 2015, 145.
56. Lehtisaari 2015, 146.
57. Tommila – Salokangas 1998, 313.

capacity, transmits television programmes, and offers services to various companies and organizations. Digita operates under various obligations and regulated pricing conditions.[58] Nationwide network services are not, however, provided by Digita alone. In 2009, DNA was granted two nationwide network licences for terrestrial television. A few years later, yet another licence was granted.[59]

18. Publishing and print media, including magazines and books, accounts for 50.7% of media consumption in Finland, whereas, electronic mass communication (radio, TV, web) accounts for 44.2%, and recorded media (i.e., phonograms, movie theatres) 5.0% (2018). Only electronic communication has experienced a clear upward trend.[60] Regarding television, Yleisradio's channels account for 43.6% of the viewing rates while MTV Media covers 23.1% and Nelonen Media 15.4%. Other channels account for a total of 18% (10%/2011).[61]

From a Nordic perspective, Finland currently has a comparatively strong radio scene. One of the possible reasons for the robust state of radio is the fairly competitive climate that has prevailed from early on.[62] Listening to the radio was split equally between Yle (49%) and commercial channels (51%). Age distinguishes between commercial and public channel listeners. Three-quarters of those who are under 45 years old listen to commercial channels while 59% of those who are over 45 years listen to YLE's channels.[63] The biggest actors in commercial radio include the nationwide operators Bauer Media and Nelonen Media. Nevertheless, local radio stations are often dominant in their respective coverage areas.

III. Infrastructure

19. Various means of distributing audiovisual mass media are used in Finland. Due to the country's large surface area, there are areas that are catered for by antennas and areas that are reached by cable. However, converged networks are on the increase, which means, in particular, the delivery of both television and internet via cable or internet-enabled television. Provision of linear television via IP-networks largely corresponds to cable television. IPTV services which include, among others, on-demand and recording services function in cable operators' own networks.[64]

---

58. *See* http://www.digita.fi/in_english (28.8.2019).
59. Communications Policy Programme for Electronic Media (2012), 54.
60. Tilastokeskus: Joukkoviestinnän markkinatrendit ennallaan vuonna 2018 (Statistics Finland: Mass media market trends remain unchanged in 2018) https://www.stat.fi/til/jvie/2018/jvie_2018_2019-11-22_tie_001_fi.html (13.8.2020).
61. Finnpanel: https://www.finnpanel.fi/tulokset/tv/vuosi/sharev/viimeisin/ (28.9.2019); old information from Communications Policy Programme for Electronic Media (2012), 55.
62. Radion tulevaisuus. Liikenne- ja viestintäministeriön julkaisuja 8/2014 (The Future of Radio. Publications of the Ministry of Transport and Communications 8/2014), 9: http://julkaisut.valtioneuvosto.fi/bitstream/handle/10024/77910/Julkaisuja_8-2014.pdf?sequence=1&isAllowed=y (28.8.2019).
63. RadioMedia: 'Radiovuosi 2018' (Radio year 2018): https://www.radiomedia.fi/radiomainonta/tutkimustietoa-radiosta/radion-kuuntelu/radiovuosi-2018 (28.9.2019).
64. *See, e.g.*, IPTV:n lähitulevaisuus – työryhmän väliraportti. Liikenne- ja viestintäministeriö (The Near Future of IPTV – Interim Report of the Working Party. Ministry of Transport and Communications),

Cable television activity started in the early 1970s, with the cable retransmission of Swedish television programmes within apartment buildings proving popular on the west coast. This development was followed by regulation of cable activities.[65] According to FICORA's (now TRAFICOM, Finnish Transport and Communications Agency) consumer survey (2018), 42% of population watched TV via antenna network, 46% via cable, 11% through IPTV, 6% via satellite reception and 5% did not watch TV or watched TV only on the internet.[66]

20. Around 27% of the households (705,000 households) subscribed to pay-television channels in 2018. If we take into account video services like Netflix, in 2017, 42% of TV households subscribed to pay-television content.[67]

21. In order to answer the increasing demands of spectrum for new types of content services and to provide 'broadband for all', the State intervened in the creation of a broadband network, with its action plan and strategy.[68] The high-speed broadband strategy aimed to establish over 99% coverage for 100 Mb/s broadband connections by the end of 2015. Public support was therefore made available for remote areas which were unlikely to be catered for on a commercial basis. At present, the objective of over 99% population coverage has been reached for wireless broadband networks (3G and 4G). However, access to high-speed broadband connections may still greatly vary by region or area and depending on the demand for such connections. According to the digital infrastructure strategy, which is in line with the broadband targets set by the European Commission, all households in Finland should have the opportunity to access connections with transfer rate of at least 100 Mb/s by 2025.[69]

The project around broadband connections was launched by a Government Resolution at the end of 2008, and relevant regulation is provided in Act 1186/2009 on public support for broadband construction in remote areas.[70] Areas eligible for support are defined and mapped in the Decree of the Ministry of Transport and Communications (246/2010). Support is granted, upon successful application, by the

2010, 5–6: https://julkaisut.valtioneuvosto.fi/bitstream/handle/10024/78176/IPTV-tyoryhman_valiraportti.pdf?sequence=1&isAllowed=y (28.8.2019).

65. For a historical account, *see* Saressalo – Tulin 2008.
66. Televisiot lähetyskanavittain ja katselutavoittain (Televisions by broadcast channel and viewing mode): https://www.ficom.fi/ict-ala/tilastot/televisiot-lähetyskanavittain-ja-katselutavoittain (28.9.2019).
67. Maksu-tv (Pay-TV): https://www.ficom.fi/ict-ala/tilastot/maksu-tv (8.10.2020).
68. Nieminen 2013, 126.
69. *See,* Turning Finland into the world leader in communication networks – Digital Infrastructure Strategy 2025. Publications of the Ministry of Transport and Communications 2019:7, 9, 17. *See also*, the press release by the Ministry of Transport and Communications 'Telecom companies and the state to accelerate construction of high-speed broadband connections with new commitment' (12.11.2020): https://vnk.fi/en/-/10184/telecom-companies-and-the-state-to-accelerate-construction-of-high-speed-broadband-connections-with-new-commitment (13.12.2020).
70. *See also* the assessments of compatibility of the Finnish measures with Art. 107(3)(c) TFEU by the European Commission C(2010) 3062 final, Brussels 6.5.2010: http://ec.europa.eu/competition/state_aid/cases/235159/235159_1106591_26_1.pdf (28.8.2019) and C(2012) 6182 final, Brussels 7.9.2012: http://ec.europa.eu/competition/state_aid/cases/243482/243482_1396581_81_2.pdf (28.8.2019).

Finnish Transport and Communications Agency ((TRAFICOM) (§ 7 of the Act), and high-speed broadband networks are under construction in many regions.[71] Moreover, mobile broadband is being advanced by transferring frequencies from television operations to mobile broadband.

IV. Developments on the Media Markets

22. The Finnish media landscape shows various signs of what can be described as media convergence. On a technological level, the landscape has witnessed digitalization and the proliferation of channels and platforms of communication, while on the industry level, media players, telecommunications, and information technology sectors have widened their range of activities. Moreover, the social media landscape is developing quickly. As a result, surveys have been conducted into such issues as multichannel distribution[72] and net neutrality,[73] among others. At the same time, economic rationale has arguably begun to depress democratic and social ideals in the field of media.

Traditional actors in the Finnish media scene have also adjusted to or embraced the opportunities offered by new media and information technologies. The newspaper industry in particular has been under tremendous pressure, whereas the television industry's transformation into the audiovisual media services industry has been somewhat more comfortable. All in all, radio and television have managed quite well compared to newspapers – even if local content production has also diminished within the radio sector.[74]

The newspaper industry still features print, but there is a strong need for new business models, as traditional ways of attracting revenue are no longer as effective

---

71. For the advancing of the high-speed broadband project, *see* 'Hankkeen eteneminen': http://pilvi.viestintavirasto.fi/ohjausjavalvonta/laajakaista2015/hankkeenetenenminen.html (28.8.2019).
72. *See* the reports on multichannel distribution: Monikanavajakelua selvittävän työryhmän raportti 2008:18: https://julkaisut.valtioneuvosto.fi/bitstream/handle/10024/79380/tr18.pdf?sequence=1 (28.8.2019 and Monikanavajakelun jatkoselvitys. Opetusministeriön työryhmämuistioita ja selvityksiä 2009:20: http://julkaisut.valtioneuvosto.fi/bitstream/handle/10024/78894/tr20.pdf?sequence=1&isAllowed=y (28.8.2019).
73. *See* the net neutrality memorandum: Viestintäviraston muistio 1800/69/20: Verkkoneutraliteetin (net neutrality) sääntelytilanteesta, Suomi ja EU. Helsinki, 4.10.2012: http://pilvi.viestintavirasto.fi/attachments/NetNeutralityMuistioLoka2012.pdf (28.8.2019).
74. Ala-Fossi et al. 2018, 68–70, 212–213, 216–223; Lehtisaari et al. 2012, 7–8. *See also* English summary in Ala-Fossi et al. 2020: "Digital distribution platforms have gained popularity while traditional distribution channels have lost ground. The change in consumer media usage has changed advertisers' investments and, consequently, the media landscape. As a result, the industry is further concentrated. The number of companies and personnel in the main media sub-sectors is also declining. Although access to recorded media seems to be fairly stable, the declining volume of letter mail threatens also the distribution of printed newspapers. In telecommunications, the development of access has been positive but with focus on mobile and slower when compared to other Nordic countries. While television's heyday in broadcasting is over, households are still eager to buy new HD receivers. Newspapers, radio and television are all highly concentrated media sectors. The highest degree of concentration is in the radio industry, which is dominated by three key players, while the lowest concentration is in the press. Although the use of traditional media is decreasing at the expense of the internet, citizens are still using many media channels at least for some time in a week." *See also* pp. 11, 15 and 43.

as they have been and other advertising revenue is more dispersed (e.g., web advertising). However, local newspapers have been able to rely on local advertisers and subscribers, which has made print to survive. Some companies also aim for expansion in other sectors. In any case, Finland still seems to be a newspaper country in the sense that printed newspapers have, in general, persisted despite the pressures of convergence.[75]

23. Finland was among the first countries to introduce digital television transmissions. The Government Resolution on digitalization dates back to 1996, while the first digital transmissions were aired in 2001. Coverage for digital television increased gradually, and the digital transition, supported by another resolution in 2004, was completed in the antenna network in September 2007 and the cable network in 2008. Television channels have increased since,[76] and over a dozen terrestrial television channels are currently available throughout the country, while the supply by cable has grown manyfold.

In contrast, analogue distribution of radio transmissions continues. It is the mainstream method even in 2014, and current licences for FM radio are valid until 2020. The digitalization of radio has been discussed since the 1980s. With a few exceptions, digitalization seems to occur by a gradual shift to internet radio, with a long transition phase. In 2012, Yleisradio operated six FM channels while commercial FM channels amounted to sixty-six. National DVB distribution covered two Yleisradio channels. Internet radio has, however, been available since the 1990s. There are many channels on the internet, and traditional radio channels (with an FM licence) have websites offering content. Podcasting and streaming radio over the internet are both growing areas.[77]

The public broadcasting company, Yleisradio, began to provide live web streaming of its television programmes in April 2013. In late 2014, Yleisradio announced its intention to invest more in Yle Areena (internet television and radio) at the expense of traditional broadcasting. The intention is to combine television and internet as part of a comprehensive reform spanning several years.

The telecommunication sector has also experienced major changes and pressures for convergence. Wireless communication has developed rapidly in terms of both speed and technologies.[78] A broadband connection of 1 Mb/s has been part of the universal services to which Finnish citizens must have access since July 2010. Moreover, major telecommunication operators previously confined to the provision

75. Lehtisaari 2015, 145; Lehtisaari et al. 2012, 43–45; Nieminen – Nordenstreng – Harjuniemi 2013, 179–182.
76. For the transition, *see* the report on the transition to digital TV 'Digitaaliseen televisioon siirtyminen'. Seurantaryhmän loppuraportti. Liikenne- ja viestintäministeriön julkaisuja 12/2008, Helsinki, 27.2.2008: http://www.lvm.fi/documents/20181/819315/1_LVM12_2008.pdf/ce10f460-aa7b-40ff-a0d2-4189883b8b9b?version=1.0 (28.8.2019).
77. Radion tulevaisuus. Liikenne- ja viestintäministeriön julkaisuja 8/2014 (The Future of Radio. Publications of the Ministry of Transport and Communications 8/2014), 7, 10, 39, 41–44, 56.
78. Lehtisaari et al. 2012, 8.

of internet connections and related services have widened their operations to the provision of content. This means provision of various channel packages and pay-per-view audiovisual services.[79]

24. Regarding media convergence and the legal landscape, a legislative reform entitled the Act on Electronic Communications Services (*tietoyhteiskuntakaari* 917/2014)[80] was enacted by Parliament in late 2014. The Code was recently renamed as the Act on Electronic Communications Services. The Act codifies and repeals such laws as the Communications Market Act (393/2003), the Act on Television and Radio Operations (744/1998), the Act on Radio Frequencies and Telecommunications Equipment (1015/2001), the Domain Name Act (228/2003), the Act on Provision of Information Society Services (458/2002) (so-called e-Commerce Act), and the Act on the Protection of Privacy in Electronic Communications (516/2004). The Act also introduced various amendments to previously existing legislation as well as some new provisions and concepts.

The gradual shift to high definition has faced some obstacles. Television frequency planning aimed to ensure that DVB-T2 broadcasting would have become the main broadcasting technology before 2020, while the date 31 March 2020 was agreed as the deadline for all free television channels. It was estimated that the reception of all free television channels using current standard technology would be possible until 2026, which means using parallel technologies (multicast).[81] To oversee the project, the Ministry of Transport and Communications appointed a working group, which published its report in late 2013,[82] and the planning of the schedule for transfer to high definition was conducted in cooperation with the television industry. A sufficiently long transition phase has been deemed necessary from the citizens' perspective.[83] The procurement procedure by the Finnish Broadcasting Company (Yle) regarding transmission services for HD channels was appealed to

79. Lehtisaari et al. 2012, 9.
80. For English translation, *see* the unofficial translation by the Ministry of Transport and Communications at https://www.finlex.fi/en/laki/kaannokset/2014/en20140917.pdf (28.8.2019).
81. Communications Policy Programme for Electronic Media (2012), 81; Report of the Transport and Communications Committee (LiVM 10/2014 vp). *See also* Suomen antennitelevision teknologiasiirtymä viivästyy (Delays in the technological transition for Finnish terrestrial television), 26.10.2018: https://legacy.viestintavirasto.fi/viestintavirasto/ajankohtaista/2018/suomenantennitelevisionteknologiasiirtymaviivastyy.html (25.10.2019).
82. Työryhmän väliraportti: Maanpäällisen televisiotoiminnan seuraava teknologiasiirtymä (Interim report of the Working group: The next technological transition in terrestrial television broadcasting), 26.11.2013: http://www.lvm.fi/documents/20181/799435/Julkaisuja+33-2013/fc7fc8e0-f6a3-4184-bd70-a51ad36abc3e?version=1.0 (28.8.2019).
83. Työryhmän väliraportti: Maanpäällisen televisiotoiminnan seuraava teknologiasiirtymä (Interim report of the Working group: The next technological transition in terrestrial television broadcasting), 26.11.2013: http://www.lvm.fi/documents/20181/799435/Julkaisuja+33-2013/fc7fc8e0-f6a3-4184-bd70-a51ad36abc3e?version=1.0 (28.8.2019). 5, 10–11, 45 et seq.; Report of the Transport and Communications Committee (LiVM 10/2014 vp).

the Market Court since the conditions include a requirement of not incurring significant costs to households relying on antenna transmission. The Market Court prohibited Yle from proceeding with the procurement. The dispute over the costs for customers has thus prolonged the process.[84]

There was no move to initiate the digitalization of radio in the Communications Policy Programme for Electronic Media adopted by the Government in 2012.[85]

V. The Social Media Landscape

25. One of the first social networking sites, IRC-Galleria, was founded by Finnish enthusiasts in 2000. Facebook, in particular, however, soon took over, both on a global scale and in Finland. Today, over a half (61%) of Finns, between the ages of 16 and 89, have followed social networking services during the past three months. The percentage is even higher for young people, those aged 16 to 24, at around 93% (2018).[86] Finns use social media to generate and share content. Popular social media platforms include Facebook and YouTube as well as the Finnish site called Suomi24.[87] WhatsApp has grown in popularity all the way to the top position, followed by Facebook and Instagram (2018).[88] In 2015 more than 75% of Finnish who are at the age of 15–55 had been using those services (79.3% and 76.8%).[89]

84. Suomen antennitelevision teknologiasiirtymä viivästyy (Delays in the technological transition for Finnish terrestrial television) (26.10.2018): https://legacy.viestintavirasto.fi/viestintavirasto/ajankohtaista/2018/suomenantennitelevisionteknologiasiirtymaviivastyy.html; Yle Uutiset: 'Yle hakee valituslupaa markkinaoikeuden päätökseen HD-jakelukilpailutuksesta' (Yle is applying for leave to appeal against the Market Court's decision on the competitive HD distribution tender) 21.3.2019: https://yle.fi/aihe/artikkeli/2019/03/21/yle-hakee-valituslupaa-markkinaoikeuden-paatokseen-hd-jakelukilpailutuksesta (25.10.2019). *See* the decision of the Market Court of Finland (MAO:68/19). At the time of writing, Yle's application for leave to appeal was pending at the Supreme Administrative Court.
85. Communications Policy Programme for Electronic Media (2012), 4.
86. *See* Tilastokeskus: 'Suomalaisten internetin käyttö 2018 – viestintää, asiointia, tiedonhakua ja medioiden seuraamista' (Statistics Finland: How Finns use the Internet in 2018 – communication, transactions, information retrieval and media monitoring): http://www.stat.fi/til/sutivi/2018/sutivi_2018_2018-12-04_kat_001_fi.html (28.8.2019).
87. *See also* Khaldarova – Laaksonen – Matikainen 2012, 5: http://www.helsinki.fi/crc/Julkaisut/SoMe_Elections.pdf (28.8.2019).
88. *See, e.g.*, Yle Uutiset: 'Whatsappia käytetään eniten, Instagramia suosivat naiset' (Whatsapp is used the most, Instagram is preferred by women) 7.4.2018: https://yle.fi/uutiset/3-10148277 (25.10.2019).
89. MTV White paper 001/0015, 'Suomalaisten sosiaalisen median käyttö 2015' (Finns' social media usage 2015); a research made by MTV, Kurio, the Social Media Age(ncy) and Laurea ammattikoulu, http://im.mtv.fi/blob/4941078/6c812d65a85598db50814610bd1da47b/suomalaisten-sosiaalisen-median-kaytto-2015-mtv-white-paper-data.pdf?utm_campaign=NTF_pdf_Some2015:eimarklupa&utm_medium=email&utm_source=Eloqua (28.8.2019).

§3. Sources of Media Law

I. Legislation: Finland

26. In Finland, legislative power is vested in Parliament, in conjunction with the President of the Republic. Legislative bills are prepared by the ministries and drafted by the Government. Draft bills (Hallituksen esitys; HE) emanate from the ministry with responsibility for the matter in question. Those laws with wider general significance are often prepared in committees with representatives from ministries, universities, political parties, those who apply the law in practice such as attorneys and lawyers, and other interest groups. Interest groups and experts are also often invited to comment upon draft legislation.

Finally, it is the Parliament's task to pass legislation, which is then ratified by the President. However, if the President refuses to ratify a law, it is returned to the Parliament, and if Parliament does not change its opinion, the Act enters into force even without presidential ratification.

Amending the Constitution is more difficult than amending an ordinary parliamentary law. When the constitution is changed, two parliamentary votings are needed. When parliament decides to change the constitution, the changes have to be accepted by a simple majority. Thereafter, if two-thirds of MPs in the new Parliament vote in favour of the amendment, it will come into force. There is also a possibility to change the constitution faster. In this case, changing the constitution has to be declared urgently by a majority of five-sixths and, after that, it requires that a majority of two-thirds votes for the proposal.[90]

Legislation is published in the Statute Book of Finland. Acts enter into force after publication on the date laid down in the Act or when it is ordered in a separate decree. Current legislation is available for review in an electronic database of Finnish legislation (Finlex, www.finlex.fi). There are also translations of the most significant laws. However, it is worth noting that the translations are not regularly updated; therefore when relying on translated law, one must check if any legislative changes have occurred after translation.

A. *Constitution*

27. The Finnish Constitution (*Suomen perustuslaki* 731/1999) entered into force on 1 March 2000.[91] According to Chapter 1, section 1(1), Finland is a sovereign republic. According to subsection (2) of the above-mentioned section, the constitution shall guarantee the inviolability of human dignity and the freedom and rights of the individual and promote justice in society. The second chapter of the Constitution includes sections on basic rights and liberties. The 1995/2000 Constitutional

---

90. For a more detailed description of the Finnish legislative process *see* Saraviita 2012, 38–55.
91. Unofficial translation by the Ministry of Justice; amendments up to 1112/2011 included: http://www.finlex.fi/fi/laki/kaannokset/1999/en19990731.pdf (28.8.2019).

reform of basic rights harmonized Finnish constitutional rights with the European Convention on Human Rights (ECHR).[92]

The principle of legality in criminal cases is guaranteed in Chapter 2, section 8, according to which:

> No one shall be found guilty of a criminal offence or be sentenced to a punishment on the basis of a deed which has not been determined punishable by an Act at the time of its commission. The penalty imposed for an offence shall not be more severe than that provided by an Act at the time of commission of the offence.[93]

This principle of *nullum crime sine lege, nulla poena sine lege* is also stated in section 1 of Chapter 3 of the Criminal Code (*rikoslaki* 39/1889;[94] 11.6.2003/515).[95]

The private life, dignity, and sanctity of the home of every citizen are guaranteed in section 10 of the Finnish Constitution. According to the same section '[m]ore detailed provisions on the protection of personal data are to be laid down by an Act'. This means that certain rights concerning personal data protection are also guaranteed at the constitutional level. Freedom of religion and conscience is guaranteed in section 11, and freedom of expression and right of access to information are guaranteed in section 12. Freedom of assembly and freedom of association (§ 13) and electoral and participatory rights (§ 14) are also guaranteed in the Constitution. In addition, the Constitution also supports media business by guaranteeing the protection of property (§ 15) and the right to work and the freedom to engage in commercial activity (§ 18).

According to section 22 the public authorities shall guarantee the observance of basic rights, liberties, and human rights. Basic and human rights have significance between the state and the individual and also between private parties.

B. Legislation

28. There is much legislation concerning media and communication law in Finland. The material limits of freedom of expression are stated, for example, in the Criminal Code of Finland (39/1889), which includes provisions on such offences as defamation, dissemination of private information, blasphemy, incitement to racial hatred and the distribution of sexually offensive pictures.

One of the most significant laws in the field of media law is the Act on the Exercise of Freedom of Expression in Mass Media (460/2003). The Act contains more detailed provisions on the exercise of freedom of expression in the mass media. It

---

92. For more, *see* Hallberg 2011, 29–59 in Hallberg et al. 2011 and Saraviita 2012, 262–265.
93. Unofficial translation by the Ministry of Justice. *See also* Saraviita 2012, 269–270.
94. *See* the unofficial translation by the Ministry of Justice; amendments up to 927/2012 included: https://www.finlex.fi/fi/laki/kaannokset/1889/en18890039.pdf (28.8.2019).
95. *See* 3:1 of the Criminal Code: 'The principle of legality: (1) A person may be found guilty of an offence only on the basis of an act that has been specifically criminalized in law at the time of its commission. (2) The punishment and other sanctions under criminal law shall be based on law.' For more on the principle of legality *see* Utriainen 2019, 37–39.

states that when applying the Act, interference with communication and the activities of the media is legitimate only in so far as is essential, taking into account the importance of freedom of expression in a democratic society (§ 1(2)). The Act offers no definition of the kind of content permitted, but it sets out how legal responsibility is allocated and implemented if the content is illegal. It also contains provisions on the right to reply and correction.

29. Definitions are included in section 2 of the Act: *network message* means information, opinion, or other types of message communicated to a freely determined group of recipients (i.e., the public) via technical means (e.g., radio waves, networks) (points 1–2). A *programme* is a uniform complex of network messages consisting mainly of sound or moving images (point 3) while *programme activity* means the provision of programmes for reception by the public (point 8). The Act applies to both publishing and broadcasting or programme activity in Finland (§ 3(1)). Moreover, the maintenance of webpages by private persons is subject to sections 12, 14, 16, 18, 19, 22, and 24 of the Act (§ 3(2)), which address criminal and tort liability, confidentiality of sources, cease and destroy orders, as well as the right to prosecution. Technical production, transmission, distribution, or intermediation are covered only by sections 17–20 and 22 (§ 3(3)) as in provisions concerning the obligation to submit identification data, seizure, and orders to cease and destroy. The regulation of information society services pursuant to the Act on Electronic Communications Services applies as such (§ 3(4) FEA).

30. A large-scale legal reform was implemented on 15 October 2014, when the new Information Society Code (917/2014) was passed in the Finnish Parliament. The Act largely entered into force at the beginning of 2015. However, some provisions were applicable only after the Domain Name Act (228/2003) expired on 4 September 2016. Moreover, applicability of some provisions was delayed (§ 351). The Act replaced eight different Acts and brought together provisions on electronic communications services, communication networks and services. A further objective of the Act is to secure the efficient and uninterrupted use of radio frequencies, to foster competition, and to ensure that communications networks and services are technologically advanced, of high quality, reliable, safe, and inexpensive. Moreover, the Act aims to ensure the confidentiality of electronic communications and the protection of privacy. In 2018, the Code was renamed as the Act on Electronic Communications Services (ECSA).

Since the Code, later the Act on Electronic Communications Services, was largely intended to function as a codification of existing legislation, no major fundamental rights problems were anticipated, as many of the proposed provisions did not significantly differ from existing legislation enacted with the contribution of the Constitutional Law Committee. Moreover, assessments were made in light of the Committee's praxis. However, a statement of the Constitutional Law Committee was deemed desirable. In Finland, it is the Constitutional Law Committee that supervises the safeguarding of human and fundamental rights during the legislative process, as opposed to a Constitutional Court. The Committee assessed the proposed code and individual provisions in relation to, among others, privacy, freedom to conduct business, and freedom of expression.[96] Indeed, due to subsequent developments at the EU level, the draft code and bill had come to include various questionable elements from the perspective of fundamental rights. After the CJEU's April 2014 ruling in Joined Cases C-293/12 and C-594/12, Chapter 19 of the draft code required particular reassessment, as it was mainly based on the Data Retention Directive (2006/24/EC), which the CJEU had declared invalid.

31. The Copyright Act (*tekijänoikeuslaki* 404/1961)[97] defines the economic and moral rights of copyright holders. It also contains many exceptions and limitations to exclusive rights. These exceptions include provisions on the so-called short news reporting right.

The Act on the Openness of Government Activities (*laki viranomaisten toiminnan julkisuudesta* 621/1999)[98] sets out the principle of openness, according to which official documents are in the public domain unless specifically provided otherwise in that or another Act (§ 1(1)). The Act aims on the one hand to promote openness and good practice in governmental information management. On the other hand, the objectives are to enable individuals and corporations to monitor and influence the exercise of public authority and the use of public resources as well as to form opinions and protect their rights and interests (§ 3). According to section 2 on the scope of application, the Act includes provisions on the right of access to official documents in the public domain, document secrecy and other restrictions, as well as officials' duties related to non-disclosure and other objectives of the Act.

32. The Act on the Public Disclosure and Confidentiality of Tax Information[99] (*laki verotustietojen julkisuudesta ja salssapidosta* 1346/1999) applies to documents concerning individual taxpayers which are submitted to or prepared by the tax administration (taxation documents) and the information contained therein (taxation information).

33. The Act on Television and Radio Operations (*laki televisio- ja radiotoiminnasta* 744/1998) was repealed by the Act on Electronic Communications Services (917/2014), which entered into force on 1 January 2015. Its Chapter 3 contains provisions on network licences and Chapter 4 contains provisions on programming licences for digital television or radio broadcasting operations. According to section 22 of the Act on Electronic Communications Services, a programming licence is required for television and radio broadcasting in a digital terrestrial mass communications network excluding operations in which:

---

96. *See* Statement of the Constitutional Law Committee (PeVL 18/2014 vp).
97. Unofficial translation by the Ministry of Education and Culture; amendments up to 608/2015 included: http://www.finlex.fi/fi/laki/kaannokset/1961/en19610404.pdf (28.8.2019).
98. Unofficial translation by the Ministry of Justice; amendments up to 907/2015 included: http://www.finlex.fi/fi/laki/kaannokset/1999/en19990621.pdf (28.8.2019).
99. Laki verotustietojen julkisuudesta ja salassapidosta (Act on the public disclosure and confidentiality of tax information, 1346/1999), unofficial translation; amendments up to 1156/2005 included: http://www.finlex.fi/fi/laki/kaannokset/1999/en19991346.pdf (28.8.2019).

1. audiovisual content services or radio broadcasts can only be received in an educational institution, hospital, hotel or similar institution; or
2. considering the number of programmes or the recurrence of broadcasts, the provision of audiovisual content is not regular and is not the main purpose of the service.

Chapter 5 contains provisions on programming licences for analogue radio broadcasting operations. According to section 34, programming licences are required for radio broadcasting operations conducted using analogue terrestrial mass communications networks. Programming licences are granted, upon successful application, by TRAFICOM. Analogue radio broadcasting operations that last a maximum of three months do not require a programming licence. In addition, minor radio broadcasting operations in a limited area may be carried out without a programming licence. Furthermore, the Finnish Broadcasting Company Ltd (Yle) has the right to carry out analogue public service radio broadcasting, as determined in section 7 of the Act on Yleisradio Oy (Finnish Broadcasting Company) (1380/1993), without a licence. Yle may carry out digital public service television and radio broadcasting without a license (§ 22(2) ECSA).

34. Public service broadcasting is regulated by the Act on Yleisradio Oy (1380/1993). Yleisradio Oy is the Finnish public service broadcasting company. According to Chapter 3 section 7, Yleisradio Oy shall be responsible for the provision of diverse and comprehensive television and radio programming with the related additional services for all citizens under equal conditions. These and other content services related to public service shall be provided in public communications networks nationally and regionally (436/2017). The Act on Broadcasting Tax (484/2012) also states that the activities of Yleisradio Oy are to be funded by a tax collected by the Finnish tax authorities. Among the benefits of Yle tax are that the license fee evasion ceased to exist as the tax is collected from everyone (except those who have a very low income), the collection costs are low, and the level of funding is easy to estimate. The purpose of the Finnish Yle tax model is to give sustainable guarantees with respect to the level of funding and the protection of the independence of the public service broadcaster.[100]

In August 2015, a Working Group was set up by the Minister of Transport and Communications for assessing the Finnish media market. It delivered its report late the same year.[101] For further investigation into Finnish public service broadcasting, the public service remit and financing PSB, a Parliamentary Working Group, was set up in late 2015. It had an original term until the end of May 2016, but it was

100. Om Vox Publica: 'Skatt istedenfor TV-lisens: Erfaringer fra Finland' (Tax instead of the TV license: Experiences from Finland), http://voxpublica.no/2016/06/skatt-istedenfor-tv-lisens-erfaringer-fra-finland/ (28.8.2019).

101. *See* the report 'Pätevät pärjäävät – Kotimaisia mediamarkkinoita arvioivan työryhmän raportti'. Liikenne- ja viestintäministeriö, raportit ja selvitykset 2/2015 (The competent will thrive. Report by the working group assessing the Finnish media market. Ministry of Transport and Communications, Reports 2/2015): http://www.lvm.fi/documents/20181/514507/Raportit+ja+selvitykset+2-2015/032b6455-2e62-4b55-af49-62c2f2caa772?version=1.0 (28.8.2019). More details in Alén-Savikko 2016.

extended by one month and results were delivered by mid-June.[102] A gradual increase in purchases from independent producers was put forward. Moreover, among the proposals of the Parliamentary Working Group (2016) were amendments or clarifications to the Yle's mission as stated in law: instead of tolerance and multiculturalism the core of the mission was safeguarding Finnish cultural heritage and promoting tolerance, equality and cultural pluralism.[103]

C. International Conventions

35. Finland joined the EU in 1995, and accession had an immediate legal impact on the country. European Union regulation is applicable within the jurisdiction of Finland, and Community law enjoys primacy. Moreover, decisions of the European Court of Justice have a significant effect as a source of law.

Finland is also a member of the European Council, and therefore Finland is also obliged to adhere to the ECHR. Finnish legislators and Finnish courts pay close attention to European Court of Human Rights (ECtHR) practice. Finland has also ratified many other international conventions on human rights, including the United Nation's Universal Declaration of Human Rights.[104]

As already mentioned, section 22 of the Finnish Constitution obliges the public authorities to guarantee the observance of human rights, which is why they and the courts must consider all human rights norms when interpreting Finnish legislation. The significance of the ECtHR has been remarkable during the past ten years. In freedom of expression cases, hardly a judgment can be found without reference to the decisions of the ECtHR.

---

102. *See* the press release by the Ministry of Transport and Communications 'Working group: Parliamentary consensus on the duties and funding of Yle' (16.6.2016): http://www.lvm.fi/en/-/working-group-parliamentary-consensus-on-the-duties-and-funding-of-y-1 (28.8.2019). *See also* the Report 'Yleisradio Oy:n julkisen palvelun tehtävät ja siihen liittyvät muut uudistukset' (Yleisradio Oy's public service remit and other related reforms): http://www.lvm.fi/lvm-site62-mahti-portlet/download?did=207240 (28.8.2019).
103. *See* the Report 'Yleisradio Oy:n julkisen palvelun tehtävät ja siihen liittyvät muut uudistukset', Annex 2 (proposal for amendments to the Yle Act): https://www.lvm.fi/asiat-aikajarjestyksessa/-/mahti/asia/71530 (29.8.2019) and the press release by the Ministry of Transport and Communications 'Working group: Parliamentary consensus on the duties and funding of Yle' 16.6.2016: http://www.lvm.fi/en/-/working-group-parliamentary-consensus-on-the-duties-and-funding-of-y-1 (29.8.2019).
104. As Saraviita writes in *IEL Constitution of Finland* (2012), 119, 'The acceptance of Parliament is required for treaties and other international obligations that contain provisions of a legislative nature, are otherwise significant, or for special reasons require approval by the Parliament under the Constitution. The acceptance of Parliament is required also for the denouncement of such obligations.'

D. *Court Practice*

1. General Information

36. According to section 3, subsection 3 of the Finnish Constitution, judicial powers are exercised by independent courts of law, with the Supreme Court and the Supreme Administrative Court as the highest instances. In Finland there is no Constitutional Court. Instead, the conformity of a law with the constitution is evaluated by the Finnish Parliament's Constitutional Law Committee before the law is passed. According to section 106 of the Finnish Constitution, if, in a matter being tried by a court of law, the application of an Act is in evident conflict with the Constitution, the court of law shall give primacy to the provision in the Constitution. According to section 107, in turn, if a provision in a Decree or other statute lower than an Act is in conflict with the Constitution or another Act, it cannot be applied by a court of law or by any other public authority. Therefore a law's conformity with the constitution can also be determined in general courts or in administrative courts.[105]

2. Supreme Court

37. According to section 99, subsection 1 of the Finnish Constitution, 'justice in civil, commercial and criminal matters is in the final instance administered by the Supreme Court'. Moreover, according to the Supreme Court Act (*laki korkeimmasta oikeudesta* 665/2005) section 1 subsection 1, 'Supreme jurisdiction in legal matters shall in Finland be exercised by the Supreme Court.' The Supreme Court's most important function is to establish judicial precedents in leading cases, thus ensuring uniformity in the administration of justice by the lower courts: 'Decisions of the courts of appeal and land courts, as well as certain decisions of the District Courts, Insurance Court and Market Court may be appealed against to the Supreme Court, provided that the Supreme Court grants leave to appeal.'[106]

38. Rulings are usually given in cases that are significant for the entire legal order, guiding thereby the administration of justice in future cases. These precedents are often established when the applicable Acts of Parliament and Decrees fail to provide a clear solution on a question of law or when there is room for interpretation. The number of such rulings is approximately 100–150 each year.

A judicial precedent is not binding, but the precedents of the Supreme Court are normally followed. If a district court departs from earlier decisions made by the Supreme Court, it is highly probable that the Court of Appeal will change the judgment. Of course, court practice can also change in the Supreme Court if, for example, the social circumstances have changed considerably or if Finnish court practice has been found to be in breach of the ECHR in the ECtHR. If the Supreme

105. For more information *see* Saraviita 2012, 200–224.
106. The quotation is from the Finnish Supreme Court's website: http://korkeinoikeus.fi/en/index.html (28.8.2019). *See* closer Code of Judicial Procedure (4/1734) Ch. 30.

Court departs from its earlier precedents, the case has to be decided by an enlarged chamber (eleven members) or by a full court.

39. Precedents in Supreme Court cases are available in the FINLEX database, and access is free of charge (www.finlex.fi). The Act on the Publicity of Court Proceedings in General Courts (*laki oikeudenkäynnin julkisuudesta yleisissä tuomioistuimissa* 370/2007)[107] states that court proceedings and trial documents are public unless provided otherwise in this or another Act.

During the ten-year period from 2005 to 2014, the Supreme Court gave fifteen judgments on defamation. This is a very large number considering the fact that the Supreme Court grants leave to appeal in just about 5% of criminal cases.[108] Moreover, in most of these cases, the Supreme Court overturned the ruling of lower courts and dismissed the charges of defamation. The Supreme Court has also decided many cases concerning dissemination of private information, and in those cases the tendency has also been to find no breach of the law. Here, the effect of rulings by the ECtHR can be clearly seen: Finland had received many condemnatory judgments in freedom of expression cases from the ECtHR, and it seems that the courts have learned their lesson and have begun ruling in favour of wider freedom of expression. The problem in the Finnish judicial system has been a 'slavish' and overly literal application of the Criminal Code, without consideration of whether the consequent limitation of freedom of expression is truly necessary in a democratic society, which is the ECHR requirement for such action.[109] Since 2014 the Supreme Court has not given precedents on defamation. Two judgments concerning disseminating private information has been delivered since 2014 (KKO 2018:81 and KKO 2018:51). In both cases the Supreme Court is convicted of disseminating private information.

3. Supreme Administrative Court

40. According to the Finnish Constitution, section 99 of Chapter 1, justice in administrative matters is, in the final instance, administered by the Supreme Administrative Court. The Constitution requires that the use of public powers be based on law. Moreover, the Administrative Judicial Procedure Act (*laki oikeudenkäynnistä hallintoasioissa* 808/2019),[110] which is the main act covering the right to appeal, states that, administrative decisions may be appealed pursuant to the act (§ 7) while decisions of administrative courts may be subject to appeal before the Supreme

107. Unofficial translation by the Ministry of Justice, amendments up to 742/2015 included: https://www.finlex.fi/fi/laki/kaannokset/2007/en20070370.pdf (28.8.2019).
108. This information is from the Supreme Court's communications officer Pia Sive. The Supreme Court got 2,611 new cases in 2014. About 1,280 of them concerned civil cases and 1,030 complaints were about criminal cases. A leave to appeal was given only in 122 cases year 2014. The number of precedents in 2014 was 104.
109. Regarding defamation and dissemination of private information, the Criminal Code has been changed by a legislative amendment, which came into force at the beginning of 2014.
110. Unofficial translation by the Ministry of Justice: https://www.finlex.fi/en/laki/kaannokset/2019/en20190808.pdf (28.8.2019).

Administrative Court (§ 109). As opposed to the Supreme Court, appellants in the administrative line do not generally require leave to appeal in the highest instance; rather, as a rule, they have the *right* to appeal. There are, however, restrictions to the right of appeal and sometimes a leave to appeal is required as determined by another act; this is the case, for instance, in alien matters (*see* § 13; § 196 Aliens Act 301/2004). Where leave to appeal is required by law, it must be granted if necessary for uniformity of case law or if particular reasons, due to an error in the matter, or some other weighty reasons so require (§ 111 of Administrative Judicial Procedure Act). Leave may also be granted only to a part of the decision under appeal (§ 111).

In the field of freedom of expression and freedom of information, the Supreme Administrative Court decides, for example, on complaints concerning the Act on the Openness of Government Activities. It can also decide on cases concerning civil servants' freedom of expression.

The Act on the Publicity of Administrative Court Proceedings (*laki oikeudenkäynnin julkisuudesta hallintotuomioistuimissa* 381/2007)[111] states, in section 1, that court proceedings and trial documents are public unless provided otherwise in the Act. The Act contains exceptions intended to protect such things as privacy or trade secrets.

4. The Parliamentary Ombudsman

41. According to section 38 of the Finnish Constitution, Parliament appoints, for a term of four years, a Parliamentary Ombudsman and two Deputy Ombudsmen, who shall have outstanding knowledge of law. The aim of their task is to ensure good administration and observance of constitutional and human rights. The Ombudsmen shall ensure that the courts of law, the other authorities and civil servants, public employees and other persons, when they are performing a public task, obey the law and fulfil their obligations. As part of their duties, they write an annual report to Parliament which includes observations on the administration of justice and any shortcomings in legislation.

Anyone can file a complaint with the Parliamentary Ombudsman if they feel that a public authority or an official failed to observe the law or fulfil a duty, or if the complainant suspects that fundamental or human rights have not been appropriately implemented. The complaint process is free of charge, and the average time to deal with a complaint is six months.

In the case of a serious breach of the law, the Ombudsman may initiate a prosecution and can also inform the public authority concerned of his/her opinion as to the appropriate course of legal action or draw the attention of a particular public authority to the requirements of good governance or aspects that promote the implementation of fundamental and human rights. The Ombudsman may also make a proposal that the authority rectifies an error or redresses a shortcoming. Finally, the

111. Unofficial translation by the Ministry of Justice: https://www.finlex.fi/fi/laki/kaannokset/2007/en20070381.pdf (28.8.2019).

Ombudsman can also draw the attention of the Government to flaws in legislative provisions or regulations and make proposals as to how shortcomings should be redressed.[112]

42. The Ombudsman cannot change or overturn decisions made by the authorities or courts or order payment of compensation. Ombudsmen have given many decisions on the freedom of expression of public officials.

> For example, in his decision of 7 January 2015 (5342/2013), the Parliamentary Ombudsman stated that the city of Tampere had violated a teacher's freedom of speech when it had issued him a written warning for contributing to a discussion on educators' role in supporting students in the performance-oriented, fast-paced world of the school. According to the teacher's comments, which were published in the newspaper *Aamulehti,* some professional educators were unsuited to the profession because they were mentally unstable.
>
> The teacher's comments were regarded as having a negative impact on the school's working atmosphere and well-being at work. According to the Parliamentary Ombudsman, the issuing of the warning was a violation of the complainant's freedom of speech, and it constituted a breach of the ECHR and the Finnish Constitution, because the teacher's employer had failed to find a balance between a public servant's freedom of speech and duty of loyalty. As a result, the city of Tampere was told to report by 16 February 2015 on the actions it had taken as a result of the Parliamentary Ombudsman's decision.
>
> The headmaster of the school in question was of the opinion that the teacher had publicly criticized the actions of his colleagues and undermined the trust between guardians and teachers when he had expressed his concern that professional educators unsuited to the profession were exacerbating the problems experienced by young people and that no one was intervening in the problem. His comments were as follows: 'to what extent are the anxieties of a young person struggling with growing pains increased by a teacher or a guidance counsellor with a personality disorder who acts illogically and makes the students pay for his or her own mistakes?'
>
> The Parliamentary Ombudsman considered that the teacher had a right to make public his concerns and critical views concerning problems in his branch of administration. The teacher's comments were part of the wider discussion on child welfare, which was a topic of high societal importance. According to the Ombudsman there must be a high threshold for intervening in letters and of additional relevance was the fact that no specific school or person had been identified in the teacher's comments, and that the criticism had been directed at public servants rather than private persons. The negative adjectives used in the writing were also deemed unavoidable in order to convey the message.
>
> Furthermore, the Parliamentary Ombudsman also considered that the teacher's comments had not caused significant damage to the school's reputation:

112. This text is from Parliamentary Ombudsman's website at https://www.oikeusasiamies.fi/en_GB/web/selkosuomi/what-does-the-parliamentary-ombudsman-do- (28.10.2019).

> 'The fact that a letter may be embarrassing to the employer and result in parents contacting the school alone is insufficient grounds for interfering with the freedom of speech. Even when assessing the limits of public servants' freedom of speech, the aim must be to reinforce fundamental rights.'[113]

5. Finnish Legal Science

43. There were no such fields of law as media law or communication law in Finland in the 1990s. Legal problems relating to the mass media or freedom of expression were discussed under constitutional law, administrative law, criminal law and tort law. However, interest in media law increased following some high-profile court cases with extremely high compensation awards, and when Finland received its first ECtHR judgments for breaches of human rights in mass media cases in 2004. Since then, media and communication law and various questions concerning the scope and dimensions of freedom of expression have attracted much interest in the Finnish legal literature. The first Yearbook of Media Law was published in 2004 by a research group led by professor (now dean) Pia Letto-Vanamo, and it was the first step towards the institutionalization of media and communication law.

A number of doctoral theses have been published since then. These and other legal writings on this topic have made an important contribution to Finnish legal science and jurisprudence.[114] The first professorship in communication law was established in 2013 and the post was filled in 2014.

113. The full text in Finnish is here http://www.eduskunta.fi/eoaratkaisut/eoae+5342/2013 (28.8.2019).
114. Some theses: Ollila 2001; Tiilikka 2007 (today Korpisaari); Hoikka 2009; Neuvonen 2012; Rautiainen 2012; Alén-Savikko 2014. Paukku's (today Fromond) licenciate thesis (Paukku 2005) is also worth mentioning as well as professor (Copyright Law) Pihlajarinne's production (for example her thesis 2010) and Savola's thesis (Savola 2015).

Part I. Freedom of Expression

Chapter 1. General Introduction

44. Freedom of expression and right of access to information is guaranteed under section 12 of the Constitution of Finland (731/1999). It states:

> Everyone has the freedom of expression. Freedom of expression entails the right to express, disseminate and receive information, opinions and other communications without prior prevention by anyone. More detailed provisions on the exercise of the freedom of expression are to be laid down by an Act. Provisions on restrictions relating to audiovisual programmes that are necessary for the protection of children may be laid down by an Act.
>
> Documents and recordings in the possession of the authorities are public, unless their publication has for compelling reasons been specifically restricted by an Act. Everyone has the right of access to public documents and recordings.[115]

In Finland, as in other countries, freedom of expression has been limited by parliamentary acts. The Criminal Code (39/1889) is the most important Act when it comes to restricting freedom of expression. Liability for damages is regulated by the Tort Liability Act (*vahingonkorvauslaki* 412/1974; TLA).[116] This means that if somebody has suffered mental distress or so-called pure economic loss due to a newspaper article or image – whether published in print or on the internet – the damage is compensated for according to the conditions stated in the Tort Liability Act. The threshold for compensating for such losses is relatively high because, in addition to the basic requirement of negligence, certain other conditions must be met before compensation is granted. In addition, the Copyright Act (404/1961) and many other acts include restrictions on freedom of expression.

As Finland is a member of the Council of Europe, limitations to freedom of expression must comply with the demands of the ECHR and Finnish jurisprudence comes under the supervision of the ECtHR.

115. Unofficial translation by the Ministry of Justice.
116. Unofficial translation http://www.finlex.fi/fi/laki/kaannokset/1974/en19740412.pdf (28.8.2019).

§1. CONSTITUTIONAL FRAMEWORK

45. Freedom of expression and right of access to information are guaranteed in section 12 of the Finnish Constitution as cited above. Therefore, freedom of expression entails both the right to express and disseminate information and the right to receive information without prior restriction from anyone, be they private persons or entities or public authorities. Thus, the prohibition of prior restraints is at the core of Finnish freedom of expression. The prohibition of prior restraints includes the checking or revision of content as well as the licensing of rights included in freedom of expression or other infringements to freedom of expression. However, due to the limited range of frequencies, licensing is permitted in broadcasting, because in that way it is possible to guarantee diverse programming and provide several companies the opportunity to pursue business activity in the sector.[117]

According to the preparatory works of the Finnish Constitution, freedom of expression – as guaranteed in the Finnish Constitution – is to be given a broad interpretation, as is understood in international conventions on human rights.[118] As Finland is a member of the Council of Europe, the ECHR and its Article 10 on freedom of expression also guarantee freedom of expression. Freedom of expression and the right to information are also protected through Article 11 of the Charter of Fundamental Rights of the EU and in Article 19, subsection two of the United Nation's Universal Declaration of Human Rights. Article 13 of the Convention on the Rights of the Child also guarantees freedom of expression, which includes the freedom to seek, receive and impart information of all kinds. The above mentioned, as well as other human rights, have significance within the Finnish legal system because according to the Finnish Constitution, section 22, 'The public authorities shall guarantee the observance of basic rights and liberties and human rights.'

46. In practice, the Finnish courts pay great attention to the practice of the ECtHR and the CJEU so as to interpret freedom of expression in a manner consistent with European court practice. Unfortunately this has not always been successful, and as a result the ECtHR has ruled against Finland twenty times in cases involving freedom of expression. In 2018, not any violation of any human right was found against Finland.[119]

Freedom of expression guarantees the freedom of communication in general. It applies to all kinds of expression, be they political, scientific, artistic, religious, entertainment or commercial. It primarily guarantees a democratic society by affecting the creation of public opinion and the exercise of public power, but it also protects the individual's right to express him/herself. The main purpose of the provision concerning freedom of expression is to ensure the free formation of opinion, which is a prerequisite of a democratic society, to guarantee open public debate and to guarantee the free development and plurality of the mass media and the possibility

---

117. *See* Statements of the Constitutional Law Committee: PeVL 3/2010 vp, PeVL 61/2002 vp p. 2/I, PeVL 8/2002 vp p. 2/II, PeVL 19/1998 vp, 2–3. *See also* Ojanen – Tiilikka – Vairimaa 2012.
118. Government bill (HE 309/1993), 57.
119. European Court of Human Right: Violations by Article and by State, https://www.echr.coe.int/Documents/Stats_violation_1959_2018_ENG.pdf (30.10.2019).

of exercising public criticism.[120] Even though freedom of expression covers all kinds of expression, the protection of political debate – which is the core idea of freedom of expression – is stronger than protection of advertising or other commercial expression.[121]

Freedom of expression is not tied to any method of communication. Therefore, the scope of the provision of freedom of expression is neutral when it comes to the medium that is used.[122] Freedom of expression is thus protected in oral, written, musical and electronic communications or in any other form whatsoever. The provision also guarantees journalistic work before the message has even been published.[123]

47. According to the Finnish Constitution, fundamental rights belong to every human being. As a starting point, the protection of fundamental rights does not apply to legal entities such as companies and associations. However, when it comes to freedom of expression, the preparatory works refer to the protection of journalistic work, and therefore the provision can be interpreted in such a way that publishing and broadcasting companies, and other legal entities, also enjoy the constitutional protection of freedom of expression.

The fact that freedom of expression is a fundamental right affects Finnish jurisprudence in two ways: first, the role of freedom of expression as fundamental right must be taken into account in the legislative process, and, second, it affects the way the law is to be interpreted in every specific case. In Finland the constitutional guarantee of a fundamental right means that the potential for restricting that right is extremely limited, if not absent entirely. For example, killing or torture as breaches of the right to life is impossible under any conditions.

§2. Restrictions

48. The restriction of fundamental rights is only possible if all the following preconditions set by the Finnish Constitutional Law Committee are fulfilled:[124]

1) *The restriction is prescribed by law.* This means that legislative powers should not be delegated to a lower level than the law.

120. Government bill (HE 309/1993 vp), 56 and Fundamental Rights Committee Report (Perusoikeuskomitean mietintö, KM 2/1993), 82–83.
121. *See, e.g.* Statements of the Constitutional Law Committee: PeVL 3/1976 vp, PeVL 4/1976 vp, PeVL 2/1986 vp, PeVL 23/2000 vp, 6, PeVL 60/2001 vp, 3–4, PeVL 19/2002 vp, 2–3, PeVL 9/2004 vp, 7, PeVL 37/2005 vp, 4 and PeVL 54/2006 vp, 1 and KM 1992:3, 249, 252. On freedom of expression and advertising *see* Sami Manninen 1995b, 571–606, Ollila 2009, 276–291. On freedom of speech and artistic expression *see* Manninen 1995a, 361–371.
122. Government bill (HE 309/1993 vp), 5–6.
123. Government bill (HE 309/1993 vp), 57.
124. Constitutional Law Committee Report (PeVM 25/1994). *See also* Viljanen's doctoral thesis (Viljanen 2001), and the guide for law makers: 'Lainkirjoittajan opas, kansallisten säädösten kirjoittamista koskevat ohjeet' Ministry of Justice Finland: http://lainkirjoittaja.finlex.fi/4-perusoikeudet/4-1/ (28.8.2019).

2) *The law is precise and clearly defined:* the essential content of the restriction shall be indicated in the Act.
3) *The restriction is acceptable:* the basis on which the fundamental right is restricted should be acceptable in regard to the system of fundamental rights as a whole. Thus, the restriction may be based, for example, on the intention to protect some other fundamental right, or the intention to achieve some other kind of goal acceptable from the perspective of the entire fundamental rights system. When assessing the acceptability of the restriction, the European Convention on Human Rights and other international human rights treaties may also be relevant. The restriction must be not only acceptable but also in response to a weighty social need.
4) *Proportionality of the restriction:* The limitation of a fundamental right must be necessary to achieve an acceptable goal, and it must otherwise comply with the requirement of proportionality. A restriction is permissible only if the objective cannot be achieved by less intrusive means. Moreover, the restriction shall not go beyond what is justified, in view of the importance of the interest underlying the restriction when compared to that of the interest subject to the restriction. The interest of limiting a fundamental right must be balanced against the interest of protecting some other right.
5) *Immunity of the core area of a fundamental right:* the restriction of the core content of a fundamental right cannot be achieved by an ordinary law. Therefore, fundamental rights cannot be limited to the extent that it would invalidate their core content.
6) *Sufficient legal protection:* when fundamental rights are infringed, the State must guarantee adequate legal protection, such as the right to appeal.
7) *Compliance with the obligations of human rights:* infringements of fundamental rights must not be in conflict with Finland's international human rights obligations. The Finnish system of fundamental rights is closely linked to the content of international human rights conventions. Restrictions that would infringe Finland's binding international human rights treaties would be unconstitutional. Therefore, the interpretative harmonization of fundamental and human rights is considered important.

49. The right to privacy is guaranteed under section 10 of the Finnish Constitution. While the earlier 1919 Constitution already guaranteed the protection of honour, the sanctity of the home and the privacy of written correspondence and telephone communications, the right to privacy per se is one of the novelties of the new system on basic rights established by the 1995 constitutional reform and integrated into the new constitution of 2000.

According to section 10 of the Finnish Constitution:

> Everyone's private life, honour and the sanctity of the home are guaranteed. More detailed provisions on the protection of personal data are laid down by an Act.
>
> The secrecy of correspondence, telephony and other confidential communications is inviolable.

> Measures encroaching on the sanctity of the home which are necessary for the purpose of guaranteeing basic rights and liberties or for the investigation of crime may be laid down by an Act (817/2018).
>
> Limitations of the secrecy of communications may be imposed by an Act if they are necessary in the investigation of crimes that jeopardise the security of the individual or society or the sanctity of the home, at trials and security checks, during deprivation of liberty, and for the purpose of obtaining information on military activities or other such activities that pose a serious threat to national security (817/2018).[125]

The rights of freedom of expression and privacy are equal. This means that both in the legislative process and in interpreting the law, the two rights must be balanced in a way that is acceptable from a fundamental rights and human rights perspective. Today, this balancing is extremely prominent in defamation cases and cases concerning disseminating private information, where it is impossible to find a decision which fails to include the balancing and weighing of these interests.

Because the section on the right to privacy protects the home, while also concerning other aspects of privacy, it gives journalists (and also other persons) protection against several forms of police investigation and thus helps to secure the confidentiality of journalistic sources. For example, the provisions on the authorities' right to investigate private correspondence and other communications are rather strict. As *Saraviita* writes:

> The Constitutional Law Committee has given strict interpretative rules on legislation which give rights to the police and customs investigators to gather information on telecommunication, ordinary (postal) and electronic correspondence, discussions on the internet and on the use of electronic surveillance. The main rule is that in the case of surveillance which violates the sanctity of the home, investigators must have firm grounds for concrete suspicion of a serious crime and the permission for investigation must be given by a Court of Law.[126]

As *Saraviita* suggests, the protection of privacy originally protected the sanctity of the home, but today it also helps to ensure the privacy of information.[127] Privacy must be guaranteed against interference from public authorities and also in the relationship between an individual and other individuals or private entities, such as media companies. At the end of the 1990s and in the first decade of the twenty-first century, there were several court cases where journalists were fined for defamation or disseminating private information.[128] Journalists and media companies have also

125. Unofficial translation by the Ministry of Justice.
126. Saraviita 2012, 271.
127. Saraviita 2012, 272.
128. Of those cases that have finally been decided by the ECtHR *see Karhuvaara and Kustannusosakeyhtiö Iltalehti v. Finland* (16.11.2004), *Selistö v. Finland* (16.11.2004), *Eerikäinen and others v. Finland* (10.2.2009), Yleisradio and others v. Finland (12.6.2009; inadmissible), *Flinkkilä and others v. Finland* (6.4.2010), *Ruokanen v. Finland* (6.4.2010), *Tuomela and others v. Finland* (6.4.2010), *Soila v. Finland* (6.4.2010), *Jokitaipale and others v. Finland* (6.4.2010), *Niskasaari and others v. Finland* (6.7.2010), *Saaristo and others v. Finland* (12.10.2010), *Reinboth and others*

been ordered to pay compensation for the mental distress caused by articles or programmes. The level of compensation has usually ranged from EUR 3,500 to EUR 10,000, depending on the degree of falsity of the statement, the position of the victim and how easily he/she could have been recognized from the story, the severity of the statement and how widely it was disseminated.

---

v. Finland (25.1.2011), *Lahtonen v. Finland* (17.1.2012), *Ojala and Etukeno Oy v. Finland* (14.1.2014; no violation), *Ruusunen v. Finland* (14.1.2014; no violation), Pentikäinen v. Finland (GC 20.10.2015; no violation) and *Satakunnan Markkinapörssi Oy and Satamedia Oy v. Finland* (GC 7.6.2017; no violation).

Part II. Regulation of Journalism and (Print) Media

Chapter 1. The Profession of Journalism and Technology Neutrality

§1. Notion

50. Journalism is an open profession, as anyone can work as a journalist; there are no registration or notification requirements, nor is a specific education required. However, in practice, Finnish journalists are very well educated. There are nearly 15,000 members at the Union of Journalists in Finland (UJF). They work for the print media, broadcasting, publishing and new communications media. In 2017, 57% of union members were women. Women also account for over 70% of student members.[129] According to labour market research, made by Suomen Journalistiliitto (the Union of Journalists in Finland), 91% of journalists were at permanent employment relationship. The average total monthly income of a member of the union in April 2018 was EUR 3,795. The corresponding median earnings were slightly lower (EUR 3,671). Those who worked at the field of press media earned more than average (EUR 3,900).[130]

In general, no special rights are guaranteed to (professional) journalists.[131] Constitutional free speech and access to public documents are guaranteed for all while, for instance, the right to protect the confidentiality of sources is guaranteed to anyone who has published a message in public, irrespective of profession. Thereby, bloggers who write on web discussion sites have the same right as professional journalists to protect the confidentiality of their information sources. In market abuse

129. About the Union of Journalists in Finland: https://journalistiliitto.fi/en/about/about-ujf/ (30.10.2019).
130. SJL:n työmarkkinatutkimus 2018 (Labour Market Survey of the Union of Journalists in Finland 2018), made by Kantar TNS Oy/Sakari Nurmela, 2–3: https://journalistiliitto.fi/wp-content/uploads/2018/10/220401648_sjl_ty%C3%B6markkinatutkimus_2018_yhteenveto.pdf (7.10.2020).
131. In our opinion this is because the legislator has not found any reason for such special rights; everyone enjoys the same (wide) (constitutional) rights. Moreover, nowadays it would be difficult to define 'a journalist' entitled to enjoy such wider rights.

regulation of the EU,[132] Article 21, there is a special rule concerning disclosure or dissemination of information in the media.[133]

The Copyright Act (404/1961) also contains some exceptions and limitations to exclusive rights as well as other provisions which relate to media activity or journalism and which aim to protect the free flow of information necessary for freedom of expression. For example, section 25b of the Copyright Act includes provisions on including works in reports on current events on radio or television transmissions. Furthermore, provisions on extended collective licences (*see* § 26) enable mass use in the media sector, among others.[134]

§2. Subsidies to the Press

51. There are some measures providing financial support to the press. The Ministry of Culture and Education is responsible for matters concerning discretionary subsidies given to newspaper publishing.[135] The Government makes the decision to grant subsidies on the basis of proposals from the Ministry of Transport and Communications.

Discretionary subsidies may be granted to newspapers and online publications published in Swedish, Sámi, Karelian and Romanian languages as well as sign language. Also the production and publication of Sámi and Karelian material in conjunction with a Finnish and Swedish language newspapers can be supported. Subsidies are also granted to Swedish-language news services. The aim of subsidy is to promote freedom of expression and the diversity and plurality of media.

Applicants for subsidies must be newspapers or online publications within the meaning defined in the Government decree on press subsidies (*valtioneuvoston asetus sanomalehdistön tuesta* 389/2008).[136] According to the decree, a newspaper is a publication that is published at least once a week. An online publication means an electronic publication that is delivered through an open information network and to which new content is added at least three times a week. The total sum granted in press subsidies for 2018 was EUR 500,000.[137]

In previous years, the news activities of the public interest television channel MTV (a total of EUR 3 million) and the news agency STT[138] (EUR 1.5 million) have been supported.[139]

---

132. Regulation (EU) No 596/2014 of the European Parliament and of the Council of 16 April 2014 on market abuse (market abuse regulation) and repealing Directive 2003/6/EC of the European Parliament and of the Council and Commission Directives 2003/124/EC, 2003/125/EC and 2004/72/EC.
133. Before the market abuse regulation that was regulated in the Securities Markets Act (*Arvopaperimarkkinalaki* 746/2012).
134. For a detailed account from 1999, *see* Bruun 1999.
135. Earlier the responsible ministry was The Ministry of Transport and Communications.
136. The decree (in Finnish): http://www.finlex.fi/fi/laki/ajantasa/2008/20080389 (28.8.2019).
137. *See* decision OKM/2018/58 by the Ministry of Education and Culture, https://minedu.fi/paatos?decisionId=0900908f805d34d3 (28.8.2019).
138. Oy Suomen Tietotoimisto – Finska Notisbyrån Ab (Finnish News Agency STT).
139. Unpublished memorandum of the Ministry of Transport and Communications, 3.12.2020, VN/9067/2020.

52. The development of new digital services aimed at the Finnish public was promoted with the media innovation support.[140] In spring 2014, the Government decided on fixed-term innovation support to the sum of EUR 30 million divided over the following three years. The support represented temporary transition assistance, the goal of which was to ease the media sector's transition to the new digital age. Between 2015 and 2018, the support was administered and granted by Business Finland (prior to 2018 called TEKES, the Finnish Funding Agency for Technology and Innovation).[141]

53. Finnish political parties receive party subsidies, which are provided for in the Act on Political Parties (*puoluelaki* 10/1969).[142] Party subsidies are granted by the Government in accordance with the number of seats in Parliament, and the use of the subsidy is supervised by the Ministry of Justice. In the past, a certain part of party subsidies were earmarked for the newspapers of political parties, but today the parties can use the party subsidies as they wish.[143] In practice, however, a part of the subsidies goes to the support of parties' communications activities.[144]

Due to COVID-19 pandemic, the Finnish government will grant EUR 7.5 million subsidies to Finnish journalism.[145] The purpose of the subsidy is to support journalistic media that has suffered because of COVID-19 pandemia. The aim of the subsidy is to support diverse journalistic content and its supply especially at local and regional level.[146] The committee agrees that the content of journalism will not be assessed when the subsidies are provided. The committee is also preparing a more permanent support model for journalism.

---

140. *See* press release of The Ministry of Transport and Communications, http://www.lvm.fi/pressreleases/4421900/minister-kiuru-media-support-for-new-digital-services (28.8.2019).
141. The final report of the project (4Front and Gaia Consulting / Business Finland: 'Median innovaatiotuen arviointi. Loppuraportti.' Raportti 6/2018) is here https://www.businessfinland.fi/globalassets/julkaisut/median_innovaatiotuen_arviointi.pdf (31.10.2019).
142. Unofficial English translation; amendments up to 653/1992 included: http://www.finlex.fi/fi/laki/kaannokset/1969/en19690010.pdf (28.8.2019).
143. *See* Laki puoluelain muuttamisesta 1688/2015.
144. Yle Uutiset: 'Puolueille myönnettiin puolueavustuksia liki 30 miljoonaa euroa' (Nearly EUR 30 million of subsidies was granted to parties) 26.1.2016 https://yle.fi/uutiset/3-8626255 (13.8.2020).
145. https://valtioneuvosto.fi/hanke?tunnus=LVM040:00/2020 (13.8.2020). The author of this book, Päivi Korpisaari, is a member at the committee that sets out the eligibility criteria. *See also* the press release of the Ministry of Transport and Communications: COVID-19 support to help the media, https://www.lvm.fi/-/covid-19-support-to-help-the-media-1233741 (accessed 3.12.2020).
146. Valtioneuvoston asetus valtionavustuksesta journalistisen sisällön edistämiseen. Liikenne- ja viestintäministeriön muistio (Government decree regarding government aid for promoting journalistic contents. Memorandum of the Ministry of Transport and Communications) 15.6.2020, VN/9067/2020, https://api.hankeikkuna.fi/asiakirjat/28728680-1fc0-44dc-a366-2b4d3e6f6ac9/403f7144-b676-4890-bebc-8d23a6b97288/LIITE_20200618071017.pdf (20.8.2020).

Chapter 2. The Rights of Journalists

§1. Role of Journalists as Watchdogs of Society

54. Even though journalists have no special rights in Finland, Finland has been consistently ranked top in international comparison of press freedom. According to the Press Freedom Index, compiled by the association Reporters Without Borders, Finland was the top country for press freedom in 2016, a ranking it has held for the sixth year running. In 2017 Finland was third, in 2018 fourth and in 2019 second at the Press Freedom ranking.[147]

55. Even though there is no special legislation guaranteeing journalists the right to practise their profession to the best of their abilities, in recent years, Finnish jurisprudence and court practice has emphasized the importance of freedom of expression and the right to receive information when published information has a wider societal significance or concerns a matter of public interest. Thus, in court cases involving, for example, defamation, freedom of speech and the importance of free and independent journalism are taken into consideration.

The function of the press as a watchdog entails, for example, that the journalists have the right to criticize politicians and those who exercise economic, political or administrative power. However, as mentioned earlier, at the level of statutes journalists have no special rights; freedom of speech is equally guaranteed for everyone. The decisive factor is not if the author is a journalist or not but, whether the matter is of wider societal interest and whether the statement is true, or there are reasonable grounds for statements. If the matter concerns disseminating private information, whether the information relates to a person's public role as a politician or holder of another powerful position is also of relevance.

56. The Finnish case *Pentikäinen v. Finland* (application 11882/10; judgment 20.10.2015; split decision 13-4), concerning the rights of a newspaper photographer was judged at the Grand Chamber of the ECtHR. The applicant alleged, in particular, that the police attempted to prevent him from practising his profession as a journalist and photographer and thus violated his freedom of expression when he was arrested at a mildly violent demonstration and subsequently convicted of disobeying the police, who had sealed off the area of the demonstration and ordered the protesters to disperse when the demonstration had turned violent.

Despite the conviction, not any sanctions were imposed on the photographer. The only result was finding him guilty of disobeying the police. Both the Chamber and Grand Chamber found no violation of freedom of expression, as the domestic courts

147. According to the website of Reporters Without Borders, the World Press Freedom Index 'ranks the performance of 180 countries according to a range of criteria that include media pluralism and independence, respect for the safety and freedom of journalists, and the legislative, institutional and infrastructural environment in which the media operate.' *See* closer https://index.rsf.org/#!/presentation (28.8.2019) and https://rsf.org/en/finland (28.8.2019). Part of the information is from https://rsf.org/index2014/en-index2014.php. The site was accessed 28.8.2019, but it does not exist anymore. It is worth mentioning that the way the index has been compiled has also been criticized. For example, no information is provided on who the country reporters are.

had ruled that there were justifiable reasons for the police to seal off the area and order the dispersal of the protesters. Since these legitimate orders were not obeyed, the police were thus entitled to arrest and detain the demonstrators. The Court also noted that the police had given the media the opportunity to move outside the police line. Two other photographers who were in the sealed-off area had indeed left the scene at this point, but the applicant had declined to enter the separated, secured area for the press, choosing to stay among the demonstrators even after the order to disperse. Moreover, it was not entirely clear at what stage the police learned that the applicant was a journalist.

The court also paid attention to the fact that the prosecution was directed against altogether eighty-six defendants who were accused of several types of offences, so the photographer was not the only one charged. The Court stated that journalists may sometimes face a conflict between the general duty to abide by ordinary criminal law, of which journalists are not absolved, and their professional duty to obtain and disseminate information. When balancing all the facts, the Court also emphasized that, while in some cases, the fact of a person's conviction may be more important than the minor nature of the penalty imposed, in the present case, the applicant's conviction had no adverse material consequences for him. Because no sanction was imposed, the conviction was not even entered in his criminal record. The applicant's conviction amounted only to a formal finding of the offence committed by him and this, as such, could hardly, if at all, have any 'chilling effect' on persons taking part in protest actions or on the work of journalists at large. Also taking into account the margin of appreciation, the Court concluded that the domestic authorities had based their decisions on relevant and sufficient reasons and struck a fair balance between the competing interests at stake. The authorities had not deliberately prevented or hindered the media from covering the demonstration. Indeed, the applicant was not prevented from carrying out his work as a journalist. The Court therefore concluded that the interference with the applicant's right to freedom of expression could have been 'necessary in a democratic society' within the meaning of Article 10 of the Convention.

This is also an example of the police trying to guarantee the press the opportunity to practise their profession when reporting a violent demonstration, because the police had provided a separated, secured area for the press. Thus, police's actions illustrate that even though we have no special legislation guaranteeing the freedom of the press, the Finnish public authorities and courts usually understand the value of press freedom and take it into consideration in their actions.

As the detention of the photographer shows, however, the Finnish authorities demand that the rules are followed. It may also be noted, that even if the presence in the sealed-off area of a single photographer can be viewed as relatively harmless, if many journalists had stayed among violent demonstrators, it would have been difficult for the police to guarantee their safety. Moreover, the police would have been unable to use force, as it would have targeted demonstrators and journalists alike. Thus, it would be difficult to have a general rule that the journalists need not obey police orders.

The outcome can, however, also be criticized. It is, for example, worth notifying that the detention lasted nearly eighteen hours, which is a relatively long time. Some of the dissenting judges in Grand Chamber stated that: the 'Grand Chamber judgment is a missed opportunity for the Court to reinforce, in line with its consistent case law, the special nature and importance of the press in providing transparency and accountability for the exercise of governmental power by upholding the rights of journalists to observe public demonstrations or other Article 11 activities effectively and unimpeded, so long as they do not take a direct and active part in hostilities. Recent events in many European countries demonstrate, more than ever, the necessity of safeguarding the fundamental role of the press in obtaining and disseminating to the public information on all aspects of governmental activity. That is, after all, one of the crucial elements of the democratic ideal protected by the European Convention on Human Rights.'

§2. The Independence of Journalists

57. The Act on the Exercise of Freedom of Expression in Mass Media (460/2003; later Freedom of expression Act or FEA) contains more detailed provisions on the exercise of the freedom of expression in the mass media. It applies to all forms of mass media: print, radio, television and the internet.

There are, however, some special rules that apply only to periodicals, network publications[148] and television and radio programmes.[149] For example, according to section 4(1) of the FEA, the duty to designate a responsible editor only exists for periodicals, network publications and programmes. Several responsible editors may also be designated, but the parts of the publication or network publication or the programmes for which the editor-in-chief is responsible must be clearly defined. Persons of 15 or more years of age who have not been declared bankrupt and whose mental capacity is unimpaired are eligible as responsible editors.

According to section 4(2) of the FEA, it is the duty of the responsible editor to direct and supervise editorial work, decide on the content of a periodical, network publication or programme, and perform the other tasks assigned to him or her by that Act. The provision that it is the editor-in-chief who decides on media content, guarantees the independence of editorial work. Not even the media owners can order the editor-in-chief to publish certain content; although in reality the editor-in-chief would be changed if the owners were constantly dissatisfied with the content of the publication or programme.

According to Chapter 2, section 4 of the Consumer Protection Act (*kuluttajansuojalaki* 38/1978),[150] marketing must clearly show its commercial purpose and on whose behalf the product or service is being marketed. Chapter 26 of the Act on

148. Here, with regard to the FEA, network publication and online publication are used as synonyms.
149. According to s. 2, subss 5 and 6 a periodical means a publication intended to be issued regularly, at least four times per year and a network publication means a set of network messages, arranged into a coherent whole comparable to a periodical from material produced or processed by the publisher, and intended to be issued regularly.
150. *See* the unofficial and not-updated English translation by the Ministry of Justice; amendments up to 29/2005 included (17.5.2019): https://www.finlex.fi/fi/laki/kaannokset/1978/en19780038.pdf (28.8.2019).

Electronic Communications Services (917/2014) also contains some provisions concerning marketing, for example, on product placement and sponsorship. According to section 214(1), marketing must be recognizable; thus, hidden advertising is prohibited by law. The ideal is that the work of marketing and publishing professionals remains clearly delineated in order to prevent the companies from advertising in newspapers, magazines and radio from affecting journalistic content. Unfortunately, today the media is in dire need of additional income, and consequently neither the editorial process nor journalistic content have always remained independent from advertisers. Consequently, there has been hidden advertising in newspapers, magazines and radio programmes. This is why the self-regulatory body, the Council for Mass Media (CMM), has issued so many notifications to different media actors:[151]

> For example, a notice (5723/SL/15) finding breach of good journalistic practice concerns an advertisement in the form of an article in a newspaper. No express indication of the material being an advertisement was included. Reader feedback was immediately received but it had been published alongside the paper's reply only after a few days. Cf. a decision (5729/AL/15) where no breach was found where advertorials were concerned: Two advertorials in a magazine imitated stories, but the word 'ad' (in Finn. *mainos*) and the logos of the advertisers were shown. They were separable from editorial content.
>
> *See also* a notice (5610/AL/14) where breach was found as the online content of a magazine did not clearly separate commercial and editorial content. Advertisements were integrated in a story among pictorial links whereby an express indication of advertisements should have been included also with regard to the links, not only in the beginning and end of the story. Cf. no breach was found (5014/SL/12) where online content of a newspaper provided both editorial and commercial material related to elections: alongside information gathered by the editorial staff the candidates could have additional information published in return for payment. An indication was provided (in Finn. *ilmoitus*). The CMM however noted that the public would have been served better had the separation been clearer; this was also important for the maintenance of confidence in the media.

58. The Guidelines for Journalists also contain provisions on journalists' professional status and independence. According to section 1, a journalist is primarily responsible to readers, listeners and viewers, who have the right to know about events occurring in society. Section 2 states that '[d]ecisions concerning the content of media must be made in accordance with journalistic principles. The power to make such decisions must not under any circumstances be surrendered to any party outside the editorial office'. The third section states that a 'journalist has the right and obligation to resist pressure or persuasion that attempts to steer, prevent or limit

151. For examples of radio stations: 5459/R/14; 5360/R/13; 5357/R/13; 5327/R/13; 6787/R/18; papers, magazines and television: 5623/SL/14; 5615/AL/14; 5610/AL/14; 5472/SL/14; 5345/SL/13; 5312/SL/13; 5140/AL/13; 5107/AL/13; 5069/SL/12, and 4988/SL/12; 7012/SL/18; 6874/SL/18; 6738/SL/17; 6689/SL/17 and online publication and web blog 5499/SL/14; 7027/MTV/18. All decisions are published at Council for Mass Media's website https://www.jsn.fi/en/ (28.9.2019).

communications'. In 2017 the Council for Mass Media decided a case concerning the independence of journalistic decision-making (6398/YLE/16 JA 6401/YLE/16). The public broadcasting company Yle had reported on its website about the Prime Minister's connection to a company that had received an order from a company, which was sponsored by the state of Finland. The headline of the story was 'Company owned by the relatives of Prime Minister have an order of 500 000 euros from Terrafame company' (Pääministerin sukulaisten omistamalla yrityksellä noin puolen miljoonan euron tilaus Terrafamesta). After the story was published, the Prime Minister Juha Sipilä had sent several text messages to YLE's editor-in-chief. He had sent the first message before he had even read the story. In it, he criticized the perspective of the story, based on the questions asked by the journalist, who had interviewed him. Only in one of the messages that was addressed to the editor-in-chief, he referred to a matter he considered to be a factual error. In addition, he sent several emails to the editor-in-chief of Yle and to the journalist, who had asked him for comments, where he criticized Yle in general. Later the same day he forwarded more than a dozen emails he had received from citizens as feedback.

59. According to Council for Mass Media, there were no mistakes or very negative publicity in the story. Nevertheless, after the Prime Minister had contacted the editor-in-chief, Yle made some changes to the story. Yle also prohibited the journalist who had written the story, to present her views in television main news programme and also declined publishing two further stories about the matter, which had already been planned to be published. Editor-in-chief and Prime Minister also agreed, that the Prime Minister will not attend the television programme where he had earlier agreed to come, and that no further reporting on the matter will be published. After these occurrences some journalists of Yle wrote some articles on what had happened. Some persons then made a complaint to the Council for Mass Media, arguing that guidelines 1–3 had been breached.[152]

60. The CMM stated that the editor-in-chief has the power and responsibility to decide on publication. This means that he can also decide on publishing restrictions, and this is not a restriction on journalists' freedom of expression. The CMM emphasized that while the editor-in-chief has the power to decide on the content of the media, he also bears the responsibility to ensuring that his media follows the Guidelines for Journalists. According to the guidelines, the editor-in-chief must not delegate the power of journalistic decision-making to outsiders, and all decisions regarding the content of the media must be made on journalistic grounds. The Council noted that in this case there were indications that the editor-in-chief had yielded to pressure. Yle had the right to make changes to the story even though there were

152.

1. A journalist is primarily responsible to the readers, listeners and viewers, who have the right to know what is happening in society.
2. Decisions concerning the content of media must be made in accordance with journalistic principles. The power to make such decisions must not under any circumstances be surrendered to any party outside the editorial office.
3. The journalist has the right and obligation to resist pressure or persuasion that attempts to steer, prevent or limit communications.

no errors on facts. However, according to CMM, it was obvious that the Prime Minister's feedback was not dealt with in the usual manner, since the story did not contain false information nor was the Prime Minister put in a bad light in order to cause negative publicity. Nevertheless, the editor-in-chief of Yle made a number of changes quickly even though there was no journalistic justification for those. The CMM voted 6-6, and the Chairman's vote was decisive. The Council considered that good journalistic practice had been breached.

Probably this occasion was one of the most important reasons why Finland fell to fourth place in press freedom index from the first place. But one can also argue that the actions of journalists under the pressure in this case and decision of CMM show that the journalistic independence is a very important value in Finnish journalism.

According to section 4 of the Guidelines for Journalists, journalists are not allowed to misuse their position or deal with issues that may lead to potential personal gain. They must also not demand or receive benefits that are likely to compromise their personal independence or professional ethics.[153] The next section states that journalists are entitled to refuse assignments that conflict with the law, their personal convictions, or good journalistic practice. Finally, section 6 states that if a journalist is handling issues concerning their own media (in a wide sense) or their owners, the context should be made clear to the public.

§3. Journalists' Right to Protect Their Information Sources

61. Journalists' right to use confidential information and anonymous sources is considered as one of the cornerstones of press freedom and democracy.[154] The aim of the *reporter's privilege* – the protection from being compelled to testify about confidential information or sources – is to safeguard the public's right to information on matters of social importance.[155] In Finland, freedom of expression and access to information is guaranteed in section 12 of the Constitution of Finland (731/1999). Although the Constitution does not explicitly mention the right to protect sources of information, the confidentiality of sources can nevertheless be regarded as an essential part of freedom of expression.[156]

62. In the era of traditional media (print, television, radio), it was relatively easy to define the 'reporter' entitled to this privilege, i.e., which individuals and media

153. For condemnatory decisions, *see* 6969/AL/18, 6686/YLE/17 and 6512/PL/17 and acquittals 6872&SL/18 and 6831//PL/18.

154. *See, e.g.*, ECtHR cases *Goodwin v. United Kingdom* (GC, 27.3.1996); *Financial Times Ltd et al. v. United Kingdom* (15.12.2009; vote 11-7) and *Sanoma Uitgevers B.V. v. the Netherlands* (GC 14.9.2010).

155. This chapter on Journalists' right to protect their sources of information is based on the presentation *Reporter's Privilege in the Era of the Internet*, which the author (at the time, named Päivi Tiilikka) and Dr (Soc.Sci.) Tuomo Mörä gave at the Research Conference on Communication, Information and Internet Policy in Arlington, Virginia, 22.9.2012. The eleven-page presentation is available at the following address: http://hq.ssrn.com/submissions/MyPapers.cfm?partid=1820352 (28.8.2019).

156. *See* closer Tiilikka 2008, 34.

were granted protection under the law. However, the internet has challenged traditional conceptions, and it is no longer clear who is to be qualified as a journalist and who or what should be protected by the reporter's privilege. For these reasons, lawmakers in Finland have decided to give the right to protect the confidentiality of sources of information to any author of a message provided to the public irrespective of that person's profession.

The right to protect the confidentiality of sources of information is regulated in section 16 of the Act on the Exercise of Freedom of Expression in Mass Media (460/2003), and it reads as follows:

> *Section 16 – Confidentiality of sources and the right to anonymous expression*
> The originator of a message provided to the public, the publisher and the broadcaster are entitled to preserve the confidentiality of the source of the information in the message. In addition, the publisher and the broadcaster are entitled to maintain the confidentiality of the identity of the originator of the message.
>
> Also a person who has become aware of the confidential information referred to in subsection (1) while in the service of the originator of the message, the publisher or the broadcaster is similarly entitled to maintain that confidentiality.
>
> Separate provisions apply to the duty to disclose confidential information referred to in subsection (1) in a pre-trial investigation or court proceedings.[157]

As stated in the above-mentioned provision, the right to protect the confidentiality of information sources applies to anyone who has authored a message or delivered it to the public, regardless of whether that person is a journalist. Moreover, if a person becomes aware of confidential information while in the service of the author of the message, the publisher, or the broadcaster, that person has an equal right to protect the source of that information. The confidentiality of sources is thus not a right that belongs to the sources of information themselves. Consequently, it is not a crime or breach of regulations for journalists or other authors of a message to reveal their sources. Of course, in practice, journalists seldom reveal their sources because this would hamper the acquisition of information in the future. In addition, revealing the sources would in most of the cases be against good journalistic ethics as stated in the Guidelines for Journalists and interpreted by the Council for Mass Media. Section 14 of the Guidelines for Journalists reads as follows:

> The journalist is entitled and duty-bound to conceal the identity of any person who has provided confidential information by agreement with the source. If the publication of information that is in the public interest results in highly negative publicity, it is desirable that the editorial office makes public how the reliability of the anonymous source and the information obtained from it has been assured.[158]

157. Unofficial translation by the Ministry of Justice.
158. *See* http://www.jsn.fi/en/guidelines_for_journalists/ (28.8.2019).

63. The previous editions of the Guidelines (prior to 2011) had only imposed on journalists the duty to conceal the identity of information sources. Now, however, journalists have the right and duty to conceal their information sources. Revelation of information sources might be appropriate in exceptional cases where, for example, the source of information has deliberately misled the journalist. However, no such case has come to the attention of the CMM. Interestingly, the CMM has discussed an alleged breach of confidentiality in a case where an anonymous official had been ready to leak information against payment and the media reported on the issue in its news coverage; however, no breach was found since confidentiality had not been agreed upon (*see* 5660/TV/14).[159]

The right to preserve the confidentiality of sources can be removed, under certain conditions, in either a pre-trial investigation or trial. These exceptions are defined in the Criminal Investigation Act (*esitutkintalaki* 449/1987[160]), currently section 7:8, and the Code of Judicial Procedure (*oikeudenkäymiskaari* 4/1734),[161] section 17:20. In a pre-trial investigation, the confidentiality of a source of information can only be broken in the case of serious crimes, which means crimes where the maximum penalty is at least six years of imprisonment. In a trial, this can also occur when the information has been given in breach of an obligation to maintain secrecy that carries a legal sanction. The conditions for removing the protection are, and have been, broader in court proceedings than in pre-trial investigations. However, such 'secrecy-cases' have been very seldom in courts, as the police have rarely been able to investigate them so as to identify the person concerned, and therefore no charges have been raised.[162]

The provisions on confidentiality of sources were amended in June 2015 with entry into force timed at 1 January 2016.[163] In general, obligations and rights of witnesses to refrain from testimony in the Criminal Investigation Act correspond to the ones provided in Chapter 17 of the Code of Judicial Procedure (7:8(1) Criminal Investigation Act). Notwithstanding this, a witness is obliged to testify where the investigated crime or attempt or accessory thereto has a maximum penalty of at least six years of imprisonment in addition to which the court must be able to oblige the witness to testify pursuant to *inter alia* section 17:20(2) of the Code of Judicial Procedure (7:8(2), point 2 Criminal Investigation Act).

64. According to the Code of Judicial Procedure, the originator of a message, publisher, and programme provider in the meaning of the FEA are entitled to refrain

159. Available at http://www.jsn.fi/sisalto/5660-tv-14/?search=l%C3%A4hdesuoja (28.8.2019).
160. Unofficial translation by the Ministry of Justice; amendments up to 733/2015 included: http://www.finlex.fi/fi/laki/kaannokset/1997/en19970689.pdf (28.8.2019).
161. Unofficial translation by the Ministry of Justice; amendments up to 732/2015 included: https://www.finlex.fi/fi/laki/kaannokset/1734/en17340004.pdf (28.8.2019).
162. For more, *see* Tiilikka 2008, 36–38; Tiilikka 2010, 50–51; cf. Report of the Legal Affairs Committee (LaVM 9/1986 vp).
163. For more on the 2016 reform, *see* Government bill (HE 46/2014 vp). *See also* Government bill (HE 245/2014 vp). The reform was reported by Anette Alén-Savikko in the context of the 'Study on Investigative Journalism' in July 2015 (*see* European Centre for Press and Media Freedom: https://ec.europa.eu/digital-agenda/en/media-freedom-pilot-projects) (28.8.2019).

from testifying on the identity of sources or creators (17:20(1)). Those in their service and assistance are provided the same right (§ 22(2)) while the right persists even if the position is lost (§ 22(1)). However, the above-mentioned persons may be obliged to answer if the prosecuted crime is one with a maximum penalty of at least six years of imprisonment or one that concerns a duty to non-disclosure being infringed in a punishable manner (17:20(2)).

Furthermore, an exception to a right or duty to refrain from testifying is included in 17:9(3) of the Code of Judicial Procedure concerning information on the unjustified obtaining, revelation, or utilization of which is under charges. It was deemed necessary to obtain such information in order to impose criminal liability. However, in pre-trial investigation, an exception to the general rule on witnessing which concerns investigated crimes where there is no duty or right to refrain from testimony in court pursuant to the above section (17:9(3)) does not apply to persons referred to in 17:20(1) of the Code of Judicial Procedure (7:8(2), point 3 Criminal Investigation Act). This means, for instance, publishers and programme providers. According to the preparatory works, section 17:9(3) applies where industrial espionage or secrecy offences are concerned whereas the derogation was tailored for confidentiality of sources.[164]

The 2016 reform basically preserves the substance as provided by the law previously in force; minor changes were made to the wording and numbering as well as to the division of provisions into sections. Previously, attempt and accessory to a crime were also mentioned in the Code of Judicial Procedure while the reference to secrecy offences was different in wording. For its part, the right of assistants was provided together with the main persons. The Government bill notes a purpose to update and clarify the provisions as well as to include express references to the Code of Judicial Procedure where provisions of the Criminal Investigation Act are concerned.[165] Even if derogations from the rights and duties of witnesses are in principle similar in scope in both the act and the code in question, the confidentiality of sources remains an important exception. Changes have however been discussed: indeed, the Government bill (HE 46/2014 vp) notes a previous Committee Report (2009:2) which was inclined to weaken the protection of confidentiality, albeit under strict conditions, where secrecy offences were concerned. No proposal on the matter was subsequently included in Government bill (HE 222/2010 vp). The preparatory works of the 2016 reform point to the fact that there has been no reason for reassessment since.[166] Indeed, the CMM gave its statement (4152/L/09) on the 2009 Report whereby it declared a negative stance on weakening the confidentiality of sources.[167]

164. Government bill (HE 46/2014 vp), 58–59, 146.
165. Government bill (HE 46/2014 vp), 79–81, 144–146, 147–149.
166. *See* Government bill (HE 46/2014 vp), 144 ff., esp. 145; *see also* Government bill (HE 222/2010 vp), 159.
167. Available in Finnish at http://www.jsn.fi/sisalto/4152-l-09/?search=l%C3%A4hdesuoja (28.8.2019).

65. It should also be noted that restrictions on confiscation and copying are included in Chapter 7 of the Coercive Measures Act (*pakkokeinolaki* 806/2011):[168] section 3(1)–(2) note that a document may not be confiscated or copied to be used as evidence if it can be assumed to contain material, in which a person entitled to protect his/her information sources may refuse to testify, and the document is in the possession of that person or in the possession of a person in whose benefit the obligation or the right to remain silent has been provided. However, the ban does not apply where a person referred to in 17:20(1) of the Code of Judicial Procedure *consents* or where the crime fulfils the above-mentioned requirements regarding punishment (minimum six years of imprisonment as a maximum penalty) and the court could oblige to testify, *inter alia*, pursuant to 17:20(2) of the Code. However, the exception to the ban in cases referred to in 17:9(3) of the Code of Judicial Procedure (breaches of duty to non-disclosure) does not apply where persons referred to in 17:20(1) of the Code are concerned, that is where objects are in their possession (7:3(3), points 2–4).[169]

Moreover, Chapter 8 of the Coercive Measures Act contains provisions on searches of homes, premises and devices, among others. A special search of a domicile, defined in section 1(3), targets premises in which the object assumedly reveals information for which there is a duty or right not to testify pursuant to 17:10–14, 16, 20–21 of the Code of Judicial Procedure and in respect of which confiscation or copying is denied pursuant to 7:3 of the Coercive Measures Act. Thus, this also applies where confidentiality of sources is concerned.[170] The prerequisites for such a search also include suspicion of a crime with at least six months of imprisonment, among others (8:2 Coercive Measures Act). Moreover, a search ombudsman (*etsintävaltuutettu*) must be appointed to oversee the search so that information referred to in section 1(3) is not targeted (8:7).[171]

Alongside the amendments concerning criminal investigations and proceedings in general courts, the previous Administrative Judicial Procedure Act (currently Administrative Procedure Act) came to include an express provision on the witnesses' right to refuse statement, including where confidentiality of sources is concerned. Previously, a reference was made to selected provisions of the Code of Judicial Procedure. The new section 39b includes provisions whereby a witness does not have to testify if information pursuant to section 16 FEA is targeted (§ 39 b(3), point 2). The amending Act 799/2015 was timed to enter into force on 1 January 2016.[172]

---

168. Unofficial translation by the Ministry of Justice; amendments up to 1146/2013 included: http://www.finlex.fi/fi/laki/kaannokset/2011/en20110806.pdf (28.8.2019).
169. Section 3 was amended by Act 737/2015 in the context of the 2016 reform with entry into force 1.1.2016. For more, *see* Government bill (HE 46/2014 vp), 147–149. Points 3–4 correspond to provisions of 7:8(2) of the Criminal Investigation Act; previously, a severe crime (point 3) provided an exception while point 2 on the consent is new.
170. Paragraph 3 was amended by Act 737/2015 in the context of the 2016 reform with entry into force 1 Jan. 2016. For more, *see* Government bill (HE 46/2014 vp), 149.
171. For more, *see* Government bill (HE 222/2010 vp). Already prior to the 2016 reform the provisions on searches were renewed so as to have an increased emphasis on the protection of homes and private data.
172. *See* Government bill (HE 245/2014 vp), 12–13.

Furthermore, the Act on Electronic Communications Services includes provisions related to data protection in electronic communications as well as provisions on the rights of corporate subscribers with regard to business secrets (*see* paragraph 173 on *Lex Nokia*). Restrictions to the right to process data for tracking disclosures of business secrets exist with regard to automated searches and processing of traffic data where confidentiality of sources is concerned; namely, section 151(1) includes a ban to target information referred to in 17:20(1) of the Code of Judicial Procedure. An employer as a corporate subscriber may also retrace disclosure of business secrets only with regard to persons who have been granted access to such secrets by the former (§ 151(2)). Information referred to in 17:20(1) of the Code of Judicial Procedure is also excluded where rights of access to data are granted to public authorities, i.e., Finnish Transport and Communications Agency TRAFICOM and the Data Ombudsman (*tietosuojavaltuutettu*), pursuant to section 316 of the Act on Electronic Communications Services (§ 316(5)).[173] The aforementioned provisions of the Act on Electronic Communications Services were previously included in the Act on the Protection of Privacy in Electronic Communications (*sähköisen viestinnän tietosuojalaki* 516/2004)[174] (§§ 13 f(1); 33(6) respectively).[175]

66. Court cases concerning the breach of journalistic sources have been rare. However, breaking the confidentiality of sources was considered in Supreme Court Case KKO 2004:30. The case concerned the anonymous publication of a defamatory book and the prosecutor's attempts to discover its author, who was suspected of being a business consultant. Nevertheless, according to the Supreme Court, the managing director of the book's publisher had the right to refrain from answering questions that would reveal the identity of either the author or the main source of information in the book. That was because the maximum penalty of aggravated defamation does not amount to six years of imprisonment. Another case concerning aggravated defamation (KKO 2009:88) was decided in a similar manner. In the case concerning an online publication, letters relating to a subsequent printed book on the same subject were not to be used as evidence to establish the identity of the online author.

At Case KKO 2019:112 Supreme Court of Finland found that memory stick seized from the reporter's home was not allowed to be examined or used in the preliminary investigation. In this case the biggest Finnish newspaper, *Helsingin Sanomat*, had revealed confidential documents concerning Finnish Defence Forces. The journalists were under preliminary investigation and suspected of crime called *disclosure of a national secret.*[176] The course of events was very unusual. First of

173. Sections 151(1) and 316(5) were amended by Act 758/2015 in the context of the 2016 reform with entry into force 1 Jan. 2016; the references were updated so as to correspond to the amendment in the Code of Judicial Procedure. *See* Government bill (HE 46/2014 vp), 155.
174. Unofficial translation by the Ministry of Transport and Communications; amendments up to 365/2011 included: http://www.finlex.fi/en/laki/kaannokset/2004/en20040516.pdf (28.8.2019).
175. *See* Government bill (HE 221/2013 vp), 192 (on exceptions for authorities' networks) and 225; s. 316 also includes some amendments as well as provisions of the repealed Radio Act (1015/2001; cf. § 37 of the act).
176. It is criminalised in Ch. 12 section 7 in penal code and reads as follows:

all, other media in general considered that revealing the documents was bad journalism, because the story at newspaper did not reveal any abuse or malpractice that would have justified publishing secret documents relating to Finnish military secrets. One journalist even called this "red-stamp-porn", because the secret documents contained red stamps notifying that they are secret.[177]

When it was informed that the police will investigate the case, one of the two journalists who had written the story tried to destroy her laptop by crushing it to pieces, in order to destroy the information it contained. Then her laptop caught fire and she called to emergency number and said that her laptop caught fire while she was destroying it. She also said, that she is the journalist who revealed military documents in *Helsingin Sanomat* newspaper. Then the fire brigade and police were sent to her place, and the police seized her home and confiscated her laptop. The Court of Appeal of Helsinki ruled that the police can use the information. The decision is secret. The journalist complained to the Supreme Court.

What is also special in this case is that a big Finnish news agency Suomen tietotoimisto (STT) traced the identity of the information source and revealed it. That was a person who had worked at the military service in a very high position. Revealing sources to other media is not usual, but in this case it was a newsworthy thing that who was the leaker. The newspaper article that was published in *Helsingin Sanomat* had revealed such details that it was not very difficult to trace the identity of information source.

In Case KKO 2019:112, the search ombudsman had objected to the seizure of memory stick because it possibly contained information which belong under the reporter's privilege.[178] As a result, the memory stick had been sealed and its investigation and recovery had been brought before a court. The Supreme Court held an oral hearing on the matter, in which a review of the sealed material was made. The Court considered that examining the file that was found on the seized memory stick could lead to the disclosure of the information source. The sealed material could therefore not be seized or reproduced for use as evidence in criminal proceedings. However, the material could be seized and kept sealed to secure a possible confiscation.[179]

---

(1) A person who unlawfully publishes or relays, delivers or discloses to another or, for such purpose, unlawfully obtains information on a matter that has been classified as secret by statute or by administrative order so as to safeguard the Finnish national security, or that to the knowledge of the perpetrator is conducive to causing serious damage to the Finnish defence, national security, foreign relations or economy, shall be sentenced for disclosure of a national secret to imprisonment for at least four months and at most four years.

(2) An attempt is punishable.

177. *See* the Finnish media company MTV's News 'MTV:n rikostoimittaja kiteyttää Helsingin Sanomien kohujutun ongelman ytimen: "Punaleimapornoa" 17.12.2017: https://www.mtvuutiset.fi/artikkeli/mtv-n-rikostoimittaja-kiteyttaa-helsingin-sanomien-kohujutun-ongelman-ytimen-punaleimapornoa/6700272#gs.dd6tty (30-10.2019).

178. Also Supreme Court case KKO 2019:67 related to the same course of events, but as it goes deep into procedural matters it is not discussed further here. More closely on that *see* Viitanen's Comment on Supreme Court case KKO 2019:67.

179. More closely, *see* Comment on Supreme Court case KKO 2019:112 by professor Tolvanen.

To conclude, Finnish legislation on the protection of sources is neutral regarding the medium in which the message is published, as it treats all forms of communication uniformly so long as the information is provided to the public. Thus, the press, radio, and television, and the journalists working in these media, enjoy no better or wider protection than other forms of communication or ordinary citizens. From a legal perspective, there is a right to maintain the confidentiality of sources of information but not an obligation to protect the source of information. However, the Guidelines for Journalists also require the preservation of the confidentiality of sources. Then again, only publishers and providers of programme activity, and those in their service, are entitled to maintain confidentiality in the identity of an originator of a message pursuant to section 16(1) FEA; this is an element counterbalanced by a tailored liability.[180]

180. *See* Tiilikka 2008, 35.

Chapter 3. The Liability of Journalists

§1. Normal Criminal Liability

67. According to section 12 of the Act on the Exercise of Freedom of Expression in Mass Media (460/2003), '[c]riminal liability for an offence arising from the contents of a message provided to the public shall lie with the perpetrator or accomplice, as defined in the Penal Code of Finland (39/1889)'. This means that the journalist is subject to normal criminal liability in the same way as persons in other positions or professions. There is neither a cascade liability system similar to that of Belgium[181] nor a system built on exclusive responsibility, such as the Swedish system.[182]

In Finnish criminal jurisprudence, an offence is defined in formal terms as an act for which a sanction is prescribed in law. In Finland, the age of criminal liability is 15 years. Offences committed by persons younger than this are nevertheless investigated and the offenders may be required to pay damages. Penalties for offenders between the ages of 15 and 17 years are determined using a reduced scale.[183]

According to the principle of instrumental neutrality, which is one of the leading principles in the FEA, the criminal and civil legal liability rules are the same regardless of the technology that has been used for publishing the message. This means that liability is the same whether a message is published in a newspaper, periodical, or on radio, television, a blog or web discussion site. The responsible person is the one who has committed a crime according to the Criminal Code or other legislation. In practice, this is usually a person who has written or otherwise created the message and/or the person who has decided to publish it. Moreover, photographers can also be liable, as in cases where they knowingly publish photographs that violate the right to private life or provide such photographs for publication (24:8–8 a Criminal Code). Providing a photograph for a defamatory newspaper article and thereby helping to identify the victim can also be regarded as contributing to defamation.

68. Several persons can also be liable for the same newspaper article or programme, depending on the description of the crime and how each person has contributed to it. It may be that each person has committed a separate crime or that they have acted together in the perpetration of one crime. If two or more persons together intentionally commit an offence, each is punished as an offender (5:3 Criminal Code).[184] Joint commission is possible only in the case of intentional offences. As

181. *See* closer Valcke – Lievens 2010, 62–63.
182. *See* Sverige's Tryckfrihetsförordning (1949:105), Ch. 8 and Yttrandefrihetsgrundlag (1991:1469) Ch. 6. The Swedish system where someone bears liability regardless of his/her own acts and guilt is problematic in terms of the principles of criminal law.
183. For a more detailed description of the Finnish criminal system *see* Utriainen 2019.
184. *See* Government bill (HE 44/2002 vp), 152–153.

Utriainen writes, although convictions are based on the same provision, the punishment received by accomplices may vary depending on the degree of guilt and special circumstances.[185]

Usually crimes involving freedom of expression are punishable only on the condition that they have been committed deliberately. This means that the act is not punishable if it is performed out of negligence. As a result, the dissemination of defamatory content by newspaper article or radio or television programme does not constitute a crime if it is a result of the negligent but unintentional acts of several individuals. This could be the case, for example, if a news item about a crime is accompanied by the wrong person's name or photograph, or if an interview where a person revealed negative things about him/herself is published alongside a photograph of the wrong person. Sometimes headlines are not formulated by the same individuals who have written the actual story, which can lead to false content due to negligence.

In practice, the threshold for intent has been rather low in defamation cases. If the perpetrator has failed to check the facts with sufficient care, the Supreme Court has often held that the false information (which constitutes defamation) had been published intentionally. For example, in Case KKO 2010:88, the Supreme Court ruled that '[a] journalist has acted intentionally if when publishing allegations and insinuations in a programme he/she must have considered it apt to cause harm and suffering to the parties involved or make them the object of contempt, and if the journalist cannot present sufficient grounds for the assertions'.[186] This means that intent is subject both to the offensive nature of the claims and to the fact that reasonable grounds in support of presenting the claim cannot be presented.

69. The statutory definition of intent is found in Chapter 3, section 6 of the Criminal Code, and it reads as follows:

> Intent. A perpetrator has intentionally caused the consequence described in the statutory definition if the causing of the consequence was the perpetrator's purpose or he or she had considered the consequence a certain or probable result of his or her actions. A consequence has also been intentionally caused if the perpetrator has considered it certainly connected with the consequence that he or she has aimed for.[187]

As is evident from the description, it applies only to the result of crimes. As there is no result in the Finnish description of defamation or disseminating private information, this description of intent does not apply to those crimes. However, the Supreme Court has also applied the same kind of 'probable intent' to crimes that do not presuppose any result, including defamation.[188]

185. Utriainen 2019, 95–102.
186. https://www.finlex.fi/fi/oikeus/kko/kko/2010/20100088?search%5Btype%5D=pika&search%5Bpika%5D=2010%3A88 .
187. Unofficial translation by the Ministry of Justice; amendments up to 766/2015 included: http://www.finlex.fi/fi/laki/kaannokset/1889/en18890039.pdf (28.8.2019).
188. *See*, *e.g.*, Supreme Court case KKO 2010:88 and for more information on intent in Finnish Criminal Law, *see* Utriainen 2019, 67–71. The unofficial translation of the Finnish Criminal Code by the

Section 1 of Chapter 4 of the Criminal Code must also be taken into consideration when deciding on the presence of intent. According to the Code: 'If at the time of the act the perpetrator was unaware of the existence of all those factors required for the completion of the statutory definition of the offence, or if he or she errs regarding such a factor, the act is not intentional. Nonetheless, liability for a negligent offence may exist pursuant to the provisions on criminal liability for negligence.'[189] This section means that if, during the commission of the offence, the perpetrator was unaware of the elements that constitute the statutory definition of the offence, or was mistaken regarding those elements, the act is not intentional. However, such cases may be considered as negligence offences if negligence is criminalized for the activity involved. In reality, however, charges are rarely dismissed on the basis of this provision.

70. Defamation and disseminating private information are not punishable acts, that is, crimes, if they have been committed through negligence. Nevertheless, in defamation cases, lack of information, that is the fact that the perpetrator was unaware of the falsity of the statement, does not exempt the perpetrator from liability; rather, the perpetrator is responsible for checking the facts in a reasonable way before publishing or disseminating them.[190] If the interpretation was different, it would be very difficult to convict anyone of defamation. In summary, deliberate ignorance offers no exemption from liability.

When it comes to the burden of proof, the prosecutor must prove that a crime has been committed. However, when a prosecutor or victim claims that a defamatory statement is false, the defendant must show or present reasonable grounds for his or her claim, or else face conviction for defamation.

§2. Dissemination of Information Violating Personal Privacy

71. Although journalists enjoy far-reaching freedom of expression, they are still bound by criminal legislation. Probably the most common criminal rules that journalists must consider are the provisions concerning defamation and aggravated defamation. However, crimes such as disseminating private information and incitement to racial hatred are also of relevance. The provisions on the dissemination of information violating personal privacy are found in the Criminal Code, Chapter 24, sections 8 and 8a (aggravated form) and provisions on defamation are in Chapter 24,

---

Ministry of Justice is here http://finlex.fi/fi/laki/kaannokset/1889/en18890039.pdf. All the Supreme Court precedent cases can be found (in Finnish or some cases in Swedish) on the website www.finlex.fi, more precisely https://www.finlex.fi/fi/oikeus/kko/kko/ (28.8.2019).

189. Unofficial translation by the Ministry of Justice.

190. *See*, i.a., Supreme Court cases KKO 2006:10, KKO 2006:62, and KKO 2010:88. For some recent articles on intent, *see*, *e.g.*, Tapani 2006, Tapani 2009, 470–481 and Tapani 2013, 787–798. *See also* a wide-ranging doctoral thesis on intent: Matikkala 2005. Because the new provisions on intent entered into force 1.1.2004, there were no precedents on intent from the Supreme Court when the dissertation was published. Turning to the recent articles is therefore recommended; court practice concerning the new regulation on intent has been taken into account.

sections 9 and 10 (aggravated form) of the same Act. Incitement to racial hatred is criminalized in Chapter 11, sections 10 and 10a (aggravated form).

The principle expressed in Chapter 1, section 1, subsection 2 of the FEA must also be taken into consideration when applying the Criminal Code, even though our old Criminal Code makes no reference to journalists. According to the above-mentioned subsection, when applying that law, interference with the activities of the media shall be legitimate only insofar as it is unavoidable, taking due note of the importance of the freedom of expression in a democracy subject to the rule of law. At the beginning of 2014, a legislative amendment came into force where provisions restricting the criminality of disseminating private information and defamation were added to those provisions. The purpose of the amendment was to highlight the importance of freedom of expression and correct the balance between freedom of expression and the right to privacy to bring it in line with ECtHR practice.[191]

The provision on disseminating private information in Chapter 24, section 8 of the Criminal Code (879/2013) reads as follows:

> *Dissemination of information violating personal privacy*
>
> 1. A person who unlawfully
>   1. through the use of the mass media, or
>   2. otherwise by making available to many persons
>
>   disseminates information, an insinuation or an image of the private life of another person, so that the act is conducive to causing that person damage or suffering, or subjecting that person to contempt, shall be sentenced for dissemination of information violating personal privacy to a fine.
> 2. The spreading of information, an insinuation or an image of the private life of a person in politics, business, public office or a public position does not constitute dissemination of information violating personal privacy if it may affect the evaluation of that person's activities in the position in question and if it is necessary for the purposes of dealing with a matter of importance to society.
> 3. Furthermore, the criteria for the dissemination of information violating personal privacy are not met if, taking into account the content of the information, the rights of others and other circumstances, the presentation of the information fails to exceed clearly the limits of what is considered acceptable.[192]

72. This provision (24:8) was amended in 2013, with the amendments entering into force on 1 January 2014. The first and second subsections are as they were in the 1 October 2000 amendment (531/2000), except that the maximum penalty was

---

191. *See* the Government bill (HE 19/2013 vp), Report of the Legal Affairs Committee (LaVM 11/2013 vp) and Statement of the Constitutional Law Committee (PeVL 16/2013 vp) on the above-mentioned Government bill. *See also* the Committee report 24/2012 concerning the same topic: Sananvapausrikokset, vainoaminen ja viestintärauhan rikkominen (Freedom of Expression crimes, persecution and breach of communications peace), Reports and statements by the Ministry of Justice.
192. Unofficial translation by the Ministry of Justice.

reduced from two years imprisonment to fines. This amendment was introduced in order to align Finnish legislation with the practice of the ECtHR, which had stated that it is usually unacceptable for journalists to be under the threat of imprisonment.[193] The third subsection is totally new. The law makers had wanted to limit the punishability of disseminating private information by adding a subsection functioning as a 'safety valve': the charge can be dismissed even if a literal reading of the first and second subsections means that the conditions for punishability are met. The problem in the Finland has been that courts have read provisions and government bills literally and have convicted when the conditions stated in the law are met, without taking into account the practice of the ECtHR and its criteria for limiting freedom of expression.[194]

Application of the third subsection essentially requires weighing and balancing between freedom of expression and other interests. If the matter in hand is an issue of wider societal interest, freedom of expression deserves much weight, but if it is not a matter of public or general interest more weight can be given to other interests.[195]

It is important to be aware of the definition of some essential criteria when interpreting this provision: these include the concept of private life and unlawfulness. First, it is necessary to elaborate on what constitutes a person's private life and what aspects are protected by this provision. According to the preliminary works of legislation, the concept of private life is not intended to be narrow or specific or limited in content.[196] Individuals must have a protected area, which includes the things they wish to remain within their circle of family and friends. Private life covers matters such as a person's family life, leisure time, health and human relations.[197] The protection of privacy also extends to disseminating truthful information.[198] Today, the Finnish courts interpret this concept in parallel with the practice of the ECtHR.[199] The concept of private life extends to aspects relating to personal identity, such as a person's name, photograph, or physical and moral integrity.[200] The concept of private life has a broad content and it is a general concept, which cannot be exhaustively defined.[201]

---

193. The scale of the penalty was from a fine to a maximum of two years imprisonment.
194. The reasons for the amendment and the existing state of the legislation are described in Government bill (HE 19/2013 vp), 37–45 and in the Committee Report 'Sananvapausrikokset, vainoaminen ja viestintärauhan rikkominen' (Freedom of Expression crimes, persecution and breach of communications peace), The Ministry of Justice reports and statements 24/2012, 91–95 and 118–126. The author of this chapter (Päivi Korpisaari, ex Tiilikka) was a member of the committee.
195. Government bill (HE 19/2013 vp), 42.
196. The Government bill of the first provision (HE 84/1974 vp, 3) and the Government bill of the next provision (HE 184/1999 vp, 31). According to the Government bill of the existing provision (HE 19/2013 vp, 38), the concept of privacy is used in the same sense as before.
197. Supreme Court case KKO 2011:72 referred to in Government bill (HE 84/1974 vp), 3.
198. Supreme Court case KKO 2011:72 with reference to Government bill (HE 184/1999), 31.
199. *See, e.g.*, Supreme Court cases KKO 2005:136 (extended chamber) and KKO 2001:72.
200. That is how the ECtHR reasoned in its Grand Chamber judgment *von Hannover 2 v. Germany* (7.2.2012).
201. Supreme Court case KKO 2011:72, where the court also referred to ECtHR case *Amann v. Switzerland*, 16.2.2000.

73. If a person has brought certain parts of their private life into the public domain, others can also comment on those matters. In that way individuals' own behaviour shapes what belongs to their protected private life.[202] Furthermore, if the information published is generally known, it is not considered as part of a person's protected private life. Moreover, the exercise of official authority or public tasks is not deemed private life.

Second, the criterion for unlawfulness states that if there is consent, publishing private information is not punishable. Every person concerned must give consent, which means that, for example, if somebody publicly discusses the termination of a relationship in a magazine article, the other party must also give consent if the article contains private information that allows him or her to be recognized and if disseminating that information is conducive to causing that person damage or suffering, or subjecting that person to contempt. The Supreme Court has interpreted the criterion for unlawfulness in such a way that even if the information is of a private nature, its publication is not unlawful if the same or similar information has already been published in a form of mass media with a wide circulation.[203]

The public availability of documents and the public nature of trials do not automatically give mass media the right to disseminate private information that is revealed in these documents or trials.[204] Therefore, the case could not be resolved solely on the basis that the information concerned came from public proceedings or judgments, which by law are public.[205]

74. In the ambiguous Case KKO 2005:136, which was decided in an extended chamber of eleven members instead of the normal five, the Supreme Court stated that it was not a crime to publish the name of an offender convicted of a crime involving aggravated assault when the crime had violated the victim's human dignity.[206] However, the Court found that although offences are themselves public matters, this did not prevent the disclosure of a convicted criminal's identity from being evaluated according to the provisions on the infringement of private life.

Consequently, the Supreme Court referred to *Sidabras and Sziautas v. Lithuania* (ECtHR, 27.7.2004), stating that provisions protecting privacy do not protect against loss of reputation, which is a foreseeable result of criminal activity. The more serious the offence of which a person is convicted, the more likely it is that the offender's name and personality will appear in the public domain one way or another. A person who intentionally commits an aggravated criminal offence should thus be prepared when committing the crime for the fact that the offence will have a news value. In addition, public interest and the need for information about the

202. Supreme Court cases KKO 2011:72 and KKO 2013:69.
203. Supreme Court case KKO 2011:72.
204. Here the Supreme Court referred to ECtHR case *P4 Radio Hele Norge v. Norway*, decision 6.5.2003, and *Z v. Finland*, judgment 25.2.1997.
205. The whole chapter is on the reasoning in Supreme Court case KKO 2005:136.
206. The Supreme Court found that committing a crime is not part of a person's private life, but disseminating information on that crime is an infringement of private life and can be evaluated on the basis of that provision. The Court of Appeal had found a violation of the perpetrator's privacy and had obliged the magazine concerned, which had published his name, to pay him EUR 2000 in compensation for mental suffering. The Supreme Court rejected the judgment.

offender's person cannot come as a surprise. The additional harm that is inevitably caused by revealing the offender's identity in such situations is thus irrelevant.

75. The Supreme Court was also of the view that the more public or socially significant the offence is, the more important it is to bring it and the offender's person into the public domain. At the same time, the severity of individual offences may have independent significance. It is natural that a serious crime in itself is perceived as a generally interesting and socially important issue. In such cases, it is often important to reveal the offender's identity in order to avoid other parties coming under undue suspicion. The fact that the article in question could have also been published without mentioning offender's identity did not indicate the illegality of revealing it.

In the case in question, it was also necessary to consider the content, headlines and illustrations of the newspaper article. It is more probable that an illegal violation of private life has occurred if other private matters have been revealed or if the information has been disseminated in an improper atmosphere of harassment, as in *von Hannover v. Germany* (21.6.2004, ECtHR).

In the Finnish case, the Supreme Court found that the general tone of the article was sound and no photographs of the offender had been published. Taking into consideration the severity of the crime and its effect on the victim's human dignity, releasing the offender's name and publishing information on the crime and punishment did not violate the offender's private life, and there was no reason to order the publishing company to pay damages.

In 2018 the Supreme Court decided another case (KKO 2018:51) concerning the right of private life of a person, who had been convicted of committing a crime. The facts of the case were, that B was convicted at the District Court of North Karelia for over two years of imprisonment for aggravated sexual abuse of a child. The judgment, perpetrators' name, age (26 years) and the age of the victim (14) and the place and time of the act were reported on several national media after his conviction. Judgment was delivered in September 2013 and the crime had been committed in April 2013. On January 2014 a person A posted a photograph of B on the open Facebook-site called 'Pedofilia's Victims', and linked it to a news article which had been published on the site of big Finnish media company, and where B's conviction was reported. A had copied B's photograph from his public Facebook profile. A added there a text saying "B apparently already released?" A lively discussion followed this posting. Also B replied, saying that he is innocent. He also asked the webmaster to remove his photograph from the publication. When this did not happen, he reported an offence to the police.

According to A, his conduct did not fulfil the criteria of crime, since the information did not relate to B's private life, but concerned public information about his crime. In addition, the information had in any case lost its private character as a result of extensive media coverage of the B crime. B, in turn, had uploaded the profile photograph of himself to his open Facebook page, and A had only linked together information that was already available (the news and B's photograph). In A's opinion, this was not likely to cause injury or distress for B or contempt for him. In any case, the publication had related to debate of general interest and social debate and did not exceed clearly of what is considered acceptable.

According to the Supreme Court, A was guilty of disseminating private information. The Supreme Court considered that the information about the crime and conviction of B, as well as B's photograph attached to the Facebook posting, concerned his private life. A sexual offence against a minor was likely to cause strong condemnation and contempt for the offender. By publishing the picture and the news link, A must have understood that the discussion on this issue would contain messages that would cause B mental suffering and contempt.

The publication of B's photograph was at the heart of his privacy, and its publication in the context of a criminal news story marked a particularly strong interference with the privacy of B. A had thus made available to many people information and a photograph of B's private life, and the act was likely to cause B suffering and harm and contempt for him. Although the information had been previously published and thus made available to the public irrespective of A's procedure, this did not mean that the information could be freely published by different parties in different contexts. Nor had B consented to the publication of his photograph. For these reasons, publishing this information was unlawful.

The Supreme Court noted that issues related to sexual offences were generally important topics of public discussion. When committing this kind of crime, B must have been prepared that this would raise public interest. On the other hand, B was a private person, who enjoyed the highest degree of privacy. His identity was of no general significance and the publication of his photograph had severely undermined his privacy.

After weighing and balancing the competing rights of freedom of expression and the right of private life, the Supreme Court found that, in the circumstances of the case, the conduct of A had clearly exceeded as what had to be considered acceptable. A's conduct thus fulfilled the crime called 'dissemination of information violating personal privacy'.

In this case, also the dismissal of charge could have been argumented for good reasons, because the crime that B had been committed was serious and the information had been obtained from public sources. The Finnish Supreme Court has recently represented a very freedom of expression-friendly line of interpretation, for example, in Cases KKO 2011:72 and KKO 2013:69. Compared to these, the outcome of this judgment is surprising.[207] Probably the Supreme Court wanted to set some limits to the discussions in social media, where "naming and shaming" is a common phenomenon. The Supreme Court also mentioned that when balancing the freedom of expression and the right of private life, it also mattered, whether the publication contained journalistic content and whether journalistic principles had been followed.

Also the personal data protection legislation sets some limits to publishing one's personal data at the web, but in this case the right of processing personal data was not questioned. The Supreme Administrative Court of Finland decided one case relating to the right to be forgotten. In KHO 2018:112, it ruled that the links to search results that revealed information on a murderer's state of health had to be

---

207. Comment on Supreme Court case KKO 2018:51 by professor Korpisaari.

removed. In this case the perpetrator had been convicted of murder (stabbing someone 60 times), but found to be with reduced criminal responsibility because of his illness.[208]

In Case KKO 2018:81 the Supreme Court decided a case concerning children's right to private life. In this case, a father of 9-year-old twins had caught on video the situation where the child welfare authorities implemented child custody at his and his children's home. The children were crying and resisting the execution. The father asked his friend to upload the video on YouTube, and blur the children's faces. When the video was uploaded, children's names were not mentioned, and their faces were slightly blurred. However, they could be recognized, because the address of their home was revealed, and their age and the fact that they were twins were mentioned. Their mother and their home yard were also seen in the video, and the name of their home town was also mentioned in the title of the video. Later, the father also spoke about this in the news, which attained more publicity for the video, and made it easier to know the children's identity. The prosecutor raised a charge against the father, and the Supreme Court found that the father was guilty of *dissemination of information violating personal privacy*. Even though there was a general interest to know how the child custody cases were executed, the decisive factor in this case was the best interest of the child. The general interest to know what is going on in the society could not override the children's interest and their right to their private life. Therefore, the publication of the video was not justified. The Supreme Court also stated that 9-year-old children could not give a valid consent for publication, because they could not understand the consequences of it.[209]

The second subsection of the provision restricts the punishability of disseminating private information. If the private matter in question is of significance when evaluating how politicians perform their duties, or if it affects the credibility of a politician or other individual exercising significant public power, then it is permissible to reveal the information. The purpose of this subsection is that the citizens as voters can assess the politicians and rulers in the light of accurate information. Some twenty-five years ago, in contrast, this subsection was interpreted literally, and if private matters that were not directly related to public tasks, the charges were invariably upheld. For example, in ECtHR case *Saaristo and others v. Finland* (12.10.2010), the Supreme Court and the ECtHR interpreted and weighed freedom of expression and the right to private life very differently.

In this case, the applicant company had published a short article during a presidential election campaign under the headline, *'The ex-husband of [R.U.] and the person in charge of communications for the Aho campaign have found each other'*. The article stated that P.N., who had separated from his wife, R.U., had found a new partner, O.T. His ex-wife, R.U., was known as a political reporter in election-related TV debates and had previously been a news reader. In the article, it was mentioned that O.T. was in charge of communications for one of the presidential candidates and that in her civilian life she was the communications manager of a pension insurance company (the name of which was specified), married and a

208. More on this case, *see* Korpisaari 2019, 47–50.
209. For a more thorough analysis, *see* Korpisaari 2019b, 36–41.

mother. In publishing the article, the paper thus revealed that O.T. was in an extra-marital relationship. Moreover, the article did not argue that the presidential candidate had known about this relationship.

The Supreme Court (KKO 2005:82) found a violation of privacy because, even when viewed as a whole, the article did not give the impression that it aimed to describe a politically important relationship. Its central aim had clearly been to spread information about the intimate relationship of public figures. In the Supreme Court's view, O.T. had served the election campaign as a hired expert without herself pursuing political office or other public function. Furthermore, the nature of her tasks as an official of the presidential campaign did not oblige in her to commit to the values advanced by the candidate in her private life. Even if the connection between O.T. and P.N. could also have had professional significance in respect to O.T.'s duties, the intimate side of their relationship had nothing to do with this. The extra-marital relationship was not a matter that could have had an impact on O.T.'s capacity to fulfil her tasks as a communications expert hired for the election campaign. Consequently, the Supreme Court considered (split decision 4-1) that the media disclosure of the extra-marital relationship of a person in O.T.'s position or exposure in public of her private morals was not justified by the public's need to receive information nor by wider societal interests. There was thus no legal right to disclose information about O.T.'s private life in the article on the basis of her duties as a campaign official.[210]

76. The ECtHR was nevertheless of a different opinion. It observed that the article in question had a direct bearing on matters of public interest, namely the presidential election campaign. Moreover, the fact that P.N.'s ex-spouse had conducted election debates on television prior to the publishing of the article and that the article had apparently been politically motivated and intended to affect the campaign were also of relevance in this respect. Taking into account that the article was published during the presidential election campaign and was thus closely linked to it in time, the Court considered that, unlike in *Von Hannover*, the article did not only satisfy the curiosity of certain readers but it also contributed to an important matter of public interest in the form of political background information.

The ECtHR also took into account 'the severity of the sanctions imposed on the applicants'. It noted that the first and second applicants were convicted under criminal law and observed that they were ordered to pay ten-day fines, amounting to EUR 270 and EUR 650, respectively. In addition, they were, together with the applicant company, jointly ordered to pay damages to O.T., amounting to a total of EUR 5,045.64 plus interest, plus her legal fees of EUR 6,500 plus interest, and witness costs of EUR 2,415.60 plus interest. The level of compensation was regarded as substantial, given that the maximum compensation afforded to victims of serious violence was approximately FIM 100,000 (EUR 17,000) at the time (*see* paragraph 28 above).[211] The ECtHR also remarked on the bringing of criminal proceedings by

210. In Finland the identity of election campaign personnel is not widely known and they themselves do not usually appear in public.

211. This justification relating to the severity of the sanctions is rather irrational because the publishing company did not contest the amount of damages at all. It simply denied that there were grounds for

a public prosecutor,[212] thus entailing the risk of a prison sentence, in the context of public debate.[213] The Court observed that the imposition of a prison sentence for a press offence would only be compatible with journalists' freedom of expression as guaranteed by Article 10 in exceptional circumstances, notably where other fundamental rights had been infringed as, for example, in the case of hate speech or incitement to violence. In conclusion, the reasons relied on by the domestic courts, although relevant, were insufficient to show that the infringement of O.T.'s right to privacy was not 'necessary in a democratic society'. Moreover, the totality of the sanctions imposed was disproportionate. Thus, the Court considered that the domestic courts had failed to strike a fair balance between the competing interests at stake and there had been a violation of Article 10 of the Convention.

In order to avoid the above-mentioned problems, the new third subsection was introduced, as it helps courts evaluate the importance of public debate in matters of general interest. Previously, it seemed the domestic courts had difficulties in dismissing charges if the criteria for criminal liability – such as those described in subsections 1 and 2 – are literally fulfilled. This new subsection gives them the means to dismiss charges wherever appropriate.

77. Along with the amendment in Chapter 24, section 8, a new aggravated form of dissemination of information violating personal privacy was introduced in Chapter 24, section 8a. It was thought that the normal form of the offence, punishable by fines (and without the possibility of imprisonment) would be applicable to journalists in the normal course of their work if it seemed that a breach of privacy had occurred. However, an aggravated form was needed because, for example, new technologies enable the widespread dissemination of sensitive information, which can violate privacy in a permanent and very visible way. It was recognized that it is not only journalists who disseminate private information, and in the worst cases a financial penalty was an insufficient sanction. The aggravated form of dissemination of information violating personal privacy reads as follows: 'If the dissemination of information violating personal privacy causes great suffering or particularly great damage and the offense as a whole is serious, the offender shall be sentenced for gross dissemination of information violating personal privacy to a fine or imprisonment not exceeding two years.'[214]

The first aggravation criterion is that the defamatory dissemination of private information causes great suffering. Here, the reference is mainly to the intensity of suffering. It is also possible to talk about the strength of suffering. Among other things, the quality of information and the way the information is disseminated may affect the extent and magnitude of the suffering. This criterion for the aggravated offence requires that it causes significantly greater suffering than it is typical of the

---

damages. In addition, it was Europe's second biggest publishing company at that time, so compensation of EUR 5,000 can hardly be viewed as 'substantial'.

212. Here the ECtHR refers to other Finnish cases: *Niskasaari and Others v. Finland* (6.7.2010) and *Ruokanen and Others v. Finland* (6.4.2010).

213. We also find this justification very odd because, in fact, there was not really any risk of imprisonment. We do not remember a case where a journalist has been imprisoned for disseminating private information.

214. Unofficial translation by the Ministry of Justice.

basic offence.[215] Another alternative criterion for the aggravated offence is that the defamatory dissemination of private information has caused particularly great damage. Here, damage refers both to economic damage and to other damage that cannot be regarded as suffering. Particularly great damage may be caused, for example, to someone whose career progression halts or becomes substantially more difficult or to someone who loses important educational opportunities or social esteem. The magnitude of the damage shall be assessed from an objective point of view.[216]

The aggravated form always requires consideration of the grievous nature of the offence as a whole. When assessing this, the criteria to be taken into account are, *inter alia*, the quality and content of the expression, how many persons have or could have recognized the individual in question, the genre of expression, the reason and purpose of disseminating the information, the insinuation or image as well as other facts relating to the offence.

§3. Defamation

78. The provisions on defamation and aggravated defamation in Chapter 24 of the Finnish Criminal Code, sections 9 and 10 read as follows:

> 9 § Defamation (879/2013)
>
> 1. A person who
>   1. spreads false information or a false insinuation about another person so that the act is conducive to causing damage or suffering to that person or subjecting that person to contempt, or
>   2. disparages another in a manner other than that referred to in the above subparagraph
>
>   shall be sentenced for defamation to a fine.
> 2. Also a person who spreads false information or a false insinuation about a deceased person, so that the act is conducive to causing suffering to a person to whom the deceased was particularly close, shall be sentenced for defamation.
> 3. Criticism that is directed at a person's activities in politics, business, public office, public position, science, art or in comparable public activity and that does not obviously overstep the limits of propriety does not constitute defamation as referred to in subsection 1(2).
> 4. Disseminating information does not constitute defamation if presenting it, taking into account the content of the information, the rights of others and other circumstances, fails to clearly exceed the limits of what is considered acceptable.

The last subsection of the provision came into force at the beginning of 2014. Its purpose is to limit the scope of punishability and emphasize the importance of

215. Government bill (HE 19/2013 vp), 44.
216. Government bill (HE 19/2013 vp), 44.

weighing and balancing expressed in the practice of the ECtHR. Prior to the amendment of the provision, the maximum penalty for defamation was six months of imprisonment, but because the ECtHR considered it unacceptable for journalists to face the risk of imprisonment, the penalty was reduced to fines.

The provision on aggravated defamation reads as follows:

> 10 § Aggravated Defamation (879/2013)
> If the defamation referred to in section 9(1) causes great suffering or particularly great damage and the offense is serious as a whole, the offender shall be sentenced for aggravated defamation to a fine or to imprisonment not exceeding two years.

79. The definition of aggravated defamation was reformulated in 2014 to remove the condition that aggravated defamation involved the use of mass media or the dissemination of information to many individuals. This qualification had led to media crimes being investigated primarily as aggravated defamation, which was considered at odds with freedom of speech as guaranteed in the practice of the ECtHR.

An important criterion for the presence of aggravation in both the dissemination of information violating personal privacy and in defamation is that the act must have caused considerable suffering or significant damage to the victim and that the crime can be viewed as aggravated when assessed as a whole. Thus, media crimes can also be considered as aggravated crimes, if they cause considerable suffering or significant damage, but use of the mass media alone is an insufficient condition. It is also important to note that the basic forms of dissemination of information violating personal privacy and defamation do not require the occurrence of actual suffering or damage; instead, it is enough that the act was conducive to causing damage or suffering. In contrast, their aggravated forms require that suffering or damage has actually occurred.

80. The victim of defamation can only be a natural person. However, if offensive claims are made about a company's functions, products or services, the injured party can be viewed as that individual (or individuals) in the company responsible for the actions, products or services targeted by the claims. For example, in Supreme Court Case KKO 2005:1, criticism of a pizza was considered to target the owner of the pizzeria, even though he had neither made the pizza nor seen or supervised its making. However, the case was dismissed because the article concerned was intended to be humorous, and the writer was seen as having the right to express his opinion on the pizza he had received.

Defamation does not require, moreover, that the target of defamation is mentioned by name; instead, it is considered sufficient that he or she can be recognized.[217] Furthermore, reference to the departmental employees of a company or

---

217. *See*, *e.g.*, Supreme Court cases KKO 2000:54 and KKO 2006:62.

organization can make every person in that department an injured party.[218] However, if the reference is directed at a very large group of people, without any more precise qualifications, the claim cannot be considered directed at a specific person and therefore defamation has not occurred.

Defamation can be committed in three ways. These are the following:

1. Presentation of false information or a false insinuation. This concerns a statement of supposed fact whose veracity, in principle, could be checked or verified.
2. Other kinds of disparagement. These concern a different kind of derogatory statement than the above. The statement can be based on facts or be an assessment. In the latter, the statement's veracity is not in question. It can involve name-calling, offensive gestures or presenting truthful statements for a derogatory purpose.
3. Spreading false information or a false insinuation about a deceased person. This provision is only applicable when the presented information is false. The other kind of disparagement mentioned in point 2 is not punishable as defamation when it involves a deceased person.

As in the dissemination of information violating personal privacy, the nature of the claim (whether it is conducive to causing damage, suffering or contempt) in defamation is also evaluated objectively, based on its content and the circumstances. A more sensitive person does not enjoy greater protection against defamation than other less sensitive individuals. In some cases, however, factors such as the victim's profession can be of significance, as some statements can be more defamatory towards a person working in a certain position.[219] For example, declaring someone to be a racist can be defamatory if that person works with immigrants,[220] but it is not defamatory in the case of a politician who has proposed amendments to laws which would worsen the rights of immigrants, or if the person in question is, for example, a member of a motorcycle club known for its anti-immigrant opinions.

81. The third subparagraph on defamation in the Finnish Criminal Code guarantees discussion in society, the right to scientific and artistic criticism and general freedom of criticism.[221] The actions of politicians, users of economic power and artists can be analysed and criticized, even if they are found to be derogatory.

The provision does not, however, protect criticism based on false premises, which are governed by subparagraph 1, point 1 on false information and false insinuation.

In its recent legal praxis, the Supreme Court has moved away from a literal interpretation of the veracity of statements towards greater emphasis on the context in

218. *See* Supreme Court case KKO 2011:71. This case involved thirty-six employers, thirty-one of whom reported the crime and acted as injured parties.
219. Government bill (HE 184/1999 vp), 31–34.
220. *See* Supreme Court case KKO 2011:71, where the charges however were dismissed because the claim was general and it thus targeted to so many persons that it could not be taken seriously towards one single individual that was working in a refugees reception centre.
221. Statement of Constitutional Law Committee (PeVL 36/1998 vp), 3.

which they are made. For example, in Case KKO 2013:70, the Supreme Court dismissed a charge of defamation even though the claims that had been presented were not completely true. The case concerned a newspaper story concerning a person suspected of three murders. The suspected murderer was identifiable from the story at least among the closest persons to him. According to the Supreme Court, the information presented in the text was not false, as it had not aimed for 'precision; rather, it was a matter of an evaluation based on facts'.

In addition, the Supreme Court did not consider that the story's headline, '*Acquaintance of suspected serial killer: He's an sycophantic scumbag!*', was 'liable to cause the kind of contempt referred to in the Criminal Code of Finland, Chapter 24, section 9, subparagraph 1, point 2', when taking into account the subject matter and the fact that he was suspected of 'killing his three male friends, partly for financial reasons'. The Supreme Court made a similar decision in Case KKO 2013:69, by considering the context of the story and the previous behaviour of the person it concerned in a case involving insinuations about a celebrity's alcohol use and infidelity in a relationship.

In recent years, the Supreme Court has dismissed many defamation charges, and this is due to the ECtHR's legal praxis. During the past few years (2016–2019) the Supreme Court has not decided any cases regarding defamation.

Defamation is punishable only if committed intentionally. Defamation is intentional if the person presenting the message considered that it could quite probably cause damage or suffering to the injured party or give rise to contempt for that person and if there were insufficient grounds for the claim.[222] Thus, intent first concerns the violating nature of the message and second whether the author of the message can present evidence or other reasonable grounds to support the truthfulness of his or her claim. Defamation only requires actual intent to defame when presenting a truthful claim for the purposes of disparagement and if subparagraph 1, point 2 of the section on defamation in the Criminal Code can be applied.[223]

§4. ETHNIC AGITATION

82. The provisions on ethnic agitation in section 10 of Chapter 11 of the Criminal Code of Finland read as follows:

> 10 § Ethnic agitation (511/2011)
> A person who makes available to the public or otherwise spreads among the public or keeps available for the public information, an expression of opinion or another message where a certain group is threatened, defamed or insulted on the basis of its race, skin colour, birth status, national or ethnic origin, religion or belief, sexual orientation or disability or a comparable basis, shall be sentenced for ethnic agitation to a fine or to imprisonment for at most two years.[224]

222. Supreme Court case KKO 2010:88.
223. Supreme Court cases KKO 2007:56 and KKO 2011:101.
224. Unofficial translation by the Ministry of Justice.

An amendment to this provision came into force in June 2011 to bring Finland in line with its international commitments. New groups of people were added to those protected by the provision, and in addition to spreading information, making racist information available to the public, and maintaining the availability of that information also became punishable.

In section 10a of Chapter 11 of the Criminal Code of Finland, there is also a provision on aggravated ethnic agitation. It is unlikely that the provision on aggravated ethnic agitation will be applied to regular media work, and therefore it is not covered here. The provision protects groups from hate crimes based on race, skin colour, birth status, national or ethnic origin, religion or belief, sexual orientation, disability or any other comparable basis. According to Government bill (HE 317/2010 vp), when evaluating what constitutes a comparable basis, attention can be paid to a group's position in society. A group's need for protection can be a justified reason for considering it worthy of protection under the provisions. For example, transsexuals, transgender individuals and immigrants fall within the remit of the provisions.

83. The provision on ethnic agitation previously applied merely to 'spreading' racist information. However, the reform made clear that the provision is also applicable to collecting links and contacts so that the material can be easily accessed by others. Because the crime of ethnic agitation requires intent, the person posting a link to racist material must be aware that the webpages concerned include material fulfilling the criteria for ethnic agitation.

According to the previous law, it was unclear whether maintaining the availability of racist information for others could be considered as spreading that information if the defendant had not himself placed the information there. Such a situation could arise, for example, if one person posted comments on another's blog, who then failed to remove them. To clarify the matter, it is now clearly mentioned that maintaining the availability of racist material is also punishable. Consequently, the administrator of a web-forum may commit the crime of ethnic agitation by failing to remove a message fulfilling the criteria for ethnic agitation after being notified or becoming aware of the presence of the message.

An annex to the Guidelines for Journalists was accepted on 5 September 2011 and entered into force on 1 October 2011. It requires that editors monitor their websites and attempt to prevent the publication of content that violates personal privacy or degrades human dignity. Content that degrades human dignity can be considered, for example, as discriminatory material, incitement to violence or material that fuels hatred against an individual or a group of people. According to the second section of the annex, once editors become aware of content that degrades human dignity and violates personal privacy, they must remove it without any delay.

84. Criminal liability requires that the disseminated message threatens, defames or insults a group of people mentioned in the provision on ethnic agitation. Threats punishable by law include the threat of violence, destruction of property or economic discrimination. Defamation or insulting is deemed to have occurred when, for example, a claim made about a group of people would be considered as defamation if it was made about a single person.[225]

Ethnic agitation is punishable only if committed intentionally, i.e., if the perpetrator is aware of the fact that spreading or keeping available his or her message threatens, defames or insults a group mentioned in the paragraph on ethnic agitation. Intention does not require that the message was disseminated or made available for the specific purpose of threatening, defaming or insulting.

85. In Supreme Court Case KKO 2012:58, a line was drawn between the crime of ethnic agitation and exercising freedom of speech. Here, the Supreme Court applied the old, now repealed provision, as it was in force at the time the act was perpetrated and because applying the new provision would not have led to a less severe outcome from the perspective of the accused. The Supreme Court stated that when applying the provision on ethnic agitation and considering the limits of its scope, it was important to consider the provision's relation to freedom of speech. Communications should not be interfered with more than what is strictly necessary when considering freedom of speech in a democratic, constitutional state. Immigration and foreign policy, or those who are responsible for it, can be strongly criticized as long as that criticism does not include threatening, defaming or insulting ethnic groups.

According to the Supreme Court, in the text in question, Somalis were described as 'a group of criminals whose social morality is below that of others'.[226] The court ruled that even if the purpose of the text was to criticize the authorities, the author was not entitled to express defamatory claims about Somalis, labelling them as criminals and parasites. For this reason, the writer was convicted of ethnic agitation. When the Supreme Court made the decision, it again took into consideration the ECtHR's legal praxis. The ECtHR has stated that expressions of racial hatred are not covered by the freedom of expression and instead fall under ECHR Article 17, which contains a prohibition on the abuse of rights.[227]

The amount of convictions concerning *ethnic agitation* has increased during the past years. In 2018, there were thirty-six convictions, while in 2017 there were sixteen. The number in earlier years were five (2016), one (2015), three (2014), four

225. For more, *see* Government bill (HE 317/2010 vp), 42.
226. Local politician (and later on a member of the parliament) had written in his blog with underlining and bolding that *'robbing passers-by and parasiting with tax money is an ethnic if not even a genetic special character to Somalians'*. With his statement he wanted to criticize so-called double standard, when the Council for Mass Media (CMM) had not taken into procedure a complaint about one magazines editorial that stated *'killing while drunk is supposedly an ethnic if not even a genetic special character to Finns'*. The writer repeated his claims about Somalians again with bolding type after displaying statistics about robberies made by Somalians and their work statistics. After that he stated that, obliviously not every Somalian robs and parasites with tax money, but not every Finn does kill while drunk.
227. *Jersild v. Denmark* 23.9.1994, *Erbakan v. Turkey* 6.7.2006, *Balsytė-Liedeikienė v. Lithuania* 4.11.2008, and *Feret v. Belgium* 16.7.2009.

(2013), fourteen (2012), one (2011), two (2010) and five (2009).[228] Currently several members of parliament are under preliminary investigation or convicted concerning ethnic agitation, which is a very peculiar phenomenon.[229] According to section 30 subsection 2 of the Finnish constitution, a member of parliament 'shall not be charged in a court of law nor be deprived of liberty owing to opinions expressed by the representative in the Parliament or owing to conduct in the consideration of a matter, unless the Parliament has consented to the same by a decision supported by at least fivesixths of the votes cast'.[230] This subsection applies only to statements that have been said in the Parliament and not to any statements said elsewhere. The Prosecutor General considered that there were grounds to accuse MP Juha Mäenpää of ethnic agitation. The Constitutional Committee of Finnish parliament (which consists of MP's) gave its statement and proposed that Parliament decides to give its consent to prosecute MP Mäenpää of ethnic agitation.[231] They considered the value of parliamentary immunity, freedom of speech and dignity and equality of human beings and considered also the practise of the ECtHR. No prosecution was filed since five-sixths majority did not vote in favour of it.[232]

§5. Editorial Misconduct

86. According to section 4 of the Act on the Exercise of Freedom of Expression in Mass Media (FEA), certain media – periodical publications, programmes, and online publications – must designate a responsible editor, who shall direct and supervise editorial work, decide on the content of a periodical, online publication or programme, and perform other tasks assigned to him or her by the FEA, and a special liability for *editorial misconduct* can follow if the responsible editor fails in that duty. However, even here, it is a question of normal criminal liability, which must be proved according to normal criminal rules and principles. Thus, in the context of the media, criminal liability is attributed according to the normal rules of criminal law. The description of *editorial misconduct* reads as follows:

228. This information is from the Information Service of the Statistics Finland (Tilastokeskus, 30.10.2019).
229. Finnish parliament consists of 200 members. MPs Päivi Räsänen and Hussein al-Taee are under preliminary investigation. MP Sebastian Tynkkynen was convicted of ethnic agitation at the court of appeal. *See*, *e.g.*, Helsingin Sanomat (News): 'Neljäs kansanedustajaa koskeva esitutkinta alkaa: Sebastian Tynkkystä epäillään kiihottamisesta kansanryhmää vastaan' 27.8.2019 (A piece of news relating to MP Sebastian Tynkkynen and his investigation for ethnic agitation): https://www.hs.fi/kotimaa/art-2000006218410.html (30.10.2019) ; *see also* Yle Uutiset: 'Kansanedustaja Sebastian Tynkkysen tuomio kiihottamisesta kansanryhmää vastaan pysyi hovissa – aikoo valittaa Euroopan ihmisoikeustuomioistuimeen' 2.7.2020 (A piece of news that relates to the judgment of Court of Appeal, according to which MP Sebastian Tynkkynen was found guilty of ethnic agitation): https://yle.fi/uutiset/3-11429491 (13.8.2020). *See also* https://yle.fi/uutiset/3-11446839 (13.8.2020).
230. An unofficial translation by the Ministry of Justice, https://www.finlex.fi/fi/laki/kaannokset/1999/en19990731.pdf (13.8.2020).
231. Report of the Constitutional Committee PeVM 21/2020 vp — M 5/2019 vp. There was a vote 13–5, which is very unusual at the constitutional committee. The author of this book, Päivi Korpisaari, gave her statement for the committee.
232. *See*, *e.g.*, https://yle.fi/uutiset/3-11418220 (13.8.2020).

> If the responsible editor intentionally or negligently fails in an essential manner in his or her duty to manage and supervise editorial work, and the failure is conducive to the occurrence of an offence arising from the contents of a message provided to the public, and the offence occurs without him or her being considered the perpetrator or accomplice, the responsible editor shall be convicted of editorial misconduct and fined.[233]

The purpose of *editorial misconduct* is to ensure that someone bears responsibility for editorial work. When drafting the law, this was considered important because articles and programmes are often created in collaboration with many persons.[234] Also the right of anonymous expression makes it difficult to prove who is the writer of a certain article that is accused of being illegal in content. However, only one (2011) editor-in-chief has been convicted of this crime during the last ten years of the FEA from 2009–2018.[235] The number is so less because the crime requires, at the very least, gross negligence, and if the editor-in-chief has organized the editorial work and supervision in a normal and proper manner there is no gross negligence or intent even if the content of the article or programme is illegal.

87. Second, even if the editor-in-chief's failure to act in proper manner amounted to gross negligence or intent and even if the content of the publication or programme were clearly defamatory or otherwise criminal, it would not constitute *editorial misconduct* if no one in the editorial team could be shown to have committed a crime. This can be difficult to prove because, as was mentioned above, crimes connected with freedom of speech usually require intent, and thus there is no crime if the criminal content of a publication or programme is the result of many persons' negligent acts, or if intent cannot be proven because, for example, the writer or author of a programme is anonymous.[236]

In a way, this is slightly contradictory, because the liability of the editor-in-chief was introduced to provide a necessary counterweight to the right of anonymous expression. This sanction has nevertheless failed to function in the desired manner, as even when an editor-in-chief neglects to perform his duties and even when the content of a newspaper's article or programme is criminal the editor-in-chief is not guilty of editorial misconduct unless the criminal content is the result of someone's intentional act. However, editors-in-chief have been convicted of a crime (e.g., defamation, dissemination of private information, or incitement to racial hatred) because they have read a defamatory text or seen an insulting programme and nevertheless decided to publish or disseminate it. Instigation and abetting may also be considered when deciding whether to convict. For example in KKO 2009:3 editor-in-chief was convicted of abetting in the disclosure of confidential information.[237]

233. Unofficial translation by the Ministry of Justice.
234. *See* Government bill (HE 54/2002 vp), 69–70 and Tiilikka 2007, 351 and Niiranen – Sotamaa – Tiilikka 2013, 34–36 and 104–110.
235. This information is from the Information Service of the Statistics Finland (Tilastokeskus).
236. For more information, *see* Tiilikka 2007, 354–358.
237. More on Supreme Court case KKO 2009:3 at Ch. 3 s. 7.

§6. Web Discussion Forums

88. Web discussion forums are governed by the same legislation as all other forms of expression. Normally the criteria for a network publication, which are defined in section 2, subsection 1, paragraph 6 of the FEA, are not met, because a network publication is defined as 'a set of network messages, arranged into a coherent whole comparable to a periodical from material produced or processed by the publisher, and intended to be issued regularly'; however, if there has been no prior monitoring before the messages are published, one cannot talk of material produced or processed by the publisher. Furthermore, even if some prior monitoring has occurred, the criteria are not met if the function was only to remove the offending words and not to produce editorial content. Moreover, web discussion comments cannot be said to form a 'coherent whole', because content is posted in a haphazard manner.[238] The definition of a network publication produced by the Constitutional Law Committee was intended to limit the liability of websites administrators. The committee stated that web discussion forums are only parts of online publications if the material that is published there is editorially handled.[239]

As a result of this, the writer of a web discussion comment bears responsibility for its content. If the writer is anonymous, it is difficult to attribute responsibility, but there are no rules, which would shift responsibility to the editors or editor-in-chief in case of anonymous expression.

Whether someone else besides the author is responsible depends on the description of the crime. The common interpretation is that the crimes of defamation and disseminating private information can only be committed via active acts, and failure to remove a defamatory or privacy-breaching message does not constitute a crime because such behaviour is not included in the description of the crime; furthermore, the preconditions for the offence of omission are not met.[240] Nevertheless, this has yet to be tested in the court.

In contrast, the description of incitement to racial hatred in Chapter 11, section 10 also includes 'keep[ing] [the information] available to the public', which means that if website administrators knows that such material is on their forums (blog, discussion forum, Facebook page or whatsoever) they have a duty to remove it. The requirement of knowing that the criminal material is there, comes from the fact that

238. For more on web discussion sites and the responsibility of the editor-in-chief, *see* Tiilikka 2012b, 53–78.

239. *See* the Report of the Constitutional Law Committee (PeVM 14/2002 vp).

240. About offences of omission in Finnish criminal law *see* Utriainen 2019, 58–62. Ch. 3, s. 3, subs. 2 of the Criminal Code of Finland sets out the statutory definition for punishing non-genuine omission: 'An omission is punishable if the perpetrator has neglected to prevent the causing of a consequence that accords with the statutory definition, even though he or she had a special legal duty to prevent the causing of the consequence. Such a duty may be based on: (1) an office, function or position, (2) the relationship between the perpetrator and the victim, (3) the assumption of an assignment or a contract, (4) the action of the perpetrator in creating danger, or (5) another reason comparable to these.'

the crime of incitement to racial hatred is punishable only if it has been committed intentionally; thus ignorance of the presence of unlawful material rules out intent.[241]

89. Consequently, there is no *general* obligation to remove defamatory or otherwise offensive material. This is understandable, because it would often be extremely difficult for a website administrator to judge whether the information was criminal. This could easily limit freedom of expression, because in uncertain situations it would be safer to remove the text or expression. There is one more point to note: in many cases the defamatory nature of content depends on the truthfulness[242] of the statement, and that is often impossible for the administrator to know.

Then again, the Act on Electronic Communications Services (917/2014) includes provisions on the liability of internet intermediaries and service providers. Conditions and restrictions on liability thereby concern various types of services – although even without such provisions general provisions and principles concerning criminal or civil liability would have to be applied. Section 182 of the Act covers services related to network connection and transfer of data, section 183 covers caching activity, and section 184 applies to hosting services. As regards the latter, liability does not exist if the service provider acts immediately after receiving knowledge of a court order concerning the stored material.

90. In copyright related matters, a specific procedure applies pursuant to sections 189–194 of the Act on Electronic Communications Services (cf. § 184(1), point 1). According to section 189, the copyright holder may request the content provider and the service provider (if the content provider is unknown or does not act) to prevent access to allegedly infringing material. The form and content of the notification is regulated in section 191 while the procedure follows sections 192–193 as regards informing the content provider, the possibility of a plea, and continued availability of the material in question. Section 184 also includes provisions for cases involving hate speech or child pornography, among others. The hosting service provider is not liable if it acts immediately after receiving *actual knowledge* that the stored material clearly contradicts section 10 or 10a of Chapter 11 (ethnic agitation or incitement to racial hatred; aggravated) or section 18 or 18a of Chapter 17 (distribution of sexually offensive pictures; aggravated) of the Criminal Code (§ 184(1), point 2).

The possibility of a court order regarding an access block is regulated in section 185 of the Act on Electronic Communications Services. Request for such an order may be made, among others, by a public prosecutor.

---

241. For more information, *see* the Government bill (HE 317/2010 vp), 39–41.
242. Or actually, whether the writer could have reasonably assumed that he/she could present reasonable grounds for what he/she wrote.

Similar provisions concerning intermediaries were previously included in the so-called e-Commerce Act (458/2002) which implemented the e-Commerce Directive (2000/31/EC): Chapter 4 included restrictions on the liability of service providers and the order to block access while Chapter 5 included sections governing the notice and take down procedure in copyright matters.[243]

§7. Instigation and Abetting

91. In some cases the journalist or editor-in-chief may be convicted as an instigator or abettor. According to Chapter 5 of the Criminal Code, section 5: 'A person who intentionally persuades another person to commit an intentional offence or to make a punishable attempt at such an act is punishable for incitement to the offence as if he or she were the perpetrator.'[244] Section 6 of the same Chapter for its part concerns abetting, and it reads as follows:

(1) A person who, before or during the commission of an offence, intentionally furthers the commission by another of an intentional act or of its punishable attempt, through advice, action or otherwise, shall be sentenced for abetting on the basis of the same legal provision as the perpetrator. The provisions of Chapter 6, Section 8, Subsection 1(3), Subsection 2 and Subsection 4 apply nonetheless to the sentence.
(2) Incitement to punishable aiding and abetting is punishable as aiding and abetting.[245]

As *Utriainen* writes in the *International Encyclopaedia of Criminal Law*, the liability of an instigator and abettor in the Finnish system is that of an accessory, which means that it is bound to the principal offence. If there is no punishable principal offence, no punishment can be imposed for instigation or abetting either. Attempted instigation cannot be punishable, because there is no principal offence. In certain situations, however, criminalization has been considered necessary even where the act does not result in a punishable principal offence. Thus, incitement to a false statement has been criminalized (15:5), as has public incitement to commit an offence (17:1).[246]

The Supreme Court convicted a journalist on instigation and an editor-in-chief on abetting in the disclosure of confidential information in Case KKO 2009:3. Here, a person interviewed in a television programme revealed confidential information about the investigation and ruling of a case of sexual abuse involving the interviewee's children. The interviewee was guilty of disclosing confidential information and the editor-in-chief, who had seen the interview before broadcasting it, was guilty of abetting. The editor who had interviewed the interviewee and persuaded him to reveal the information and appear in person using his real name was found

243. For more, *see*, *e.g.*, Tiilikka 2012b; Pihlajarinne 2011; 2012.
244. Unofficial translation by the Ministry of Justice.
245. Unofficial translation by the Ministry of Justice.
246. *See* Utriainen 2019, 85. For more information on instigation and abetting in Government bill (HE 44/2002 vp), 22 and 154–158.

guilty of instigation. In this case only the interviewee was guilty of disclosing confidential information, because he was the only one under the obligation of secrecy. If the journalist and editor-in-chief had been under the obligation of secrecy they would probably have been convicted of committing the same offence.

Chapter 4. Right of Reply

§1. General Introduction

92. Reply and correction are regulated under the Act on the Exercise of Freedom of Expression in Mass Media (460/2003, later FEA or Freedom of Expression Act). The right of reply and correction concern all regular publishing and programme activity.

To our knowledge, however, the FEA has yet to be used to resolve matters relating to the right of reply or correction, since self-regulation, based on the Guidelines for Journalists and the decision-making practice of Council for Mass Media (CMM), functions well.

§2. Right of Reply

93. The right of reply is regulated in section 8 of the Act on the Exercise of Freedom of Expression in Mass Media. According to the said section, a private individual who has justified reason for considering a message contained in a periodical, network publication, or comparable programmes provided on a repeated basis as offensive has the right to have a reply published in the same publication or programme.

The right of reply can only concern a private person. It requires the experience of offence, and this is evaluated objectively; i.e., the mere subjective experience of offence does not establish the right of reply.[247] Thus, in the assessment, consideration is given to whether a third person could also consider the message offensive.

94. Public opinions expressed in social, economic, political or other debate do not establish a person's right of reply. An argument presented in the mass media should personally concern a private person before that person is entitled to the right of reply as provided in the Act.

In the interpretation of the provision, consideration should also be given to the person to whom the message concerns. For a politician, prominent entrepreneur or other public figure, the threshold for deeming that a justifiable reason for offence exists is higher than for ordinary persons, because individuals performing public duties, or who are otherwise in high-profile positions, are obliged to tolerate greater criticism. Moreover, they usually have better opportunities for publicly expressing their views than ordinary citizens. When assessing justified reason for offence, consideration must also be given to the genre of the message concerned. A person is less likely to be granted the right of reply for claim presented in a column, piece of

247. What is stated in this section on reply and correction, is based not only on law but also on Government bill (HE 54/2002 vp), 61–68 and the Report of the Constitutional Law Committee (PeVM 14/2002 vp) on the same Act. On the right of reply and correction *see also* Niiranen – Sotamaa – Tiilikka 2013, 50–72.

satire, work of scientific or artistic criticism or similar text or programme than when the claim is presented in a conventional, formal style, such as in a regular newspaper article.

The right of reply is only related to repeat publications or broadcasts. Consequently, the right of reply does not apply in the case of a *single* printed product, network message, or programme.

§3. Correction

95. The right to correction is regulated in section 9 of the Act on the Exercise of Freedom of Expression in Mass Media. According to this section, private individuals, corporations, foundations and public authorities have the right to have the false information concerning them or their operations contained in a periodical, network publication, or programme corrected in the same publication or programme unless such correction is manifestly unnecessary due to the minor significance of the error.

The potential offensiveness of the message is irrelevant to the right to correction, as the issue simply concerns the correction of false information. The person demanding correction must demonstrate that the information presented in a publication is false in terms of objective evaluation. Corrections are to be issued in such a way that the corrected information reaches the same audience who originally received the false information. In addition to natural persons, companies, foundations, public authorities or any other legal persons have the right to correction. Thus, the right to correction is available to all whom the false information concerns, regardless of their legal form.

Entitlement to the right to the correction of false information requires that said information personally concerns the claimant or the operations of an organization or authority which the claimant represents. A private person cannot demand correction on behalf of another person, nor can a company demand correction on behalf of another company, subsidiary or associated partner. The right to correction does not exist if the false information has already been corrected at the magazine's own initiative.

96. If the matter is open to interpretation, it is the task of the editor-in-chief to consider whether the matter concerns false information. Where there is disagreement over the conditions for the right to correction, the interested parties may request a court ruling on the matter. To our knowledge, no matters relating to correction have been resolved in court during the present Act on the Exercise of Freedom of Expression in Mass Media. In contrast, the CMM has decided many cases concerning the right to reply and correction and their method of implementation.

Since the right to correction extends only to regular mass communications, the right to correction does not apply to individual publications, such as a book or a single network message. The right to correction does not exist if correction is manifestly unnecessary taking into consideration the minor significance of the mistake.

Evaluation of the necessity of correction is primarily the responsibility of the editor-in-chief. If the complainant is dissatisfied with the editor-in-chief's decision, the complainant may request a ruling on the issue from a court or the Council for Mass Media.

According to section 10 of the Act on the Exercise of Freedom of Expression in Mass Media, the responsible editor shall publish a reply or correction free of charge and without undue delay, in appropriate scale and in the same manner as the message on which the demand for a reply or correction is based. Moreover, the content of the reply or correction shall not be illegal or offensive. If necessary, the responsible editor shall assist in the technical realization of the reply.

The editor-in-chief is obliged to publish the reply or the correction if the conditions of section 8 or 9 of the Act on the Exercise of Freedom of Expression in Mass Media are fulfilled. Reply and correction shall be published free of charge and without undue delay. The Act does not include more detailed provisions on the precise timing of the correction or reply.

§4. Common Issues on Right of Reply and Correction

97. The reply or correction need not be provided more space or programme time than that given to the original message. Furthermore, the reply or correction should be placed in the media in same manner as the message in which the demand is based. If, for example, a private person is entitled to the right of reply on the basis of a message in a magazine's editorial, the reply cannot be placed among advertisements or promotional material, nor would a correction be deemed to have been placed in a similar way to the original message if a correction in an online publication were hidden behind multi-level link chains. Regarding television and radio programmes, 'same manner' means that if the message establishing the right of reply or correction is presented or broadcast during daytime programming, the reply or correction should not be broadcast at night. In addition, it is essential that the reply or correction reaches a sufficiently similar audience.

The editor-in-chief's duty is to ensure that a reply or correction published in a periodical, network publication, or programme is not itself illegal or offensive. Illegality means that the content of the message represents a breach of criminal law. Such crimes are mainly regulated under the Criminal Code (39/1889). Offensiveness, in turn, means that the nature of the message is sufficient to establish the right of reply for a private person.

The responsibilities of the editor-in-chief include assisting in the technical realization of the reply. In practice, the provision mainly refers to the duty of the responsible editor of online publications and programmes to use his or her editorial expertise in communications to ensure that the reply is in a condition suitable for publication or broadcast.

98. According to section 11 of the FEA, a demand for the right to reply or correction shall be presented to the responsible editor within fourteen days of the publication of the message in which the demand is based, irrespective of when the complainant became aware of the offensive message or erroneous information. The claim shall be presented either in writing or electronically, provided that its contents cannot be unilaterally altered. If the demand for the right of reply or correction is rejected, the complainant shall be notified of the rejection and the reasons for it within seven days of the reception of the demand. Upon request, the reasons for the rejection shall be provided in writing. Moreover, in the case of a rejection, the complainant has the right to submit the issue for consideration to the District Court of his or her domicile, or to the District Court of Helsinki, no later than thirty days after reception of a written notification of the reasons for the rejection.

In the event that the District Court orders the responsible editor to comply with his or her duties under section 10, the court may reinforce the order under threat of fine. The court order on the imposition of the threat of fine shall be open to appeal as a separate matter.

§5. The Guidelines for Journalists and the Right of Reply and Correction

99. Sections 20–25 of the Guidelines for Journalists include guidance on the right to reply and correction.[248] At the time of the guidelines' formulation, it was widely claimed that the courts had used the previous guidelines and the practice of the Council for Mass Media as the basis for their judgments in a number of cases.[249] However, more detailed research has revealed the falsity of the claim. In fact, the notion that the courts were using press ethics standards as a basis for legal responsibility was a misunderstanding based on a small number of cases where the court evaluated negligence with terms reminiscent of those included in the evaluation of press ethics.[250] Nevertheless, these claims are the reason why in the Finnish language version of the Guidelines for Journalists the concepts of 'reply' and 'correction' are not used. Instead, to avoid using similar terminology to the law (FEA), the Guidelines for Journalists mention 'own statement' and 'correction of incorrect information'.

100. According to section 20 of the Guidelines, essentially incorrect information must be corrected without delay and so as to reach, to the highest extent possible, the attention of those who have had access to the incorrect information. Moreover, the correction must be published on the editorial website of the media in

248. *See* http://www.jsn.fi/en/guidelines_for_journalists/ (28.8.2019).
249. CMM gave a statement on the relation between the law and ethical guidelines, *see* 'Lausuma lain ja eettisten ohjeiden suhdetta koskevassa asiassa 2002', 3206/L/02: http://www.jsn.fi/lausumat/lausuma-lain-ja-eettisten-ohjeiden-suhdetta-koskevassa-asiassa-2002/ (30.10.2019). *See also* statement on the same topic plus an opinion, whether journalists may in some situations breach the law in the name of freedom of expression and without breaching good journalistic ethics. Of course the statement has no legal significance. *See* 'Kannanotto sananvapauden merkityksestä sekä journalistin ohjeiden ja lainsäädännön suhteesta 2018' (Statement on the Importance of Freedom of Expression and the Relationship Between the Journalist's Guidelines and Legislation in 2018) 2.8.2018 / 6736/L/17: http://www.jsn.fi/lausumat/kannanotto-sananvapauden-merkityksesta-seka-journalistin-ohjeiden-ja-lainsaadannon-suhteesta-2018/ (30.10.2019).
250. *See* Tiilikka 2007, 246–266.

question, as well as in the publication or broadcast in which the incorrect information was originally published. This proviso was added because it was considered that in cases of monthly periodicals too long period would elapse before publication of the correction in the next issue. Therefore, the correction must be made on the publication's editorial website as soon as possible.

According to the same section in the Guidelines, the degree of attention brought to the correction must correspond to the seriousness of the error. If there are multiple factual errors in an article, or if the incorrect information might result in significant damage, the editors must publish a new article in which the incorrect information is identified and corrected.

In terms of the correction of essential information on the internet, it is insufficient for the incorrect information or article simply to be removed; rather, the public must also be informed of the error and how and when the correction was made.

According to the Guidelines for Journalists, it is also advisable that the media in question makes clear to the public those practices and principles by which they correct their own errors. In that way, trust in those media governed by the self-regulation system is promoted and a clear distinction is made between them and other modes of communication, such as blogs, web discussion forums, and those media who have not committed themselves to the self-regulation system.[251]

101. The CMM has issued many notices concerning the right of reply and correction, particularly concerning correction on websites, which has been a difficult issue for the mass media. As was earlier mentioned, the CMM does not consider it acceptable simply to remove false information or correct it without mention of the former mistake. Instead, the correction must be accompanied by a note that false information has been corrected. Moreover, if the correction is made by way of a new story, there must be a link from the old story to the new story so that each reader can see the correction when they read the false information.

In Case 5598/YLE/14, for example, the CMM issued a notice to the public broadcasting company Yleisradio regarding the correction of false information it had disseminated on its website and in a radio programme about the number of Russian people in Estonia. The correction on the website had been unclear, and it was impossible to ascertain what had been corrected and when. In addition, Yleisradio had failed to make any correction in the radio programme.[252]

According to section 21 of the Guidelines for Journalists, if the intention is to present information about the activities of a clearly identifiable person, company or organization in a manner that would present them in a very negative light, they must be granted the right of reply on the issue in question.

According to section 22, if it is impossible to simultaneously hear the views of the parties involved, it may be necessary to provide the recipient of extremely negative publicity the opportunity to comment at a later date.

---

251. As mentioned before, all the major media are involved in the self-regulatory system.
252. Some other adverse decisions: 5618/SL/14, 5654/SL/14, 5640/SL/14, 5606/SL/14, 5588/SL/145571/SL/14, 5570/SL/14 and 5569/YLE/14, 6071/SL/16, 6599/MTV/17, 7072/SL/19 and 6650/Yle/17 (SL means that the defendant is a newspaper). Cf. exculpatory decisions: 5722/SL/15, 5694/SL/14, 5648/SL/14, 5641/YLE/14, 5577/SL/14, 5574/SL 14 and 5551/SL14, 6016/SL/15, 6025/SL/15, 6028/SL/15 and 5987/SL15. The decisions are at www.jsn.fi (29.8.2019).

102. In Case 5684/SL/14, for example, the CMM issued a notice to a newspaper which had reported on rumours concerning a special audit that had been made at the workplace of an interviewee. The interviewee, who was a complainant in the case, refuted the rumours and was portrayed in a negative light in the newspaper article. The newspaper had first promised to publish the complainant's statement on the matter, but later refused to do so. The CMM stated that it was not the task of a newspaper to publish rumours without first checking their veracity. Instead, newspapers should verify the facts of a story and refute rumours if they prove to be false. The newspaper had thus been acting against good journalistic ethics. Concerning the same claimant but a different newspaper, the CMM decided there was no breach of journalistic ethics in Case 5678/SL/14, where the newspaper concerned would have published the claimant's statement if he had changed it to a form unlikely to give rise to offence. Because the claimant did not change the statement, the CMM saw that the paper had the right to refuse its publication.

According to section 23, the right of reply should be exercised as soon as possible without any irrelevant additions. Section 24 states that conventional cultural critique, political, economic or societal evaluation or similar expression of opinion does not provide entitlement to the right of reply. Naturally, the media in question can also publish a reply in such cases in order to stimulate debate.

According to section 25, if a reply is unsuitable for publication as such, changes should be discussed with the writer. Even if agreement cannot be reached, it is advisable to publish the essential content in an objective manner. The right of reply (i.e., right to issue one's own statement, as the Finnish language version reads) belongs to both natural and legal persons, such as companies, associations and foundations. Thus, journalistic self-regulation guarantees a broader right of reply than the legislation.

Chapter 5. Access to Public Information

§1. Public Documents

I. Historical Background

103. In 1776, Finland, along with Sweden, enacted the world's first freedom of information act, which abolished political censorship and gave the public access to government documents. This freedom of information legislation was adopted by the Swedish parliament in 1766. At that time, Finland was part of Sweden, and the Finnish enlightenment thinker and politician Anders Chydenius (1729–1803) played a crucial role in creating the new law. In its original formulation, the Swedish Freedom of the Press Decree[253] was short-lived, a mere six years, but its effect on notions of freedom of expression and information rights was indelible, and it returned in new forms. With the exclusion of religious and foreign printed materials, the Freedom of the Press Decree released all printed documents from prior censorship.

The 1766 Freedom of the Press Decree served as a starting point for many subsequent principles on printing and freedom of expression, such as, for example, access to public documents.

II. Present Legal State

104. Section 12 of the Finnish constitution guarantees freedom of expression and public access to the acts of authorities. The first section guarantees freedom of expression. The second subsection reads as follows:

> Documents and recordings in the possession of the authorities are public, unless their publication has for compelling reasons been specifically restricted by an Act. Everyone has the right of access to public documents and recordings.

Further provisions on the transparency of the activities of public authorities are found in the Act on the Openness of Government Activities (Openness Act 621/1999; later OA).[254]

105. Journalists have no special rights regarding access to information; rather, this right belongs to everyone. Nevertheless, journalists have appealed quite actively

253. It was a decree but at a constitutional level.

254. *See also* the website of the Ministry of Justice: https://oikeusministerio.fi/en/act-on-the-openness-of-government-activities (29.8.2019). For further information, *see* Mäenpää 2016 and Kulla – Koillinen 2014.

against decisions denying access to information.[255] Such cases are decided in administrative courts and not in general courts. Furthermore, the Parliamentary Ombudsman has given many decisions concerning access to information.

According to Chapter 1, section 1(1) of the OA, official documents shall be in the public domain unless otherwise specifically provided in that or another Act. According to Chapter 1, section 3, the objectives behind the right of access and the duties of the authorities include promotion of openness in government, and to provide private individuals and corporations with an opportunity to monitor the exercise of public authority and the use of public resources, to freely form an opinion, to influence the exercise of public authority, and to protect their rights and interests.

The concept of authorities is to be understood widely when interpreting the Openness Act. According to Chapter 1, section 4(1), the category of authorities includes:

1. State administrative authorities and other State agencies and institutions;
2. courts of law and the other bodies for the administration of the law;
3. State enterprises;
4. municipal authorities;
5. the Bank of Finland, including the Finance Supervision Authority, the National Pensions Institution and other independent institutions subject to public law with some exceptions;
6. Parliamentary agencies and institutions;
7. authorities of the province of Åland, when performing the duties of State authorities in Åland; and
8. independent boards, consultative bodies, commissions, committees, working groups, investigators, as well as auditors of municipalities and federations of municipalities, and other comparable organs appointed for the performance of a given task on the basis of an Act, a Decree or a decision of an authority referred to in subparagraph (1), (2) or (7).

According to the second subsection of Chapter 1, section 4, the provisions on an authority also apply to corporations, institutions, foundations, and private individuals appointed for the performance of a public task on the basis of an Act, a Decree or a provision or order issued by virtue of an Act or a Decree, when they exercise public authority.

106. The Act applies both to documents delivered to a public authority, such as letters and applications, and to the documents that it produces, including, for example, decisions and statements. Some documents relating to the internal activities of a public authority are excluded from the scope of application of the Act.[256]

---

255. *See*, *e.g.*, Supreme Administrative Court cases (including also other claimants than journalists) KHO 2002:90, KHO 2003:77, KHO 2004:25, KHO 2005:26, KHO 2007:83, KHO 2008:52, KHO 2010:31, KHO 2011:27, KHO 2012:3, KHO 2013:90 and KHO 2012:124, KHO 2018:25, KHO 2018:154, KHO 2018:164.
256. *See* closer the Government bill (HE 30/1998 vp).

According to section 5, a document means not only traditional documents on paper but also electronic messages and documents that are stored in electronic information systems. Information can be obtained in several ways. For instance it can be available on the website of the relevant or it can be provided on request. Access to information shall be granted in the manner requested unless this would unreasonably inconvenience the activity of the authority.

As regards access, public authorities can only charge for the actual costs incurred, such as the cost of printing the document. Normally, they cannot charge for the working time spent seeking for the document or information. If the information is provided in oral or electronic form, it is free of charge. The authorities are duty bound to assist those who request information. Moreover, they must organize files and documents in such a way that they are easy to find. If it takes them excessive time to find a document or information because the information system has been poorly organized, they are not entitled to charge extra. However, if the request for information is exceptionally wide in scale, they can charge for reasonable costs.[257]

107. The person requesting the document or information is not required to identify himself or herself or provide reasons for the request. However, in some exceptional cases, such as when the information is only available to those party to a particular case, it might be necessary to enquire about a person's identity and the purpose of obtaining the information.

The starting point is that everyone has the right to obtain information from official documents in the public domain. According to the principle of openness, official documents are in the public domain unless otherwise specifically provided. Section 24 contains thirty-two exceptions to the principle of openness. These provisions protect important public and private interests such as:

- international relations;
- prevention and prosecution of crimes;
- security arrangements and preparations for emergency conditions;
- state security;
- income, financial, monetary and currency policy;
- the credibility and functioning of financial and capital markets;
- protection of natural values;
- efficiency of the authorities' inspection and supervisory tasks;
- protection of the confidentiality of information;
- public and private economic interests;,
- interests of research and development and education;
- the security of asylum seekers as well as the protection of privacy.[258]

108. According to section 14, public authorities must consider a request for a document without delay. Access to a document in the public domain must be granted as soon as possible, and in any event within two weeks from the date when

257. This means the cost corresponds the actual costs of searching the information.
258. The list is from the webpage of Ministry of Justice: https://oikeusministerio.fi/en/brochure-about-the-act-on-the-openness-of-government-activities (29.8.2019).

the authority received the access request. The deadline is extended to a month if the number of requested documents is large, if they contain secret parts or if there is any other comparable reason and the decision of the matter requires special measures or otherwise exceptional work.

According to section 14, a decision refusing access to a document shall contain the reasons for the refusal. The public authority concerned is required to provide a written decision if so requested by the person asking for the document. Appeals against such decisions are usually made to the Administrative Court. The decision is accompanied by further instructions on appeal (*see* closer § 33).

§2. Court Hearings and Documents

I. General Issues

109. The publicity of court proceedings is part of the constitutional protection for fair trial (§ 21): Section 21(2) of the Finnish Constitution notes that the publicity of proceedings alongside other elements of fair trial is to be laid down by a parliamentary act.

Separate laws exist for the general courts and the administrative courts: the Act on the Publicity of Court Proceedings in General Courts and the Act on the Publicity of Administrative Court Proceedings. The former applies to court proceedings and trial documents in the High Court of Impeachment, the Supreme Court, the Court of Appeal, the District Court, the Labour Court, and the Military Court. It also applies to cases before the Market Court where the Administrative Judicial Procedure Act (808/2019) does not apply (§ 2). The latter applies to proceedings in administrative judicial cases as well as to trial documents in administrative courts which means the Supreme Administrative Court, administrative courts, and the insurance court, as well as the Market Court and boards established for appeals handled in accordance with the Administrative Judicial Procedure Act (§ 2). The provisions of the OA apply where not provided otherwise in the Acts on the Publicity of Court Proceedings (§ 2(3); § 3 resp.). Publicity is the main principle whereas derogations thereto must be provided in the law (§ 1; § 1 resp.).

It should be noted that the highest instances, as in the Supreme Court and the Supreme Administrative Court, as well as the administrative line in general largely rely on written proceedings.[259]

II. General Courts

110. According to the Act on the Publicity of Court Proceedings in General Courts[260] court proceedings and trial documents are public unless otherwise legislated (1:1). The basic information of a trial is public, including the name of the court

259. *See also* Neuvonen 2014, 171.
260. For more information, *see also* District courts' website at http://oikeus.fi/tuomioistuimet/karajaoikeudet/en/index/openness/basicinformationoncourtproceedings.html (29.8.2019).

handling the case, the nature of the matter, the stages of the process, the time and the place of the hearing, and information to identify the party (2:4). However, in a criminal case the court may declare the identity of the complainant as a secret where the case concerns a particularly sensitive aspect of his/her private life. The court may also order that the identity of an asylum seeker is kept secret in custody cases, unless apparent that the information would not endanger the safety of the person or someone close to him or her (2:6). Basic information referred to in section 4 becomes public immediately (2:5(1)) with exceptions concerning covert activity (2:5(2–3)).

Provisions on testimony as an anonymous witness were enacted in June 2015 (Act 742/2015) and entered into force on 1 January 2016. A new paragraph 4 was added to section 2 so as to refer to the Criminal Procedure Act (*laki oikeudenkäynnistä rikosasioissa* 689/1997)[261] where publicity of trial documents concerning the decision of anonymity or revealing the identity of an anonymous witness or trial publicity in the latter case are concerned. Moreover, provisions on hearing such a witness without a public are included in the Code of Judicial Procedure.[262]

111. As a main rule, trial documents are public and everyone has the right to receive information thereof (3:7). The documents become public pursuant to section 8: the moment in time basically depends on the nature of the document so that, for instance, a document handed to the court becomes public after oral hearing or after deciding the principle claim while preparatory material of the court (e.g., memorandum) becomes public after the matter has been brought to an end in that court and a ruling when it has been delivered or when available to parties (points 2, 4–5). In some situations, parts of documents are confidential by virtue of law. This applies to the extent the documents contain (3:9(1)):

- information which could endanger the external security or cause significant damage or detriment to the international relations of Finland or the state's ability to engage in international cooperation;
- sensitive information about an individual's private life, health, disability, or social welfare;
- information about a victim of a crime where the victim's rights, memory, or close ones would be infringed;
- information on a psychiatric examination, a character examination of a young offender, or a study of the feasibility for community service, and statements relating to community service, supervision punishment, conditional imprisonment for committing an offence after the age of 21, and statements issued for the procedure of release of a life prisoner or a probation period of combined punishment and criminal record;
- secret contact information where safety of a person is concerned (*see* § 11(2), point 7; § 24(1), point 31 OA); or
- information on the court's deliberations (3:9(1)).

261. Unofficial translation by the Ministry of Justice; amendments up to 733/2015 included: https://www.finlex.fi/en/laki/kaannokset/1997/en19970689_20150733.pdf (29.8.2019).

262. For more, *see* the Government bill (HE 46/2014 vp).

On the one hand, the court may however decide on partial or full publicity on the basis of a weighty public or private interest or on the request of the person whom the information concerns, excluding where state concerns or its own negotiations are the ground for secrecy (3:9(2)). On the other hand, the court may, on the request of a party or due to particular reasons, declare a trial document secret to the extent necessary where documents contain information under secrecy pursuant to another act. It must also be probable that the revelation would cause significant detriment or harm to the interests which the secrecy provisions aim to protect (3:10). The period of secrecy varies from twenty-five to eighty years depending on the ground of secrecy (3:11(1)–(2)). The period may be prolonged (3:11(4)).

According to section 14, oral proceedings are public; the court may however declare them or parts of them to be held without the presence of the public pursuant to section 15, on request or for particular reasons. The grounds for the latter partly correspond to those of section 9 while a trial may also be held behind closed doors, *inter alia*, where minors are accused of crimes or where someone is obliged to answer questions that can otherwise be refused (4:15(1), points 5, 7). Section 16 includes some special rules concerning publicity of coercive measures cases.

Everyone has the right to be present at public proceedings, unless legislated to the contrary (4:14(2)). Section 20 notes that the court may restrict the presence of the public during public proceedings where necessary to protect the security of, for instance, a witness. The chairperson may also restrict the presence to avoid crowding (4:20(1)) and prohibit the presence of a minor below the age of 15 if the presence may be detrimental to the person (4:20(2)).

112. Recording, including photography, and transmitting video and audio signals is allowed only with the permission of and following the instructions given by the chairman (4:21(1)). Permission for recording before the hearing and during the pronouncement of the judgment may be granted if no significant detriment to privacy of a party is caused, their safety is not endangered, and no other weighty reasons exist comparable to those referred to (4:21(2)). Regarding other parts of the trial, recording may be permitted where the above-mentioned conditions are met, the proceedings are not disturbed, and the participants consent to the recording (4:21(3)). All in all, permitting recording during the entirety of a trial is exceptional.[263]

The Parliamentary Ombudsman has issued a decision (3149/4/10) on a case where photography in a court lobby was forbidden. The Ombudsman found that issuing such a ban fell outside the scope of section 21 of the Act on the Publicity of Court Proceedings in General Courts; that provision was limited to the court room. Neither was it a question of illicit observation pursuant to 24:6 of the Criminal Code since mere recording in a court lobby (enjoying public peace) does not constitute a violation of privacy.[264]

---

263. *See* http://oikeus.fi/tuomioistuimet/karajaoikeudet/en/index/openness/oralhearing.html (29.8.2019).
264. Parliamentary Ombudsman of Finland's decision 3149/2010 available in Finnish at http://www.eduskunta.fi/triphome/bin/eoar3000.sh?HAKUSANA=3149 (29.8.2019); for more, *see* Neuvonen 2014, 172.

The judgment of the court is public, unless the court declares it partly secret pursuant to section 24 (5:22). The court may order necessary parts of the judgment secret if it contains information which is confidential by law; information which the court has declared secret; or information the secrecy of which has required oral hearing without the public's presence. However, the conclusion and the provisions applied in the judgment are always public (5:24(2)); notwithstanding this, the court may declare the identity of a party secret in a criminal case when it involves particularly sensitive information (e.g., sexual offences), or involves a request for asylum (5:24(2)).

113. Overall, the Finnish media have adopted these provisions and principles well. The Guidelines for Journalists also include provisions on the privacy of victims of crime. According to section 28, discretion is required when reporting on victims of accidents or crimes while section 30 notes that the right to privacy applies also when publishing information obtained from public documents or other public sources; public availability does not necessarily imply that information may be freely published. Particular discretion is advised in matters concerning minors (section 30).

As a main rule according to the Guidelines, the name, photograph, or other identifying facts of a convicted person may be published. Exceptions exist for minors and persons found to be criminally unaccountable or if the publication is viewed as clearly excessive in terms of the position or action of that individual (section 31). According to section 33, information about the convicted, charged, or suspected person is not to be published where this may reveal the identity of the victim in highly sensitive crimes.

However, nowadays, it is a growing tendency that names of criminals, and sometimes also names of victims, are published by ordinary citizens on web discussion forums or blogs discussing criminal cases and criminality. Also, for instance, victims of rape have faced bad publicity on the internet and some details of their private life and the rape in question have been published. This is the reverse side of publicity of documents. Some websites also publish names of sex offenders or foreign criminals. There has been some recent case law concerning the issue at hand. In Case KKO 2018:51 A had published B's name and other personal information in a Facebook group meant to defame convicted paedophiles. The Supreme Court convicted A of dissemination of information violating personal privacy (Finnish Criminal Code Chapter 24 Section 8).[265]

265. More about the case, *see* (in Finnish): https://korkeinoikeus.fi/fi/index/ennakkopaatokset/precedent/1531126320018.html (29.8.2019).

III. Administrative Courts

114. In the administrative line,[266] the following basic information is in general public regardless of secrecy provisions: the name of the administrative court handling the matter, the nature of the matter, the stages of the process, the time and the place of the hearing, the authority that has delivered the underlying decision, and the information needed to identify the party (the Act on the Publicity of Administrative Court Proceedings, 2:4). However, if the information needed to identify the party, combined with other information, would reveal specified confidential information, such as those related to privacy or business secrets, the information must be kept secret (2:5).

According to section 8, the provisions of the OA and other Acts on the publicity of documents apply to trial documents where the Act on the Publicity of Administrative Court Proceedings does not legislate to the contrary. Notwithstanding secrecy provisions, the court may provide information to the extent needed in order to ensure due process or to protect an important public or private interest. Thereby, secrecy applies, *inter alia*, to information concerning a person seeking asylum or about someone's private life, health, disability, or social welfare, or to documents of the security police concerning the maintenance of State security.

Moreover, pursuant to section 9(1), access to information is guaranteed for the parties as regards to documents possibly influencing their case. This is also required by the ECHR and ECtHR practice.[267] There are however exceptions to this right, including the parts of a document the publicity of which is under scrutiny by the court, preparatory material of the court (e.g., memorandum), the court's deliberations, and contact information of a party or other person involved in the trial where access would compromise the safety of the person concerned (3:9(2)). Further, access may be denied, without endangering due process, in cases of highly important public or private interests and official tenders (*see* § 11(2), paragraphs 2 and 6 OA) where that interest would be compromised (3:9(3)).

115. Where oral proceedings are held, section 10 notes that everyone is entitled to presence unless otherwise provided in the Act on the Publicity of Administrative Court Proceedings or some other act. The provisions on oral proceedings also apply to judicial views (4:10(3)). According to section 57 of the Administrative Judicial Procedure Act, an administrative court shall arrange an oral hearing if the court deems this necessary or if a private party requests so. However there are several exceptions to this. Exceptions apply, among others, where the facts may be established in some other way or if an oral hearing would be manifestly unnecessary, having regard to the nature and significance of the matter for the party and the requirements of a fair trial.

Should secret information be presented, oral proceedings are to be held in full or to a necessary extent without the presence of the public; the court may decide on

---

266. For more, *see* the website of the Administrative courts 'Publicity of court proceedings' at http://oikeus.fi/tuomioistuimet/hallintooikeudet/en/index/julkisuus.html (29.8.2019).
267. *See* Tiilikka 2013.

publicity where necessary for due process (4:11(1) Act on the Publicity of Administrative Court Proceedings). Then again, the court may declare the trial to be held behind closed doors on request if this is apt to enable the court to obtain information on the matter and publicity would cause particular detriment to the party in question. However, important public or private interest may require public proceedings (4:11(2)).

Even during open proceedings the court may restrict the presence of the public if necessary for protecting the life or health of a party, among others. The same applies where it is necessary to avoid crowding. The court may also prohibit the presence of a minor under the age of 15 if there is a possibility of detrimental effects (4:13).[268]

Third parties may only record with the consent of and following the instructions given by the court. Recording during the trial and transmitting video and audio signals therefrom may be allowed unless this would cause significant detriment to the privacy of a participant, endanger their safety, or otherwise disturb the proceedings. Moreover, other weighty reasons comparable to these may justify refusal (4:14).

The conclusion of the judgment and applicable provisions are always public (5:16(3)). Regarding confidential information, the judgment is secret to the extent necessary for the secrecy interest (5:16(2)). The court may however declare the decision public also beyond the judgment and applicable provisions where required by an important public or private interest (5:16(3)). Within the possibilities, the court must ensure that a party is informed of a decision before the contents are communicated to the public if the matter is of social significance, of considerable interest in the public eye, or if otherwise necessary (5:17).

268. Section 13 was amended by Act 800/2015 which entered into force 1 Jan. 2016. For more, *see* Government bill (HE 245/2014 vp) and further amended by Act 816/2019 which has entered into force 1.1.2020.

Chapter 6. Council for Mass Media

116. The Union for Journalists and associations representing publishers have created the Guidelines for Journalists.[269] An important point to make at the outset is that in Finland media self-regulation is real self-regulation, as the enforcement and application of the Guidelines for Journalists is carried out by media actors and kept separate from governmental regulation and government bodies. Journalists and media companies draw up the Guidelines without any outside interference. The work is performed by associations whose members are journalists and media companies.

The Guidelines apply to print, online and broadcast media. All the major actors in Finnish media have joined the self-regulation system. It cannot be applied to those media actors that have not made such a commitment. However, as no significant media players are outside the self-regulation system, this is of minor importance.

117. The Council for Mass Media (CMM) was established in 1968 by publishers and journalists in the field of mass communication.[270] It interprets good professional practice following the Guidelines for Journalists and by using its own discretion. Its task is also to defend freedom of speech and publication. However, it has no legal jurisdiction. The Council for Mass Media is totally independent of governmental organizations and consequently, as was earlier stated, the media's self-regulation is real self-regulation: the rules are made by the media and interpreted by the media and its audience. This is one reason why journalists respect the Guidelines for Journalists and the decisions on their interpretation and application given by the Council for Mass Media.

The CMM consists of a chairman and thirteen members, whose term of office is three years. Eight members represent areas of expertise in the field of media, and five are drawn from the public. The chairman is appointed by the Managing Group of the Council for Mass Media. He or she may have expertise in the field of media but can also be from another field. Representatives of the public are elected by the Council. They may not be employees or board members of any media company. The media representatives (journalists, managing editors, producers, etc.) are appointed by the Managing Group.

Anyone who considers that there has been a breach of good professional ethics by the media may take a complaint to the CMM. However, if it is a matter of privacy, the proceedings require the consent of the infringed party, because the proceedings and publication of the CMM's decision normally result in additional publicity. The CMM can also initiate cases of fundamental importance at its own

269. *See* the guidelines in English at http://www.jsn.fi/en/guidelines_for_journalists/ (29.8.2019). The current guidelines took effect from 1.1.2014 onwards. The guidelines have been revised in the course of time.

270. *See* closer http://www.jsn.fi/en/Council_for_Mass_Media/the-council-for-mass-media-in-finland/ (29.8.2019).

initiative, even though no complaint has been made. Moreover, the Council can issue statements of principles and policy statements regarding questions of professional ethics.

118. If the CMM finds a breach of good professional ethics, it issues a reprimand or severe reprimand, which the media must publish within a short time span. The severe form of reprimand may be issued if it is a question of gross violation or the media in question otherwise shows disregard in its actions.[271] Reprimands must be published in the media in question and also on that media group's website. This is the only sanction that the Council may impose. The reprimand and severe reprimand must be published without any comments that would lower the value of the decision. That is the only consequence of CMM proceeding. The reprimand is to be directed to the media company that has published the content in question. It is directed to the journalist concerned only if the complaint concerns the way in which the information was obtained.[272]

The CMM does not undertake investigations and it cannot hear witnesses. Therefore, it cannot decide on cases if there is insufficient information on the facts. The handling of complaints is free of charge, and the average timeframe for proceedings is about four months. The Chair of the Council may give independent resolutions on matters which clearly do not refer to a breach of good professional practice and are of no significant importance.

In 2019 the number of claims made was 250 (compared to 318 in 2018 and 369 in 2017). In total only 53 claims were handled in 2019 (compared to 64 in 2018). Breaches were found in 28% of the cases (compared to 37% in 2018).[273] The number of claims is much greater than the number of handled cases, because many of the claims are as inadmissible for example because they have been made after the three months' time limit or in privacy-cases there is not consent from the victim.

The Council receives two-thirds of its funding from the media, while the Ministry of Justice accounts for the remainder.

271. *See* 4 § CMM, Basic Agreement of the Council for Mass Media: http://www.jsn.fi/en/Council_for_Mass_Media/basic-agreement-of-the-council-for-mass-media/ 6.7.2020).

272. According to s. 9, The journalist is encouraged to make known his/her profession during the course of an assignment. Information should be obtained openly. If matters that are in the public interest cannot be otherwise investigated, the journalist may carry out interviews and obtain information by means that depart from standard practice.

273. *See* more from CMM's yearly report in 2018: http://www.jsn.fi/ContentFiles/6/Sisaltosivut/JSN_toimintakertomus2018[5].pdf (29.8.2019) and CMM's yearly report in 2019 http://www.jsn.fi/ContentFiles/6/Sisaltosivut/Vuosiljulkaisu%202019.pdf (25.9.2020).

Part III. Regulation of Audiovisual Media (Broadcasting)

Chapter 1. General Issues

119. Both traditional broadcasting media (radio and television) and on-demand audiovisual media services are regulated in the Act on Electronic Communications Services (971/2014). Specific provisions on audiovisual media and radio activities are included in Part VIII of the Act: Chapter 25 includes regulation of content and Chapter 26 regulates marketing. The provisions were previously included in the Act on Television and Radio Operations (744/1998),[274] which for its part implemented the TVwF Directive and the subsequent AVMS Directive (2007/65/EC). Some amendments, however, were made by the Act on Electronic Communications Services. Regulation concerning events of major importance to society included in Chapter 25 is discussed separately. Moreover, it must be noted that the reform of the AVMS Directive has led to proposed amendments concerning the scope of regulation to cover video-sharing platform services, while also increasing obligations aimed at protecting minors.[275]

Section 3 of the Act on Electronic Communications Services includes definitions of some key terms. *Audiovisual content service* is defined as television broadcasting and video-on-demand services offered as business activity to the public (point 2). *Audiovisual programme* means a movie, television programme, communication to the public of events, as well as other repertory comprised mainly of moving images and sound attached thereto (point 1). *Programme* (programming; repertory) means ‘a pre-selected composition of audiovisual programmes or radio programmes’ (point 12). *Information society service* is defined as electronic distance services provided at individual recipients’ request, usually against payment (point 29). The definition of audiovisual content services and programmes are subject to proposed changes, while some new definitions have also been proposed, including that of a *video-sharing platform service* and *user-generated video.*[276]

120. The Act on Electronic Communications Services was not intended to bring radical changes to the regulation of audiovisual content services or radio activity.

274. Unofficial translation by the Ministry of Transport and Communications; amendments up to 129/2013 included: https://www.finlex.fi/fi/laki/kaannokset/1998/en19980744.pdf (29.8.2019).
275. Government bill (HE 98/2020 vp), 1.
276. Ibid. 15, 171–174.

However, the limitations in the previous Communications Market Act (393/2003) with regard to its scope of application so as to exclude the *content* of communication had to be removed as to Act came to include provisions of the previous Act on Television and Radio Operations (744/1998).[277]

In the Act on Electronic Communications Services, a *network service* means a service whereby a network operator provides a communication network in its ownership or possession for purposes of transferring and distributing messages (§ 3, point 34). A *communications service* means a service that consists solely or mainly of transferring messages in a communications network as well as the transfer and transmission of messages in a mass communications network (point 37). The scope of application was however not affected by the codification. Thus, the definitions of network or communications services still do not cover content services. This means separating, for instance, free or pay-television programming from the means of communication.[278] Moreover, broadband connection and IPTV services are regarded as communications services whereas internet-based content may be accessible with the former. Communications networks and communications services are subjected to criteria for their quality (e.g., reliability, interoperability, capacity). These provisions are included in Chapter 29 of the Act. Following the reform of the EECC, the definition of an electronic communication service is subject to proposed amendments.[279]

121. There are electronic media-related activities that require various licences, while some other activities only carry the obligation to notify TRAFICOM. It should be noted that the same actor, such as an audiovisual media service provider or a broadcaster, may be covered by various provisions, depending on the type of activity and operations.

Chapters 25 and 26 of the Act on Electronic Communications Services are applicable to audiovisual content services provided by a natural or legal person established in Finland, provided that the service may be received in one or more countries belonging to the EEA or states party to the European Convention on Transfrontier Television. Moreover, the chapters are applicable to radio activity if the frequency is granted by Finland or a Finnish distribution network is used (§ 206). However, local television broadcasting is excluded from the scope of quotas for European works and independent producers. The same exclusion applies to transmissions which cannot be received in any EEA-country or state party to the European Convention on Transfrontier Television outside Finland (§ 208). In addition, according

277. Government bill (HE 221/2013 vp), 63, 93. According to the Government bill (HE 221/2013 vp, 79–80), the applicability of the Code with regard to the Province of Åland is determined pursuant to the Act on the Autonomy of Åland (1144/1991). National legislation applies in areas of State competence. Provincial competence concerning broadcasting and cable activity covers audiovisual content services whereby the Code is not applicable to such activities in the Province. Regarding telecommunications, national competence prevails and national legislation applies (e.g., where spectrum administration is concerned) – albeit with the requirement of consent by the Government of Åland where general telecommunications is granted permission by the State official. *See also* Government Decree (1244/2014) on the use of frequencies and the frequency plan in the Province of Åland issued pursuant to s. 95 of the Code.

278. Government bill (HE 221/2013 vp), 93.

279. Government bill (HE 98/2020 vp), 22, 174.

to section 206(3), Part VIII does not apply to services where audiovisual content or radio transmissions are only receivable in educational establishments, hospitals, hotels, or corresponding facilities, nor does it apply to analogue radio broadcasting with a maximum duration of three months or minor radio broadcasting of limited scope in the meaning of section 34(2).

Legal obligations related to impartiality and non-discrimination mostly concern the national public service broadcaster. According to section 7 of the Act on Yleisradio (1380/1993), public service programming content is to be based on such values as tolerance, multiculturalism, equality, and pluralism. It should be noted, however, that the content of audiovisual programmes is subject to classification and rating according to age suitability, and restrictions may be imposed pursuant to the Act on Audiovisual Programmes (*kuvaohjelmalaki* 710/2011).[280] This is justified by the protection of minors. In principle, content regulation does not extend to those providing *merely* technical services, such as activities related to distribution (e.g., telecommunications companies).

122. People with visual or hearing impairment are catered for by obliging content providers to provide subtitles for Finnish or Swedish television programmes, while other programmes are to be complemented by explanation or a service whereby text is converted to voice (§ 211(1)). Audio-subtitling and subtitling must be added to public service programming pursuant to the Act on Yleisradio (1380/1993). Moreover, they must be added to programming 'of public interest' pursuant to section 26 and as issued by Government Decree. However, audio-subtitling and subtitling services need not be attached to music or sports programmes (§ 211(2)). As a result of the Act on Electronic Communications Services, children's programmes are no longer outside the scope of these subtitling requirements, since there was reportedly a need for such services, which were considered beneficial for immigrant children, among others.[281] Following the reform of the AVMS Directive, the obligations related to subtitling and accessibility are subject to amendments that aim to extend and fortify them.[282]

Section 26 regulates the granting of programming licences for public interest television operations. Conditions include, *inter alia*, daily provision of Finnish and Swedish programmes as well as news and current affairs programmes. The regulation on subtitling services was previously included in section 19 a (2) of the Act on Television and Radio Operations. Audio-subtitling and subtitling obligations are further regulated in Government Decree 1245/2014, whereby they must be accompanied to programming with a nationwide licence and catering for several audiences, that is, in case they are freely available throughout the country and include Finnish and Swedish programmes on a daily basis, among others. The Ministry of Transport and Communications laid down this type of programming with its decision (§ 8).

280. Unofficial translation by the Ministry of Education and Culture: https://www.finlex.fi/fi/laki/kaannokset/2011/en20110710.pdf (29.8.2019).
281. Government bill (HE 221/2013 vp), 171; the Report of the Transport and Communications Committee (LiVM 8/2010 vp), 4.
282. Government bill (HE 98/2020 vp), 15, 253.

123. Gradually increasing quotas may be introduced by Government decree for programmes subject to subtitling obligations (§ 211(3)). For the period 2011–2016, the quota for programmes of public interest can be set at 10%–50% and for public service programmes 50%–100% of programme hours (§ 221(3)–(4)). The graduated approach was specified in Government Decree 292/2011 on subtitling services and the Annex thereto; currently, the provisions are included in Government Decree on television and radio operations (1245/2014). TRAFICOM (previously FICORA) has sent notification letters to broadcasters in cases of non-compliance. For instance, as *all* public service programmes (with translation subtitles) are to be accompanied by audio-subtitling service (*see* Annex to the decree), Yleisradio was found in breach of its obligation in 2011, when the proportion only amounted to 85%.[283]

More detailed provisions on the exercise of the constitutional freedom of expression in mass communications are included in the Act on the Exercise of Freedom of Expression in Mass Media (460/2003). The Act also applies to broadcasting and programme activity in Finland (§ 3(1)). Merely sections 17–20 and 22 (§ 3(3)) (i.e., provisions on the obligation to submit identification data, seizure, and orders to cease and destroy) apply to technical production, transmission, distribution, or intermediation. According to the definitions in section 2, a *programme* means a coherent set of network messages primarily expressed as sound or moving picture (point 3). Programmes are specific forms of network messages with a focus on sound and images. *Programme activity* means the provision of programmes for reception by the public (point 8). Besides traditional publishing and broadcasting, the act also applies to new forms of mass media, such as on-demand services.

Questions related to duties and obligations in mass communications rely on a system of responsible editors.[284] According to section 4 of the Act on the Exercise of Freedom of Expression in Mass Media, a programme provider must appoint a responsible editor for programmes. However, it is possible to appoint several such editors. The responsible editor supervises and directs editorial work and makes final decisions concerning programme content. The identity of the responsible editor(s), and the division of responsibility between several persons, must be disclosed in the programme activity. Access to information concerning the responsible editor is guaranteed for all (§ 5(2)–(4)).

124. The obligation to publish official announcements free of charge is provided in section 7 of the Act. This applies in cases concerning life and health or significant interests related to property or the environment and cases of comparable importance. Such announcements often involve danger related to explosives, poisonous substances, or dangerous animals.

Chapter 4 of the Act on the Exercise of Freedom of Expression in Mass Media contains provisions concerning responsibilities and obligations for the content of published messages, including programming content. This means provisions on criminal and tort liability and editorial misconduct. Crimes are included in the

283. FICORA's Letter No 145/9220/2012, 29.3.2012.
284. For more, *see* Neuvonen 2012, 236–242; Tiilikka 2007.

Criminal Code (39/1889), while media violation is included in section 21 of the Act. Confidentiality of sources is provided in section 16. Coercive measures are included in Chapter 5. These include the obligation to submit identification data and orders to cease the distribution of programmes.

Chapter 2. Public Service Broadcasting

§1. Mission

125. The Finnish public service broadcaster is Yleisradio. Its activity is regulated by the Act on Yleisradio (1380/1993) as well as the Act on Electronic Communications Services (917/2014) and other relevant legislation.

Public service is set out in section 7 of the Act on Yleisradio: according to the provisions, the task and mission of the company is to provide, on equal terms, comprehensive radio and television programming for all. Public service content may be offered nationally and regionally. In particular, public service programming is to support democracy and universal participation by offering a wide variety of information, opinions, and discussion as well as opportunities for interaction. It is also to produce, create, develop, and preserve national culture, art, and entertainment. Yleisradio's programming should take aspects of education and equality into account, offer opportunities for self-development as well as emphasize programming for children and the young. Religious or spiritual programming is to be offered as well (§ 7).

Moreover, Yleisradio is obliged to give equal treatment to the country's Finnish and Swedish speaking populations and produce services in Sámi, Romani, and sign languages. Where applicable, it should also offer services for the country's other language groups. Programming is to support the cherishing of Finnish cultural heritage, tolerance, equality, and cultural diversity, while also catering for minorities and special groups. It should promote cultural interaction and provide for programming targeted abroad. Finally, the public service remit includes the transmission of official announcements as issued by decree and the making of preparations for providing television and radio in states of emergency and exceptional circumstances (§ 7).

126. The journalistic activities of Yleisradio are to comply with good journalistic practices, and the public service media follows the Guidelines for Journalists. The Council for Mass Media (CMM) in Finland issues notices on compliance with the Guidelines. In addition, Yleisradio has its own guidelines on programme activity. New ethical guidelines for Yleisradio's programmes and content were adopted in 2017, after being approved by the Administrative Council.[285] These guidelines include principles similar to the general journalistic guidelines, but they also discuss the negative stance towards commercial content and advertising as well as sponsorship. Moreover, guidelines are laid down for content concerning elections. Previously, Yleisradio had its own regulations concerning its programme activity; they were replaced by the ethical guidelines in 2012. Furthermore, Yleisradio also has principles guiding social media presence and activities.[286] The principles emphasize interaction and respect for the logics of social networking, use of social

285. *See* the current guidelines from year 2017 in Finnish at https://yle.fi/aihe/artikkeli/2017/11/20/yle n-ohjelmatoiminnan-ja-sisaltojen-eettiset-ohjeet (29.8.2019).

286. *See* the principles at http://yle.fi/aihe/artikkeli/2015/01/11/sosiaalisen-median-toimintalinjaukset (29.8.2019).

media to target groups outside the range of traditional broadcasting as well as for journalistic and informative purposes. Reliability and independence are also named as the core guidelines. Moreover, content should be openly accessible and the personnel or persons involved in content production must note the difficulty of separating private and public personality in social media.

As regards the system of responsible editors, Yleisradio is subject to the provisions of the Act on the Exercise of Freedom of Expression in Mass Media (460/2003). Furthermore, the Act on the Use of Orphan Works (*laki orpoteosten käyttämisestä* 764/2013) provides the possibility for public service broadcasters to use orphan works in order to fulfil their duties under their public service remit (§ 2, point 3).

In 2012, *ex ante* testing was introduced for public service media. The Act on Yleisradio was amended to include provisions concerning prior evaluation. According to section 6a of the Act, prior evaluation is required for 'such new services and functions that have a more than insignificant influence on the available content services as a whole and that are considerable in terms of significance, duration, and cost'.[287] Then again, it is also possible to conduct an evaluation in other cases if deemed necessary. The evaluation is to include estimations of the impact of the new service or function on the market and competition as well as other impacts (§ 6 a(3)).

The initiative for such an assessment may come from the Administrative Council or it may be requested by Yleisradio Oy or a third party.[288] A form for requesting assessment is available on Yleisradio's website.[289]

§2. Organization

127. Section 5 of the Act on Yleisradio contains provisions for the company's Administrative Council (*hallintoneuvosto*). Members of the Council are elected by the Finnish Parliament in the first session of a parliamentary term. They should include representatives of science, the arts, education, business and economics and representatives from various social and language groups. The duties of the Council are listed in section 6, including responsibility for the election and dismissal of the company's Board of Directors and its Chairman. It also decides on issues concerning significant restriction or expansion of Yleisradio's activities or significant changes in the organization of the company and oversees and supervises public service activities. The Council must also execute *ex ante* tests pursuant to section 6a. Moreover, the Council supervises the administration of the company and issues statements on the company's finances.

287. Unofficial translation by the Ministry of Transport and Communications: https://www.finlex.fi/en/laki/kaannokset/1993/en19931380.pdf (20.7.2020).
288. For more, *see* Government bill (HE 29/2012 vp), 37–39. *See also* Tarhonen 2014.
289. *See* https://yle.fi/aihe/artikkeli/2015/01/11/merkittavien-palvelujen-ennakkoarviointi (29.8.2019).

Even before the provisions on testing were enacted, Yleisradio's high definition (HD) transmissions were under scrutiny. After approval from the Administrative Council, the service was launched in 2011. The evaluation was conducted pursuant to the Amsterdam Protocol and the Commission's Communication (2009/C 257/1) on the application of state aid rules to public service broadcasting, especially point 84, in which prior evaluation for new audiovisual services by PSBs is required.[290]

The first *ex ante* testing conducted on the basis of the new legislation concerned the rental of free studio capacity belonging to Yleisradio in the city of Tampere (the request also refers to plans regarding Helsinki). The Administrative Council approved the activity in April 2014. According to the assessment, rental was not considered to have a detrimental effect on competition provided market prices were imposed. Thus, rental should not unduly include related services that can be produced separately. Personnel may also be offered separately.[291]

TRAFICOM currently supervises many aspects of Yleisradio. Section 12a of the Act on Yleisradio includes the economic supervisory tasks of TRAFICOM, whereas section 12b states that Yleisradio Oy must annually submit a report to TRAFICOM on its public service. The submission of the report is the task of the Administrative Council. TRAFICOM then issues a statement on that basis to the Government.

A Parliamentary Working Group (2016) recommends strengthening the position of the Administrative Council (e.g., decisions on strategy) while also introducing a permanent procedure for hearing experts on issues, such as Yle's market effects. Moreover, representation for political parties with at least three parliament seats should be guaranteed.[292]

§3. Financing

128. Since 2013, Yleisradio has been funded from the state budget. Its financing relies on the so-called public broadcasting tax.[293] In section 2 of the Act on Public

290. *See* the Report on the assessment (17.3.2011) at http://avoinyle.fi/www/fi/liitetiedostot/Raportti_Yleisradion_teravapiirtotelevisiolahetysten_yhteiskunnallisia_vaikutuksia_koskevasta_arvioinnista_Nieminen.pdf (29.8.2019).

291. *See* 'Kilpailuvaikutusten ennakkoarviointi' (Report on the assessment of effects to competition), Borenius Attorneys at Law, 29.4.2014; *see also* information on the approval by the Administrative Council at http://yle.fi/aihe/artikkeli/2014/04/29/ylen-hallintoneuvoston-ennakkoarvioinnin-tulos-yle-saa-vuokrata (29.8.2019).

292. *See* the Report 'Yleisradio Oy:n julkisen palvelun tehtävät ja siihen liittyvät muut uudistukset' (Yleisradio Oy's public service remit and other related reforms), 2 and Annex 2 (proposal for amendments too the Yle Act): http://www.lvm.fi/lvm-site62-mahti-portlet/download?did=207240 (29.8.2019) as well as the press release by the Ministry of Transport and Communications 'Working group: Parliamentary consensus on the duties and funding of Yle' (16 Jun. 2016): http://www.lvm.fi/en/-/working-group-parliamentary-consensus-on-the-duties-and-funding-of-y-1 (29.8.2019).

293. *See* Government bill (HE 29/2012 vp). For more, *see* Tiilikka 2012a.

Broadcasting Tax (484/2012) as amended by Act 817/2017 in force from 1 December 2017, the tax is set at 2.5% of a natural person's annual earned income and capital income that exceeds EUR 14 000, with a maximum amount of EUR 163.[294] Section 3 of the Act, sets the tax for legal persons at EUR 140 plus 0.35% of taxable income exceeding EUR 50,000, with a ceiling of EUR 3,000. The Act on the State Television and Radio Fund (745/1998)[295] regulates Yle's financing and aims at promotion of TV and radio activities (§ 1). The fund is managed by TRAFICOM. Financing for PSB flows from state budget to the fund, while annual index reviews are executed pursuant to the act (§ 3; freezed in 2016 by Act 1501/2015 and in 2015 by Act 1045/2014). A report by the Parliamentary Working Group (2016) suggested freezing annual reviews until 2020, with the possibility of executing an increase for 2019.[296]

According to section 12 of the Act on Yleisradio, the company cannot transmit advertisements in connection with either its television or radio programming or other content services provided within its public service remit through various telecommunications networks. The company is also prohibited from producing sponsored content.

129. After the 2012 amendments to the Act on Yleisradio and its subsequent funding by taxation, a popular lottery show, *Lotto*, was removed from Yleisradio's programming. *Lotto* had been running on Yleisradio's channel for decades, but FICORA decided that it was a question of sponsored content (138/931/2013, 14.5.2013): TV coverage for Lotto had been the result of cooperation between Yleisradio and the Finnish gaming company Veikkaus, which had financed the show's production. Lotto was removed from Yle's programming at the end of 2013, and it now runs on the commercial channel MTV3.

FICORA also concluded that Yleisradio was in breach of section 12 when producing programmes on harness racing in cooperation with the gaming company Fintoto Oy. The decision (31/931/2014, 14.4.2014) prohibited Yle from continuing to transmit these sponsored programmes.

In December 2014 FICORA announced a decision (478/931/2014, 17.12.2014) concerning the televising of a popular Finnish singing contest, *Tangomarkkinat*. According to the decision, Yleisradio had breached the ban on transmitting advertising by showing the event's trademark for marketing purposes, which might have misled the viewers. The programme was not, however, sponsored by the event. FICORA further clarified the law by stating that giving exposure to trademarks does not, as such, correspond to advertising which is banned.

---

294. For more on taxation, *see* the Finnish Tax Administrator: https://www.vero.fi/en/About-us/newsroom/visual_aids_for_presentations_and_for_t/public_broadcasting_tax/ (29.8.2019).

295. Unofficial translation by Ministry of Transport and Communications; amendments up to 475/2012 included: https://www.finlex.fi/en/laki/kaannokset/1998/en19980745_20120475.pdf (29.8.2019).

296. *See* the Report 'Yleisradio Oy:n julkisen palvelun tehtävät ja siihen liittyvät muut uudistukset' (Yleisradio Oy's public service remit and other related reforms), 2–3: http://www.lvm.fi/lvm-site62-mahti-portlet/download?did=207240 (29.8.2019) and the press release by the Ministry of Transport and Communications 'Working group: Parliamentary consensus on the duties and funding of Yle' (16.6.2016): http://www.lvm.fi/en/-/working-group-parliamentary-consensus-on-the-duties-and-funding-of-y-1 (29.8.2019).

Chapter 3. Regulating Electronic Media Operations

130. Public service broadcasting (PSB/PSM) is covered by a dedicated Act on Yleisradio as well as other relevant legislation and Yleisradio is granted by law the right to operate digital television and radio broadcasting without a programming licence whereas operations of other actors fall within the scope of general rules and regulations.

Moreover, a new Chapter to the Act on Electronic Communications Services was introduced by Act 456/2016 which concerns Public Regulated Service (PRS) pursuant to the Galileo programme.[297] The provisions therein concern the entities entitled to be included in the service as well as production and export of related technology. Authorized users are determined by the Ministry of Transport and Communications, a board will approve production, and the Foreign Affairs decides on export while TRAFICOM may provide more detailed orders (e.g., on the management of keys), performs intermediary tasks and must be consulted on export issues (§ 271 a–c).

§1. Licensing Requirements

131. The traditional separation between press freedom and regulation of electronic mass media (TV, radio) is still somewhat apparent in the field of licensing schemes. The operation of digital terrestrial television and mobile phone networks which rely on radio frequencies require licence (network licence) and the transmission of radio or television programming in terrestrial mass communications networks is also subject to licensing (programming licence). The former enables provision of network service, possession and use of frequencies, while the latter makes possible the transmission of programming. Moreover, operations, such as television activity in a cable network, must be notified.

Notification is regulated in Chapter 2 of the Act on Electronic Communications Services. Network licences and programming licences for television and radio operations are regulated in Chapters 3–5 while provisions on radio licences are in Chapter 6 of the Act. The regulation of notifications and licences was previously provided for in the Communications Market Act (*viestintämarkkinalaki* 393/2003) and the Act on Television and Radio Operations (*laki televisio- ja radiotoiminnasta* 744/1998). Provisions on issuing licences through an auction process for certain frequency bands were laid down in the Act on Auctioning Certain Radio Frequencies (*laki eräiden radiotaajuuksien huutokaupoista* 462/2009).[298]

Previously, programming licences for TV and radio activity in terrestrial mass communications networks were regulated in the Act on Television and Radio Operations; they were granted by the Government and in some cases by TRAFICOM.

297. *See* Government bill (HE 67/2016 vp). The act entered into force 20.6.2016. Galileo is a programme establishing a European satellite navigation system. *See* PRS Decision No 1104/2011/EU and Galileo Regulation (EU) No 1285/2013.

298. For the previous system and its history (incl. separation of the types of licences in 2002), *see*, *e.g.*, Ojanen – Tiilikka – Vairimaa 2012, 7–8.

Provisions concerning the grant of network licences with a view to frequencies were included in the Communications Market Act. The previous system for granting licences largely relied on a comparative procedure where the Government assessed the appropriateness of licences in light of quality criteria. The system was complemented and revised in 2009 so as to introduce auctioning of certain frequencies.[299]

132. The proposal on the amendments concerned the granting of licences via auction for general telecommunications in the frequency band 2500–2690 MHz. The European Commission decision (2008/477/EC) concerning the harmonization of this frequency band is referred to in the preparatory works.[300] The Government's 2012 Communications Policy Programme noted that telecommunications licences have been granted through the comparative method referred to above, with the exception of the 2009 trial auction.[301] In 2013 the 800 MHz frequency band was auctioned.[302]

In 2014, the provisions concerning licences and auctions were incorporated into the Act on Electronic Communications Services (917/2014). The system for granting licences was also renewed so as to correspond to technological development and the market-oriented environment. The administration of licences was simplified, especially in cases where there is no scarcity of frequencies. Inefficiencies were also tackled: competitive tendering of network operators was deemed beneficial while frequencies already in use would be subjected to payment (*see* § 288: the market-based spectrum fee).[303] The Constitutional Law Committee assessed the proposed provisions in light of freedom of expression and freedom to conduct business. In principle, it has viewed licensing as problematic. However, as regards network licences, scarcity of frequencies still provides justification for regulation whereas programming licences in the field of television and radio activity must also be reviewed in the future as circumstances continue to develop. The Committee, however, also noted the fact that discretion would be mainly based on requirements prescribed by law and therefore more acceptable from the point of view of freedom of expression and the ban on prior censorship.[304]

---

299. *See* Government bill (HE 37/2009 vp); Government bill (HE 72/2012 vp), 4. The comparative procedure has been referred to as 'beauty contest'; the system has its strengths but there are challenges with regard to transparency and neutrality. Auction has been considered a more straightforward process in these regards (*see* HE 72/2012 vp, 4).
300. *See* Government bill (HE 37/2009 vp), 8.
301. Communications Policy Programme for Electronic Media (2012), 37. *See also* Government bill (HE 72/2012 vp), 3–5: the auction was tailored for an individual frequency band (2500–2690 MHz) reserved for wireless broadband. The Act on Auctioning Certain Radio Frequencies dated back to 2009.
302. Government bill (HE 72/2012 vp); Government bill (HE 221/2013 vp), 10–11, 57; Lehtisaari 2015, 138. The Act on Auctioning Certain Radio Frequencies was amended so as to enable auction of the frequency band.
303. Government bill (HE 221/2013 vp), 57–59; Report of the Transport and Communications Committee (LiVM 10/2014 vp). *See also* FICORA's newsletter 'Tehokkuutta toimilupien myöntämiseen' (Efficiency in licensing) (23.4.2015): http://pilvi.viestintavirasto.fi/viestintavirasto/signaali/signaali2015/tehokkuuttatoimilupienmyontamiseen.html (29.8.2019).
304. *See* Statement of the Constitutional Law Committee (PeVL 18/2014 vp); cf. Statement (PeVL 3/2010 vp).

133. According to the Act on Electronic Communications Services, network licences are mainly granted through a comparative Government procedure, while programming licences are mainly granted by TRAFICOM, following the requirements provided in law. Only if the Government is required to grant a programming licence is there a need to assess appropriateness.

Section 4(1) of the Act on Electronic Communications Services states that a telecommunications operator established in Finland must submit a *notification* to TRAFICOM before engaging in television activities other than television broadcasting subject to licence or offering on-demand audiovisual media services. Operators must also notify TRAFICOM before engaging in general telecommunications or linear pay-television services in the terrestrial digital network using a decoding system. Short-term or minor activity need not be notified (§ 4(2)). The notification obligation was extended to improve the efficiency of supervisory tasks. The notification, which may be submitted electronically, mainly serves informational purposes, as it does not create rights or responsibilities. A point of note is that there is an overlap in the case of on-demand service providers that are obliged to provide notification of their operations to both TRAFICOM and the authority responsible for supervising audiovisual programmes with a view to the protection of minors.[305] According to section 5 of the Act on Electronic Communications Services, TRAFICOM keeps a public register on the notifications it receives. The reform of the AVMS Directive has led to proposed changes so that video-sharing platform services would come under notification obligation.[306]

134. The Government announces the availability of *network licences*, with the exception of licences granted by TRAFICOM (§ 7).

As regards digital terrestrial mass communications networks, no network licence is required for the operation for a short term of a network service that uses radio frequencies, provided that its activities last a maximum of one month and the radiation power of the television transmitter does not exceed 50 W (§ 6(3), point 1). The same exception applies in cases where the radiation power is very low and its operation covers a limited area (§ 6(3), point 2). A good example is provided by television transmission in shopping malls.[307] Proposed changes to the licensing requirement include small scale local activities.[308]

Section 9 of the Act states that if operations last for a maximum of three months and the radiation power does not exceed 2 kW, a network licence is granted by TRAFICOM. According to section 8, the Government grants free-of-charge licences for telecommunications operations using radio frequencies in the digital terrestrial mass communications network (*see* § 6(1)) and for mobile networks functioning as a public authority network operating in more than one municipality (*see* § 6(2)). These licences are granted using a comparative procedure. The requirements are specified in law (§§ 8, 10).

305. Government bill (HE 221/2013 vp), 96–97.
306. Government bill (HE 98/2020 vp), 176, 178.
307. Government bill (HE 221/2013 vp), 99–100.
308. Government bill (HE 98/2020 vp), 180.

Under the *comparative procedure*, the licence must be granted where the applicant has sufficient financial resources and there is no reason to suspect breach of law and no particularly weighty reasons to suspect danger to national safety. In cases of scarcity, licences must be granted to those applicants whose activity would best serve the goals specified in section 1 of the Act (i.a., availability and quality of services, competition) (§ 10). This is an overall assessment (cf. *infra* on programming licences). In addition, the Government may grant a network licence by *auction* if new frequencies are allotted for public telecommunications operations in the mobile network. The licence must be granted to the highest bidder for the frequency band or pair in an open, unbiased, and non-discriminatory auction. The auction is arranged by TRAFICOM, which may also issue detailed instructions for the procedure (§§ 8(2), 11, 12). Proposed amendments include changing the highest bid to the winning bid.[309]

Licences for temporary operations (*see* § 9(1)) must be granted if radio frequencies can be allocated and there is no reason to suspect a breach of law (§ 9(1)–(2)). The period between two consecutive temporary licences must be at least two months (§ 9(3)). The Government grants network licences for a fixed term, with a maximum duration of twenty years. Moreover, the licence may be accompanied by conditions related to technical features and efficient use of frequencies, transmission technique and decoding, as well as terms concerning capacity reserved for a programming licence holder (§ 16). Following the reform of the EECC, proposed changes include a minimum of fifteen years duration and a shorter period respectively for certain types of activities.[310]

The 700 MHz band was allocated for mobile communications, i.e., wireless broadband from 2017 onwards, whereas the 800 MHz band was auctioned following Government Resolution and reserved for broadband use. The 4G-network is extended within these frequency bands.[311]

135. Programming licences[312] for television and radio activity in digital terrestrial mass communications networks are applied from TRAFICOM; however, exceptions apply where reception of audiovisual content services or radio transmission is possible only in certain establishments (e.g., hospital) or where audiovisual content provision is not regular nor the main purpose of the service (§§ 22–23). The national public broadcasting company, Yleisradio, also has the right to operate digital television and radio broadcasting without a licence (§ 22 Act on Electronic Communications Services; § 7 Act on Yleisradio). According to section 25, TRAFICOM must grant a programming licence to the applicant provided that the requirements

309. Government bill (HE 98/2020 vp), 182.

310. Ibid. 183.

311. *See, e.g.*, Communications Policy Programme for Electronic Media (2012), 93; for the uncertainties and the need for analysis, *see* Report of the Transport and Communications Committee (LiVM 10/2014 vp). *See also* 'Request for opinions on the 700 MHz auction' (22.6.2016): http://www.lvm.fi/en/-/request-for-opinions-on-the-700-mhz-auction (29.8.2019).

312. Regarding programming licences for Åland, competence is vested on the provincial Government. *See also* FICORA's newsletter 'Tehokkuutta toimilupien myöntämiseen' (Efficiency in licensing) (23.4.2015): http://pilvi.viestintavirasto.fi/viestintavirasto/signaali/signaali12015/tehokkuuttatoimilupienmyontamiseen.html (29.8.2019).

laid down in the same section are met. These requirements include the payment of the application fee, solvency, and a report on the organization of content distribution (§ 25(1)). The grant is transferred to the Government if the applicants are too numerous in terms of available transmission capacity or if granting the licence could have a significant effect on the development of the communications market; the application may be supplemented with plans for the content within a fortnight (§ 25(3)). In its assessment the Government must strive to promote free speech and safeguard both the diversity of programming and needs of special groups in a way that best serves the goals specified in section 1 of the Act (§ 25(5)).

Section 26 includes provisions on the granting of programming licences for the so-called public interest television operations. Capacity for these operations is designated by Government decree (*see* § 95). The procedure for granting licences follows the framework set out in sections 23 and 25(1) of the Act on Electronic Communications Services. The licence must be granted if the applicant meets the requirements laid down in section 26(3); these include the payment of the licence fee, free and nationwide reception of the transmissions (excl. Åland), as well as inclusion of subtitling services. Moreover, proposed changes include a minimum of eight-hour daily broadcasting time.[313]

Programming licences for public interest television operations are granted by TRAFICOM, unless there is scarcity of capacity or possible significant effects. In the latter case, the Government must take into account who would best meet the requirements laid down in sections 26(3) and 25(1) and (5) (§ 26(6)).

The provisions on designated capacity for public interest channels (together with those on PSB) aim at safeguarding the continuity of domestic content production as well as the quality and diversity of domestic television activity. Commercial public interest channels are to be available throughout the country.[314]

According to section 27, programming licences are granted for a fixed term, with a maximum duration of ten years. This applies both to public interest licence holders and to other programme licence holders and regardless of whether the licence is granted by the Government or TRAFICOM. Temporary programming licences for short-term radio and television operations in the digital terrestrial mass communications network are granted by TRAFICOM. The operations must last for a maximum of three months (§ 28(1), point 1) or the weekly duration must be limited to eight hours (§ 28(2), point 2). The provisions of sections 23 and 25 need not be applied. With regard to activity pursuant to point 1, licences may not be granted for the same programming for consecutive three-month periods, while activity pursuant to point 2 may be licensed for a maximum duration of one year at a time[315] (*see* § 28). Act 456/2016 brought changes to the provisions so that the weekly duration was extended to twelve hours while the licence for activity pursuant to point 1 may be re-granted for the same entity or essentially same programming earliest after two

313. Government bill (HE 98/2020 vp), 95.
314. Government bill (HE 221/2013 vp), 109.
315. Government bill (HE 221/2013 vp), 111.

months after the expiry of the previous license (excl. temporary activity; cf. similar changes in § 40 on analogue radio lasting for maximum of three months).[316]

Licences granted by the Government may be accompanied by conditions related to regional coverage, daily broadcasting time, or transmission technique and capacity. In special cases, conditions may be imposed to safeguard diversity and the needs of special groups (§§ 27(3)–(4)).

A programming licence loses its validity if no regular activity has been commenced within six months from the first date of its period or if there is an interruption lasting over thirty days (§ 31).

Furthermore, separate provisions exist for *programming licences for analogue radio*, which are issued by TRAFICOM for a maximum of ten years, in Chapter 5 of the Act on Electronic Communications Services. Analogue radio activity for a maximum duration of three months, as well as minor activity within a limited area, may be carried out without a programming licence. Yleisradio's public service analogue radio activity need not be licensed (§§ 34, 37).

136. According to section 39 of the Act on Electronic Communications Services, a *radio licence* is required for the possession and use of radio transmitters. The licence is granted by TRAFICOM for a maximum of a ten-year or twenty-year period depending on the activity (§§ 39–40). Detailed provisions on the licence, conditions, and licence terms as well as the procedure are included in Chapter 6 of the Act. The provisions are subject to proposed changes.[317]

Various fees, including the application fee, participation and licence fees regarding the auction, as well as the spectrum fee, are regulated in Chapter 36 of the Act on Electronic Communications Services (§§ 285–288). However, according to section 352(10), section 288(1), point 1 on the market-based spectrum fee for network licence holders pursuant to section 39 is applicable only to licences granted after the entry into force of the Act that is when the licences are granted anew.[318] Spectrum administration is regulated in Chapter 13 of the Act.

316. Government bill (HE 67/2016 vp); the bill also meant many other changes to various provisions of the Information Society Code due to observed needs for regulatory amendments as well as pursuant to EU law, such as the European Radio Equipment Directive 2014/53/EU and Roaming and Open Internet Regulation (EU) 2015/2120. Moreover, provisions on Galileo Public Regulated Service (PRS) are included pursuant to PRS Decision No 1104/2011/EU.

317. Government bill (HE 98/2020 vp), 190.

318. *See also* Government bill (HE 221/2013 vp), 211.

Chapter 4. Programme Standards

§1. Cultural Diversity

I. Content Obligations (quota)

137. Quotas for European works are included in section 209 of the Act on Electronic Communications Services. Accordingly, television broadcasters are to reserve the majority of their annual transmission time for European works. However, the transmission time does not cover news, sporting events, competitive entertainment shows, advertising, teletext services, or teleshopping (§ 209(1)). More detailed provisions on the definition of European works are issued by Government Decree (1245/2014).

Providers of video-on-demand audiovisual services must promote the production and availability of European works by means of financial contribution, programme acquisition, and enhanced visibility, among others (§ 209(3)). Following the reform of the AVMS Directive, proposed amendments relate to a quota of 30% extending to video-on-demand service providers with a de minimis rule.[319]

Quotas for independent producers are included in section 210(1) of the Act on Electronic Communications Services. Television broadcasters are therefore obliged to reserve 19% of their transmission time as defined in section 209(1) for programmes produced by independent producers as defined in paragraph 2. Compared to the previous act on television and radio operations, the percentage was raised from 15% to 19% in line with the Communications Policy Programme for Electronic Media adopted by the Government in 2012.[320]

Exceptions to these quotas apply for activity subject to short-term programming licence and short-term analogue radio activity (§ 206(5)).

Compliance with these quotas is supervised by the Finnish Transport and Communications Agency (TRAFICOM). It also collects statistics on the number of works by European and independent producers and reports the data to the European Commission. For instance, in 2017 Yleisradio's channel TV1 dedicated over 90% of its programming to European works and around 34% to independent producers. The corresponding figures for MTV3 are around 85% and 59%, respectively (2017).[321]

II. Requirements Related to Language and Minorities

138. Language and minorities are taken into particular account in public service broadcasting. In its programming, Yleisradio is obliged to give equal treatment to the Finnish and Swedish speaking population and to produce services in Sámi,

319. Government bill (HE 98/2020 vp), 15, 251.
320. Communications Policy Programme for Electronic Media (2012); Government bill (HE 221/2013 vp), 170.
321. *See* FICORA, statistics for the year 2017 at https://www.FICORA (TRAFICOM).fi/sites/default/files/media/file/Tv-ohjelmien_eurooppalaisuus_ja_riippumattomuus_.pdf (29.8.2019).

Romani, and sign languages, as well as cater for the needs of the country's other language groups where applicable. Yleisradio should also provide services for minorities and special groups. Yleisradio consequently provides television news and children's programmes in the Sámi language. It also maintains the website *Yle Sápmin*,[322] which reports news in Sámi. Radio is also available in Sámi both over the airwaves and streamed on the internet. Yleisradio also has Russian news both on television and the web[323] as well as news coverage in English (Yle News), sign language, and simplified Finnish. For audio-subtitling and subtitling services, *see* above. Moreover, Yleisradio's Yle Mondo provides radio coverage in many languages, as it features various international radio services in its programming. In addition, a Russian radio station, *Sputnik*, operates in Finland. It aims to cater for both the Russian speaking minority in Finland as well as Russian speaking tourists.

§2. Protection of Minors

139. Section 12 of the Constitution of Finland, which addresses freedom of speech, includes a qualified clause on subjecting audiovisual programmes to restrictions necessary for the protection of children. These restrictions require legislating at the level of law, not decrees.

The modernization of the system for regulating audiovisual programmes occurred in tandem with the fundamental rights reform of the 1990s.[324] The outcome was the Act on the Classification of Audiovisual Programmes (775/2000).[325] The supervisory body was the Finnish Board of Film Classification (*Valtion elokuvatarkastamo*) regulated by the Act of the same name (776/2000). With the reform, the focus shifted to the protection of minors. In addition, the scope of regulation was extended to programme services provided on-demand as defined in section 2, point 3 of the new act from 2000. It should also be noted that in 2008 the National Audiovisual Archive (*Kansallinen audiovisuaalinen arkisto*; KAVI) started to operate taking over the duties of the Film Archive. Regulation concerning the archive was included in the act on KAVA (1434/2007).

Later, the Act on Audiovisual Programmes[326] (710/2011) and the Act on the Finnish Centre for Media Education and Audiovisual Programmes (711/2011) were enacted so as to renew the system of classification. In 2012, the Finnish Centre for Media Education and Audiovisual Programmes (*Mediakasvatus- ja kuvaohjelmakeskus*; MEKU) replaced the Finnish Board of Film Classification. Currently, the reform of the AVMS Directive has led to proposals that aim to fortify the protection of minors, including the extension of some obligations to video-sharing platforms. These amendments would also cover the Act on Audiovisual Programmes.[327]

---

322. *See* Yle in Sámi at http://yle.fi/uutiset/sapmi/ (29.8.2019).
323. *See* Yle in Russian at http://yle.fi/uutiset/novosti/ (29.8.2019).
324. *See* Neuvonen 2012, 342. For history, *see* Neuvonen 2010; 2012, 332–341.
325. Unofficial translation by the Ministry of Education; https://www.finlex.fi/fi/laki/kaannokset/2000/en20000775.pdf amendments up to 1380/2006 are included: (29.8.2019).
326. This Act replaced the Act on the Classification of Audiovisual Programmes (775/2000).
327. Government bill (98/2020 vp), 14, 17, 281, 299, 301.

140. The 2011 reform signified a focus on content rather than the means of distribution. It also combined elements of the previous system related to both the regulation of television programmes (FICORA) and regulation of other types of audiovisual content (the Finnish Board of Film Classification). The 2000 Act had already combined video and film and brought computer and video games within the scope of the Act (even if exemptions applied). Similarly, the 2011 reform aimed at adjusting the system to the new media landscape, also by means of increased focus on media education and distribution of information. The traditional form of prior inspection was abandoned.[328]

Currently, audiovisual programmes are rated, and restrictions on their provision may be imposed for the protection of minors pursuant to the Act on Audiovisual Programmes (710/2011). The Act on the Finnish Centre for Media Education and Audiovisual Programmes (711/2011) was repealed by Act 675/2013, while the Act on Audiovisual Programmes was also correspondingly amended. The system was renewed so as to combine KAVA and MEKU. Together they formed the National Audiovisual Institute (*Kansallinen audiovisuaalinen instituutti*; KAVI), which began operating in 1 January 2014.[329]

141. KAVI operates under the Ministry of Education and Culture and is regulated by the act of the same name, as amended by the reform (1434/2007). The act includes provisions on the duties and organs of the Institute. According to section 2 (point 5) of the act, KAVI is responsible for duties related to supervision and classification pursuant to the Act on Audiovisual Programmes. KAVI's Department for Media Education and Audiovisual Media (*Mediakasvatus- ja kuvaohjelmayksikkö*; MEKU) is responsible for the area of audiovisual programmes.[330]

According to section 3 of the Act on Audiovisual Programmes, an *audiovisual programme* is a film, television programme, game, or other content intended for viewing, by technical means, as moving images (point 1). This means that mere text, sound, or still pictures (or combinations thereof) remain out of the scope; in this sense, webpages, for instance, remain out of scope. *Provision of audiovisual programmes* means offering said programmes for the public to view (§ 3, point 3).

Section 2 includes definitions on the scope of application of the act. This means that it applies to audiovisual programme provision and its supervision in Finland, if said programmes are provided by a television or on-demand service subject to the Act on Television and Radio Operations (744/1998), currently the Act on Electronic Communications Services (917/2014) (§ 2(1)). The Act also applies to *other* audiovisual programme provision and its supervision in Finland if said programmes are provided by Finnish (-based) legal or natural persons or if the decision on the provision of programmes has been made in Finland (§ 2(1), points 1–3). However, if an audiovisual programme is included in programming originating outside Finland and is provided simultaneously with the original transmission, the provision is only

328. Government bill (HE 190/2010 vp). *See also* Neuvonen 2012, 343–345.
329. Government bill (HE 48/2013 vp).
330. *See* https://kavi.fi/en/media-education/ (29.8.2019).

subject to the provisions of section 4(1)–(3) and sections 7 and 25–29 (§ 2(2)). Proposed amendments include extension to video-sharing platform services that fall under the scope of the Electronic Communications Code by means of cross-referencing a number of provisions.[331]

142. The provision of audiovisual programmes is subject to notification requirements. According to section 4 of the Act, the provider is to notify KAVI in cases where the intended activity is carried out for commercial purposes and on a regular basis. However, no notification to KAVI is needed if all the audiovisual programmes offered are exempt from classification and labelling requirements pursuant to sections 9–11 of the Act on Audiovisual Programmes.

Exemptions concern educational programmes as well as programmes solely focused on areas such as music, sports, gardening, cooking, or game shows, marketing or news material and political bulletins. Moreover, live transmissions are also exempted (§ 9). Audiovisual programmes are also exempted based on their purpose. This refers, *inter alia*, to content made available in and produced in connection to or for a network publication pursuant to the Act on the Exercise of Freedom of Expression in Mass Media, amateur content offered via dedicated services, as well as educational content made for and provided in connection to educational activities (§ 10). Furthermore, KAVI may allow provision by means of fixed-term exemptions or for a specific event (§ 11).

143. Audiovisual programmes may otherwise be provided only if they have been subjected to classification in accordance with the Act on Audiovisual Programmes and if a label indicating the age limit and content is displayed with the programme. Audiovisual programmes for adults may only be provided if clearly labelled with the age limit 18 (§ 5(1)). Labels used in the European Union may be accepted by KAVI for use in Finland (§ 16(3)).

Classification is performed by approved and trained audiovisual programme classifiers (§§ 12–14), for whom KAVI provides training and maintains a register (§ 2, point 5; § 6 a of the Act on KAVI 1434/2007). KAVI may also undertake to classify or re-classify an audiovisual programme due to suspected non-compliance or changes in societal assessments (§ 21). It may also inspect labelling (§ 23). A classifier may be withdrawn the approval as a disciplinary measure (§ 22).

Classification and rates rest on possible detrimental effects to children due to sexual or violent content, among others (§ 15 of the Act on Audiovisual Programmes). Section 16 includes detailed provisions on classification and age limits; the rates for programmes with detrimental effects to children include the age limits 7, 12, 16, and 18 (adults only). In addition, the class 'suitable for all' (S) (in Swedish 'T') is used if there is no risk to the development of children (§ 16(1)). Labels corresponding to these classes are used. Moreover, there are labels for content that contains violence, sex, or drug abuse, or may cause anxiety (Figure 1). These labels are used and shown in connection with television programmes, films, and audiovisual recordings. KAVI decides on the design of the labels (§ 5(2)).

331. Government bill (HE 98/2020 vp), 380.

Figure 1 Labels for Audiovisual Programmes[332]

Audiovisual programmes clearly intended only for adults are not subject to classification. For provision, they must be rated 18 (§ 16(2)).

Section 6(1) includes a prohibition on the provision to minors of audiovisual programmes rated 18. Such programmes may, however, be broadcast as a part of television programming late at night or as a scrambled transmission, as stated in paragraph 2.

144. According to section 6(3), the provider must ensure that an audiovisual programme with an age limit of 7, 12 or 16 is not available for younger viewers. This is to be achieved by timing unscrambled broadcasts, by offering preventive services in connection with the programme, or by checking the viewer's age in some other way.

Notification of audiovisual programmes that have been subject to classification must be given for inclusion in a database maintained by KAVI (§§ 17–18) unless already notified.

Provisions on appeal are included in Chapter 6 of the Act on Audiovisual Programmes as amended by Act 965/2014. Rectification to the decision of a classifier may be requested from KAVI while the Audiovisual Programme Board handles complaints against classification decisions by KAVI (§ 30). Further appeal on the Board's decisions is directed to the Supreme Administrative Court (33 §). KAVI's decisions concerning classifiers are to be appealed pursuant to the Administrative Judicial Procedure Act, and some Administrative Court decisions are subject to leave to appeal (§ 31). KAVI supervises compliance with the Act on Audiovisual Programmes (§ 19).

TV broadcasters have also been able to contract and streamline their practices around airing rated programmes on freely receivable channels (incl. graduated times).[333]

---

332. *See* more about age ratings at https://kavi.fi/ikarajat/ (8.10.2020).

333. *See*, *e.g.*, Neuvonen 2012, 348 and 'Televisio-ohjelmien lähetysajat ja ikärajat' (Transmission times and age limits for television programs): https://kavi.fi/ikarajat/annapalautetta/annapalautettamedia sta/ (13.12.2020).

§3. Right to Reply

145. The right to reply and correction is regulated in Chapter 3 of the Act on the Exercise of Freedom of Expression in Mass Media. Publishing replies and corrections is among the duties of the responsible editor. The replies and corrections must be published in due time, they must be appropriate in content and extent, and technical assistance must be provided where necessary (§ 10).

According to section 8, private persons have the right to have their replies published in the same programmes where the offending messages were included. The person must have a justified cause and the programme must be a regular transmission rather than a one-off event. Section 9 provides the right to correction for natural and legal persons (including corporations and public authorities). This means that erroneous information must be corrected by the programme provider in question in the same programme where the false information was presented. There is, however, no right to correction if it would be manifestly unnecessary due to the minor significance of the error.

While the previous Act was in force, the Supreme Court ruled on one case concerning the right to correction (KKO 2003:96), where it deemed that a current affairs TV programme had not broadcast incorrect information that required correction when it had used obscure hints and innuendo to imply dishonesty and inconsistencies in the public funding of a researcher and the research unit she represented. The general impressions created by the programme could not be addressed by correction; however, the person concerned could have appealed to her right of reply, which she had nevertheless failed to do.

146. Unless the same series of programmes is broadcasted again, false information must be corrected in another programme or broadcast produced by the operator, with the editor-in-chief deciding on the placement of the correction in the operator's programming. Section 10 of the Act on the Exercise of Freedom of Expression in Mass Media stipulates how and where a reply or correction shall be published or broadcasted. A 'similar space' should be reserved for the correction as for the message on which the demand is based. The correction cannot, therefore, be broadcast on late-night television or radio programme unless the original message was presented at that time. Reply or correction must be demanded in writing and within two weeks of the publication of the original message containing the offensive or erroneous content (§ 11(1)). If the right is denied, the matter may be submitted to a general court of law (§ 11(2)).

The Council for Mass Media (CMM) issues notices concerning compliance with the Guidelines for Journalists. Sections 20–25 of the Guidelines concern the right to reply and correction.

According to section 21, those criticized should be offered a chance to reply in the same connection. When this is not possible, it may be necessary to hear the party or publish their side of the story afterwards (section 22). Interestingly, section 20 notes that on the internet it is insufficient to remove the information or article containing the erroneous content. The public must be informed of the error.

During the years, the Council has assessed media activity on several occasions with regard to replies and corrections, and some cases involve radio and television.

For instance, in notice 5569/YLE/14, 10.12.2014, a television report on a long-standing local dispute was considered to have been executed contrary to the Guidelines, as it contained factual errors and the complainant (one party in the dispute in question) was not heard in the report. Moreover, there were also inadequacies in the correction, which was only issued after the second request to do so. The reporter had also published a column on the issue which made it clear that the subject was also of personal concern to the journalist (Vote 11-1; contains dissenting opinions).

In another notice (5411/TV/14, 21.5.2014), the Council concluded that a television channel had failed to follow good journalistic practice when a factual error contained in its evening news was not corrected. The error had been corrected by a news agency and a foreign newspaper.

In notice 4983/YLE/12, 13.3.2013, the Council considered that there had been no infringement of the Guidelines even though a person criticized in a TV show was later interviewed in connection with the show's extra internet content. This was because the person had considered the internet the most suitable forum for his comment on the issue, as opposed to the original medium.

Compare, however, a notice concerning the Guidelines of 2005 (4459/YLE/10, 17.2.2011), where the rules of good journalistic practice were considered to have been infringed by the publication of a correction solely on a TV programme's website rather than on the actual TV programme, as the correction should have been included in all the media used.

See also notice 4863/YLE/12, 21.11.2012, where the Guidelines were not infringed in a TV report on human relation (HR) disputes in a small municipality. Here, coverage of the other side of the story was limited due to the local authority's refusal to provide interviews.

In Case 6212/YLE/16 Yle got a notice because they corrected a factual error which they had published at the evening news, only at the news broadcast the next morning, but it did not correct the error at the web.

Chapter 5. Advertising Rules

§1. Regulation of Different Forms of Commercial Communication

In Finland, the provisions of the TVwF Directive as amended by Directive 97/36/EC were implemented by the Act on Television and Radio Operations (744/1998) while the amendments introduced by the AVMS Directive 2007/65/EC were included in the Act later.[334] Following the AVMS Directive, the Act came to extend its scope to on-demand media services with regard to the general principles of commercial communication and provisions on sponsoring, product placement, and European works. In 2014, these provisions were incorporated into the Information Society Code, now Act on Electronic Communications Services (917/2014). In some respects, advertising, teleshopping, sponsoring, and product placement are separated in the Act on Electronic Communications Services following the AVMS Directive. Some provisions in national law explicitly concern audiovisual media and/or television marketing, while others, however, also concern marketing on radio.

147. The definition of *teleshopping* is found in point 24 of section 3 of the Act on Electronic Communications Services and it means television transmission containing sales and purchase offers. *Sponsoring* is defined in point 20 of section 3 of the Act so that it means any form of financing or other support of audiovisual content services, audiovisual programmes, radio programmes, or radio broadcasting which aims at promoting the sales or reputation of the sponsor. The support is to come from a party who does not produce programmes, provide content services, or carry out radio broadcasting. *Product placement* means placing products, services, or trademarks in audiovisual programmes against payment (*see* § 220(1)).

148. The Guidelines for Journalists also include provisions on the separation of editorial content and commercial communication. Indeed, the Council for Mass Media (CMM) gave a recommendation about distinguishing between journalistic and commercial content on 20 May 2015. The reason for this was that there had been difficulties in distinguishing between these types of content, such as advertising, because the media had found new ways of cooperation, like partnership blogs, advertorials, and sponsored content. Now the CMM has recommended that the media uses the term 'advertisement' and the name of the advertiser or the trademark when the question is of advertising, and term 'trade cooperation' and the name of advertiser or trademark in the same context if the question is of other forms of trade cooperation.[335]

A more detailed account of different forms of commercial communication will be provided below.

---

334. *See* Government bill (HE 34/1998 vp); Government bill (HE 87/2009 vp).
335. *See* the statement 'Lausuma medialle mainonnan merkitsemisestä 2015' (Statement to the media on the labeling of advertising by Council for Mass Media): http://www.jsn.fi/lausumat/lausuma-medialle-mainonnan-merkitsemisesta-2015/ (29.8.2019).

In addition, the advertising of various substances is regulated in the following legislation: the Alcohol Act (1102/2017),[336] the Tobacco Act (549/2016),[337] and the Medicines Act (395/1987).[338] The Consumer Protection Act (38/1978) also applies in the context of consumer relations, while the Act on Unfair Business Practices (1061/1978) applies in business relations. Both acts include provisions on marketing. Advertising regulation represents an example of co-regulation.[339] In some respects the requirements of law and self-regulatory instruments may overlap.

The Council of Ethics in Advertising (*mainonnan eettinen neuvosto*) functions as an affiliated board of the Finnish Chamber of Commerce. As a self-regulatory body, it issues statements on advertisements and advertising in light of good practices. Consumers, entrepreneurs, officials, and organizations may request statements from the Council. Although the statements are not legally binding and advertisements cannot be banned by the Council, the Council is a major player in the field of marketing in Finland. The Board of Business Practice (*liiketapalautakunta*), in contrast, discusses marketing-related issues and disputes between entrepreneurs. It assesses compliance with good business practices and evaluates comparative advertising, among others.[340]

TRAFICOM has duties pursuant to the Act on Electronic Communications Services.[341] The protection of minors instead is assigned to the Consumer Ombudsman (*kuluttaja-asiamies*). In addition, the Consumer Disputes Board (*kuluttajariitalautakunta*) gives guidance and mediates disputes related to consumer goods and services, including the field of mobile phones and telecommunications (*see* Table 1).[342]

---

336. The law was reformed in 2017 and an unofficial translation has not been published yet. More information about the reform can be found at https://stm.fi/en/comprehensive-reform-of-alcohol-act (29.8.2019).
337. Unofficial translation by the Ministry of Social Affairs and Health; amendments up to 1374/2016 included: https://www.finlex.fi/en/laki/kaannokset/1976/en19760693.pdf (29.8.2019).
338. Unofficial translation by the Finnish Medicines Agency; amendments up to 1340/2010 included: https://www.fimea.fi/documents/160140/765540/18580_Laakelaki_englanniksi_paivitetty_5_2011.pdf (29.8.2019).
339. More in Markkanen – Nieminen 2013, 29–30. For marketing regulation in Finland, *see* Neuvonen 2012, 301–331.
340. For the Boards, *see* http://kauppakamari.fi/en/boards/council-of-ethics-in-advertising/ and http://kauppakamari.fi/en/boards/board-of-business-practice/ (29.8.2019) respectively. For more on self-regulation in the field of advertising and marketing *see* Neuvonen 2012, 322–327.
341. Markkanen – Nieminen 2013, 29–30.
342. *See* the webpage 'About the Consumer Disputes Board': http://www.kuluttajariita.fi/en/index.html (29.8.2019).

Table 1 Competence of Supervisory Bodies in the Field of Audiovisual Media and Communications

Directive	*Competent Authority in Finland*
2006/114/EC: comparative advertising	FCCA/Consumer Ombudsman
2010/13/EU: audiovisual media services	TRAFICOM/FCCA/Consumer Ombudsman
2000/31/EC: electronic commerce	TRAFICOM/FCCA/Consumer Ombudsman
2005/29/EC: unfair practices	FCCA/Consumer Ombudsman (other authorities*)
2011/83/EU: consumer rights	FCCA/Consumer Ombudsman

Cf. a more comprehensive table at 'Kuluttaja-asiamiehen valvontatehtävät': http://www.kkv.fi/Tietoa-KKVsta/kuluttaja-asiamies/kuluttaja-asiamiehen-valvontatehtavat/ (29.8.2019).

* These authorities include, *inter alia*, the Finnish Medicines Agency (Fimea) and the Financial Supervisory Authority (Fiva) in their respective fields of supervision.

TRAFICOM conducts regular surveys in order to supervise media advertising. This supervision is targeted at the recognizability, placement, duration, and time limits of advertising. TRAFICOM has, for instance, notified television broadcasters about overlay advertising and deficiencies with regard to the means of separating advertising from programmes and to exceeding the time limits permitted for advertisements.[343] The FCCA's supervision is targeted at the content of advertising. Moreover, the Council for Mass Media (CMM) issues notices concerning compliance with the Guidelines for Journalists.

§2. Advertising

I. Content Restrictions

149. Advertising or marketing regulation is included in Chapter 26 of the Act on Electronic Communications Services (917/2014). General principles are included in section 214 whereby marketing has to be 'readily recognisable' (§ 214(1)) and advertisements and teleshopping must be separated from audiovisual programmes and radio programmes by visual or acoustic means or by resorting to spatial division (§ 214(3)). Moreover, marketing, not including ideological or social advertising, may not resort to pictures or sounds of persons regularly present in news or programmes (§ 214(2)). The Constitutional Law Committee assessed the proposed provision in light of freedom of expression and deemed it necessary to

343. *See, e.g.*, FICORA decisions 918/932/2014, 5.12.2014; 917/932/2014, 5.12.2014; 1650/9220/2011, 9.3.2012.

expressly exempt ideological or social advertising in this regard (*see* § 224).[344] According to paragraph 4 of section 214, teleshopping must not exhort minors to enter into contracts of sale or rent. Further provisions on marketing that is against good practice and is targeted at children are provided in Chapter 2 of the Consumer Protection Act (§ 214(5)). Proposed amendments include extending the general principles in the field of marketing to video-sharing platform services.[345]

As a comparison, section 16 of the Guidelines for Journalists notes that editorial content and advertising are to be kept apart, while hidden advertising is to be avoided altogether.

For example, in a notice concerning the role of a reporter (4720/TV/11, 18.4.2012), the Council for Mass Media (CMM) concluded that the rules of good journalistic practice were infringed when a TV journalist both reported on motor sport competitions and also appeared during commercial breaks in the advertisements of a Finnish driver's sponsor. In these advertisements, the reporter was seen interviewing the driver while holding the reporting TV broadcaster's microphone. The line between editorial content and advertising was thus blurred and the credibility and independence of journalism and the broadcaster were called into question.

However, reporting on the acquisition of transmission rights for sports in TV sports news, including references to the company name, was not considered a breach of good journalistic practice (4495/TV/11, 4.5.2011), even though the TV broadcaster and the company which had acquired the rights were part of the same group. The Council nonetheless noted that information on the association between the two entities would have been appropriate.

The online content of TV broadcasters has also been under scrutiny by the Council. The inclusion of product testing alongside editorial content has been regarded as apt to blur the lines between different types of content (*see*, e.g., 4527/TV/11, 22.8.2011).

Recently, the Council for Mass Media concluded that a Finnish newspaper had infringed section 16 of the Guidelines (6874/SL/18). The newspaper had published an article concerning working life. The article was heavily surrounded by ads from the recruitment site called Monster, belonging to the same corporate group as the newspaper. The CMM pointed out that it is highly important to separate ads and editorial content from each other. In the case at hand, the ad links could not be properly separated from the editorial content.

Early 2016, the CJEU rendered a judgment (C-314/14) on the interpretation of the AVMS Directive in the context of 'black seconds' and 'split screens'.[346] The parties in the case were FICORA (now TRAFICOM) and Sanoma Media Finland Oy/Nelonen Media (Sanoma) while the facts derived from 2012 when Sanoma's execution of TV advertising was declared by FICORA to be infringing the Finnish law[347] implementing the AVMS Directive (at the time the TV and Radio Act).

344. *See* Statement of the Constitutional Law Committee (PeVL 18/2014 vp).
345. Government bill (HE 98/2020 vp), 87.
346. For more on the case, *see* Alén-Savikko 2016.
347. FICORA had also issued non-binding guidance (2004; updated 2011) on the duration and placement of ads as well as a non-binding stance on screen-splitting (2010) pursuant to the TV and Radio

According to FICORA, advertising and programme content were not appropriately separated since the screen was split between two types of programme content (closing credits and upcoming programmes) without an actual break-bumper. Moreover, when including 'black seconds' (excl. after programmes) and sponsor signs shown outside the sponsored programmes, the amount of time allotted to advertising exceeded the maximum time of twelve minutes per clock hour. The CJEU ruled that any means of separation, whether optical, acoustic or spatial, must meet the minimum requirements of the Directive but a combination is not required. The maximum advertising time must include sponsor signs shown elsewhere than in the sponsored programmes as well as 'black seconds' (where national law does not prescribe a shorter time limit).

150. Both the Alcohol Act and the Tobacco Act apply to advertising of the products in question, while the Medicines Act governs the marketing of medicines (§ 217 Act on Electronic Communications Services).

The provisions of the Tobacco Advertising Directive (2003/33/EC) were implemented with the Tobacco Act and the TV and Radio Act; provisions of the latter were repealed by the Act on Electronic Communications Services (*see* sections 219 and 221 ECSA which are discussed below). Implementation of the Tobacco Products Directive (2014/40/EU) brought about a new Tobacco Act with clarifications on terminology and an extended scope with regard to the products covered by marketing and other regulation. Consequently, section 217 of the Act on Electronic Communications Services nowadays also refers to 'marketing' and to the new act.[348]

According to section 68 of the new Tobacco Act (549/2016), direct and indirect advertising of tobacco products is prohibited. The word 'advertising' is defined in section 2 part 35 of the act. However, this does not apply to advertising in publications outside the European Union not targeted at European markets (§ 69(2)). An exception applies in this regard to the provision of information in marketing to those involved in the sales of tobacco products (§ 69(3)).

Section 50 of the Alcohol Act (1102/2017) forbids the direct and indirect advertising and other sales promotion of strong alcoholic beverages. Moreover, direct and indirect advertising and other sales promotion of mild alcoholic beverages and beverages with an ethyl alcohol content of least 1.2% volume is prohibited if it targets minors or creates an association with the positive effects of use (sexual, therapeutic, etc.), or establishes a connection to driving, among others (§ 50(2), points 1–10). Similarly, advertising is forbidden when a commercial entity uses content produced by consumers in its network service or makes such content or content produced by the entity itself available via this service for consumers to share (§ 50(2), point 11,

Act. *See* 'Ohjeistus. Mainonnan kesto ja sijoittelu' (Instructions. Advertising duration and placement) (31.1.2004; updated 22.3.2011): https://www.traficom.fi/sites/default/files/media/regulation/Mainonnan-kestoa-ja-sijoittelua-koskeva-ohje.pdf (29.8.2019) and 'Viestintäviraston kannanotto jaetun kuvaruudun käytöstä mainonnassa' (FICORA's statement on the use of the split screen in advertising), 1162/9220/2010, 21.12.2010: http://vivi-test.abako.fi/attachments/Viestintaviraston_kannanotto_jaetun_kuvaruudunkaytosta.pdf (26.7.2020).

348. *See* Government bill (HE 15/2016 vp).

Alcohol Act). Strong beverages may, however, be marketed, following the restrictions set out in paragraph 2, by way of presentation in a product catalogue of retail prices whether in print or online. The parties involved in sales may also be targeted (e.g., via websites for professionals), excluding the use of open networks (§ 50(4) Alcohol Act). Specific exceptions for mild beverages are included in paragraph 5 for international transport and for presentation inside and outside public houses. Moreover, paragraphs 1–3 of section 50 do not apply to publishing or broadcasting activities pursuant to the Act on the Exercise of Freedom of Expression in Mass Media (460/2003) that are carried out abroad by a company not established in Finland and whose content is intended for reception outside Finland or for reception in a similar fashion irrespective of country. The provisions do apply, however, to such marketing of alcohol in the Finnish market which is specifically targeted at Finland (§ 50(5) Alcohol Act). This means, for instance, that the websites of foreign companies, although accessible in Finland, are not subject to the regulation. The same applies to satellite channels.[349]

151. The highest competence in supervising compliance with the Alcohol Act is assigned to the Ministry of Social Affairs and Health (§ 59).

For its part, section 91a of the Medicines Act (395/1987) prohibits the marketing to the general public of medicinal products supplied by prescription or containing narcotic drugs or psychotropic substances. It is also prohibited to market a medicinal product that does not have a valid marketing authorization or registration in Finland (§ 91(2)). The general principles of marketing medical products as referred to in the Act includes encouraging appropriate use and avoiding inducement to unnecessary use (§ 91).

As regards channels exclusively dedicated to teleshopping or self-promotion, the Act on Audiovisual Programmes (710/2011) applies to content likely to be detrimental to the development of children (sex, violence, etc.) while sections 209–210 on quotas for European and independent producers' works do not apply to such channels (§ 226 ECSA).

II. Time and Frequency Restrictions

152. Section 215(1) of the Act on Electronic Communications Services states that in television activity, advertising and teleshopping spots must be inserted between audiovisual programmes. However, they may also be placed within audiovisual programmes if this can be achieved without infringing the integrity and value of the programme or rights of copyright holders. In the case of sports programmes and other audiovisual programmes consisting of independent parts and having intermissions, advertising and teleshopping spots may only be inserted between the parts or during the intermission (§ 215(2)). Isolated advertising and teleshopping spots are prohibited in paragraph 3, with the exception of sports programmes.

349. Government bill (HE 70/2013 vp), 15.

153. Section 216 of the Act on Electronic Communications Services regulates interruptions by advertising and teleshopping spots in the case of movies, news, and children's programmes transmitted on television. These may be interrupted once for each thirty minute period. For children's programmes the rule applies only if their scheduled duration is more than thirty minutes. Television transmission of religious events may not be interrupted at all. Time limits for television advertising and teleshopping are included in section 222(1) of the Act on Electronic Communications Services. The proportion of transmission time for advertising and teleshopping spots may not exceed twelve minutes per one hour (between exact hours). An exception is provided for channels that are exclusively devoted to teleshopping. Paragraph 2 of section 222 also contains a list of exceptions whereby section 222(1) does not apply to a television broadcaster's announcements concerning its own audiovisual programmes and ancillary products derived from those programmes. Moreover, the provisions do not apply to sponsorship announcements, product placement, ideological or political advertising, or teleshopping windows in the meaning of section 225. The latter refers to windows devoted to teleshopping on regular channels, which must be a minimum of fifteen uninterrupted minutes in duration and clearly identifiable (§ 225).

Sections 215(1) and 222(1) on the insertion and time limits of advertisements do not apply to channels exclusively dedicated to teleshopping or self-promotion (§ 226 ECSA).

According to section 224(1), ideological or social advertising must be kept separate from audiovisual programmes by visual or acoustic means or by splitting the screen. Such advertising may be placed between programmes or independent parts thereof. They may also be placed within programmes if this can be achieved without infringing the integrity and value of the programme or the rights of copyright holders (§ 224(2)). Religious programmes may not be interrupted by ideological or social advertising. In addition, the Act on Audiovisual Programmes applies (§ 224(3)).

Advertising mild alcohol on television or radio is forbidden between 7 a.m. and 10 p.m. The time limit was extended by one hour on 1 January 2015. The same applies to audiovisual programmes rated suitable for minors under 18 when publicly shown at a cinema (§ 50(2), point 8, Alcohol Act). Advertising is also forbidden when it involves consumer participation in games and contests (§ 50(2), point 10). The latest amendments related to time limits and games were aimed at protecting minors. Thereby, both the use of television and radio and the internet or social media for advertising was restricted.[350]

Following the reform of the AVMS Directive, some changes have been proposed to these provisions, including a 20% limit for ads and teleshopping between 6–18 and 18–24.[351]

---

350. Government bill (HE 70/2013 vp). A ban was also introduced for advertising in public places (with the exception of public events).
351. Government bill (HE 98/2020 vp), 19, 253–254.

III. Radio Advertising

154. Radio advertising is regulated in section 223. Advertising must be clearly separated from radio programmes by sound or other means. The transmission time allotted to radio advertising may not exceed 20% of the daily transmission time.

One notice from the Council for Mass Media (5580/R/14, 10.12.2014) concerned a radio station which had broadcast an interview containing references to a particular grocery wholesaler. The company was referred to by name and received praise. The topic was initially raised by the interviewee, but the journalist also participated. The Council nevertheless decided that the line between advertising and editorial content had remained sufficiently clear. It should also be noted that the company had not sponsored the radio station in question.

In another notice (5459/R/14, 18.6.2014), the Council took the view that hidden advertising was used when radio show hosts praised a car brand whose campaign was running on the channel. In the campaign, listeners had the chance to win the car in question for private use. The line between editorial content and advertising had thus been blurred and the credibility and independence of the journalists had been called into question. *See also* similar notices on hidden advertising infringing the Guidelines: 5360/R/13, 26.3.2014, 5357/R/13, 12.2.2014, 5327/R/13, 26.3.2014, 4910/R/12, 23.1.2013.

In another notice (4979/R/12, 14.3.2013), the Council found that infringement of good journalistic practice had occurred when a fictitious recording artist was interviewed and included in a news report on the radio. The fictitious character was part of a teleoperator's advertising campaign.

§3. Sponsorship

155. Sponsoring is also regulated in the Act on Electronic Communications Services. According to section 218(1), a 'sponsor may not influence the content and scheduling of sponsored [audiovisual] or radio programmes or audiovisual content services' in a manner which affects the responsibility or editorial independence of the broadcaster or audiovisual media service provider. Moreover, the name or logo of the sponsor must be clearly displayed at the beginning and end of the programme (§ 218(2)). Furthermore, sponsored audiovisual or radio programmes may in no way encourage purchasing or renting by referring to products or services in a manner which resembles advertising (§ 218(3)).

FICORA's (now TRAFICOM, Finnish Transport and Communications Agency) interpretation also indicates that the name or logo of a sponsor may not be displayed in a manner that resembles advertising. Accordingly, FICORA has issued notifications on the use of ad-like sponsor identification and required the removal of advertising features or their clear separation from programmes.[352]

The Supreme Administrative Court has ruled on sponsoring with regard to a reality TV show on the everyday activities in a large department store, its personnel and customers. The show had been run by Sanoma Entertainment Finland/Nelonen

352. *See, e.g.*, FICORA decision 603/932/2014, 30.6.2014. Cf. also CJEU C-314/14.

Media (Sanoma), and FICORA (now TRAFICOM) had already notified the company during the first season of the programme.[353] The department store had facilitated the production and allowed the location to be used, free of charge, for the show. It had also helped the production to inform about the filming and to get the permits required, as well as arranged a room for the crew to be used as an office and for storage. Finally, it had provided accommodation, full-board, free of charge and for maximum of twelve persons at a time during the filming. In its ruling (KHO 2014:87) the court was of the opinion that free accommodation on a full-board basis was sponsoring – without any consideration on its value. Sponsorship should be clearly and explicitly indicated. Section 219 includes bans on sponsorship. Programmes, audiovisual media services, and radio activity may not be sponsored by tobacco manufacturers or marketers. Furthermore, only the name or logo of a manufacturer of medicinal products may be displayed in connection with a programme. Prescription products or cures may not be mentioned. News and current affair programmes may not be sponsored.

§4. Product Placement

156. The regulation of product placement is currently found in the Act on Electronic Communications Services. Section 220(1) includes a general ban on placing products, services, or trademarks in audiovisual programmes against payment. According to paragraph 2, product placement is, however, allowed in cinematographic works, films and series produced for audiovisual media services, sports programmes, and light entertainment programmes. These exceptions do not concern children's programmes (§ 220(3)). The concept of product placement also covers provision of goods and services of significant value without payment. However, product placement in the form of production props or prices is allowed in programmes other than children's programmes (§ 220(4)). Product placement must, nevertheless, be implemented so as not to influence the content or schedule of programmes or encourage people to acquire the goods or services in question. It also must not constitute advertising or give undue prominence to the products in question (§ 221(1)). Product placement of tobacco products as well as prescription drugs and medicinal treatments is prohibited in section 221(2).

In addition, viewers must be clearly informed of product placement, as prescribed in paragraph 3 of section 221: This may be achieved by means of text or other marks commonly used by audiovisual media service providers. The information must be placed at the beginning and end of the programme as well as after each commercial break. It cannot constitute advertising (§ 221(3)). Paragraph 4 of section 221, however, provides an exception for situations where the programme has not been produced or commissioned by the provider itself or its affiliate. In such cases, information on product placement need not be given if knowledge thereof cannot be obtained without unreasonable effort.

353. *See* FICORA decision 1952/9224/2010, 17.6.2011: http://pilvi.viestintavirasto.fi/attachments/muut paatokset/Paatos_Tuuri_ja_Unitupa_JULKINEN_versio.pdf (29.8.2019).

Following the reforms of the AVMS Directive, proposed amendments include acceptance of product placement, excluding in certain types of programmes.[354]

As of 2010, the Council for Mass Media (CMM) no longer assesses questions related to hidden advertising when product placement is used. This principle has been restated by the Council, where complaints are filed concerning TV programmes. For example, in a notice concerning the presentation of a car shampoo in a TV show (5204/TV/13, 9.10.2013), questions related to hidden advertising were not discussed, as the show included product placement. The journalist and producer of the programme were, however, importers of the shampoo, and their role was considered in breach of good journalistic practice.

However, notice 4767/TV/11, 16.5.2012 concerning a TV programme could also be mentioned. The programme sponsor's products were purposefully shown with logos facing the camera. The Council concluded that hidden advertising was used. According to the channel's representative, the programme did not include product placement and the contract with the production company included a prohibition on hidden advertising.

354. Government bill (98/2020 vp), 88.

Chapter 6. Right to Information

§1. Access to Major Events

157. In Finland, the regulatory system currently prescribed by Article 14 of the AVMS Directive (2010/13/EU) was realized by amending the Act on Television and Radio Operations. In 2014, the provisions were incorporated into the Act on Electronic Communications Services (917/2014). National measures also include a decree listing the events considered of major importance to society in Finland. The concept of 'a substantial proportion of the public' is not harmonized in the directive, but in Finland the proportion of the population which should be able to receive broadcasts of major events is set at 90% (§ 212(3) ECSA).[355] The Finnish list was published according to the requirements of the directive.[356]

The first two subsections of section 212 of the Act on Electronic Communications Services read as follows:

> If a television broadcaster has purchased an exclusive right to broadcast an event which one of the Member States of the [EEA] has included in the list referred to in Article 14(1) of the [AVMS] Directive and confirmed by the Commission of the European Union, it may not exercise its exclusive right in such a way as to deprive a substantial proportion of the public in that Member State of the possibility of following the coverage of the event on free television as provided for by the Member State in question.
>
> Provisions of subsection 1 on the use of exclusive rights shall be correspondingly applied to events […] in the list referred to in Article 9(a)(2) of the Protocol of Amendment [to the ECTT].[357]

158. Article 212(3) states that 'events of major importance' in Finland may be designated by Government Decree. Such major events are considered to have reached the substantial proportion of the Finnish public when 90% of the population are covered 'without a separate charge'. In case the broadcaster with exclusive right does not transmit itself, another broadcaster must be able to do so. The former is guaranteed full compensation (§ 212(4)). Section 213 includes provisions on the procedure if the broadcasters cannot come to an agreement (cf. § 20a Act on Television and Radio Operations).

Article 3a of the TVwF Directive on 'major events' was originally implemented by section 20 of the Act on Television and Radio Operations (744/1998). However, since the list was optional, it was not drafted at that time. Only some years later it was finally considered necessary to adopt measures pursuant to the first paragraph of the article and to draw up a list of major events in Finland. The first hearing for drawing up the Finnish list was held in 2004, but preparation only commenced in

355. *See* Government bill (HE 112/2002 vp) for the amendments leading to the inclusion of the percentage in the Act.
356. *See* Commission Decision (2007/481/EC), OJ L 180/38, 25.7.2007: https://eur-lex.europa.eu/legal-content/EN/TXT/PDF/?uri=CELEX:32007D0481&from=CS (29.8.2019).
357. Unofficial translation by the Ministry of Transport and Communications.

2005. Finally, a Government decree (199/2007) on television broadcasting of events of importance to society was enacted by virtue of section 20(3) of the Act on Television and Radio Operations. The provisions of the Decree were replaced by those of a new Government Decree on television and radio operations (1245/2014). Currently, section 6 (previously section 1 of 199/2007) of the Decree 1245/2014 includes 'events of major importance for society' in Finland. These are:

- the Summer and Winter Olympic Games, organized by the IOC;
- the opening match, quarter-finals, semi-finals, and final of the Football World Cup, organized by FIFA, and the matches of the Finnish team;
- the opening match, quarter-finals, semi-finals, and final of the European Football Championships, organized by UEFA, and the matches of the Finnish team;
- the Men's Ice Hockey World Championships, organized by the IIHF;
- the Nordic World Ski Championships, organized by the FIS;
- the World Championships in Athletics, organized by the IAAF; and
- the European Athletics Championships, organized by the EAA.[358]

According to section 1(2) of the Decree, the opening match, semi-finals, and finals of the Football World Cup, and the matches of the Finnish team, the opening match, semi-finals, and finals of the European Football Championships, and the matches of the Finnish team, the semi-finals, and finals of the men's Ice Hockey World Championships, and the matches of the Finnish team are to be broadcast live in their entirety. In contrast, other above-mentioned events 'may be broadcast wholly or partially live or deferred' (§ 6(3)).[359]

159. In Finland, the intention was to draw up a narrow list including only such events that were clearly of major importance to society. No radical changes ensued from the list, since at the time of its adoption, the national public service broadcaster, Yleisradio, had been broadcasting such coverage. The events had thus already been available to the public on free television. In that regard, the Decree guaranteed continuation of free television coverage of the listed events, all of which are sporting events. However, the list is deemed to have greater importance as pay-television develops and the scope of subscription content widens.[360]

The Constitutional Law Committee issued a statement on the proposed regulation of major events from the perspective of protection of property as enshrined in section 15 of the Constitution of Finland. The Committee noted that the restrictions on the exercise of broadcasting rights concerned 'events of major importance for society' included in a list approved by the Commission. Anyone planning to acquire exclusive rights to a given major event in a given territory would be aware of the restrictions. The regulation thus had no retroactive effects, and, moreover, full compensation was guaranteed. The criteria for determining the specific events also mean

358. Translation from the English version of Commission decision (2007/481/EC), 40: https://eur-lex.europa.eu/eli/dec/2007/481/oj (29.8.2019).
359. Translation from the English version of Commission decision (2007/481/EC), 40.
360. Communications Policy Programme (2012), 21.

that public interest considerations had an important role. The proposal was not considered to be problematic in terms of the right to property.[361]

However, the level of enactment regarding the list of major events was upgraded during the constitutional reforms of the early 2000s. According to a Government bill on amending legislation on the communications market (HE 112/2002 vp), an amendment to section 20(3) of the Act on Television and Radio Operations was required because of the new Constitution of Finland (731/1999). The provision previously in force allowed the list to be enacted by Government decision, whereas the issue was subsequently considered a matter of generally binding regulation requiring designation by Government decree.[362] Simultaneously, the percentage of the population required for the obligation to be fulfilled was included in section 20(3), as the definition for the 'substantial proportion of the public' was transferred to the Act from section 4 of the decree on television and radio operations (14/1999). The obligation to transmit on free-to-air television was linked to safeguarding public access to broadcasts of major events. Therefore, provisions were required at the level of law.[363]

160. The new Government decree on television and radio operations (698/2003) entered into force in July 2003; this instrument was subsequently replaced by the Government Decree 1245/2014. Furthermore, in 2003, the Finnish provisions implementing Article 3a of the TVwF Directive were complemented by Act 394/2003, with renewed provisions on the procedure concerning the exercise of exclusive broadcasting rights. Section 20(4) of the Act on Television and Radio Operations was amended to highlight the fact that transfer occurs against payment: the provision thus came to state that a television broadcaster with an exclusive right is obliged to *assign* (but not give) to another broadcaster the right to broadcast a given event if it does not transmit it itself.[364] The latter broadcaster should request this right at least six months prior to commencement of the event. The same section also entitles the former broadcaster to full compensation for conveying the right (*see* § 212(4) ECSA). The preparatory works state that the right to broadcast a major event may be *divided* so as to enable both the original right holder and the acquiring party to broadcast the event.[365]

Moreover, section 20a of the Finnish Act on Television and Radio Operations came to include provisions on the procedure to be followed if no agreement is reached. In such an event, either one of the broadcasters may submit the matter to the regulator (FICORA, now TRAFICOM) for consideration. Submission should occur three months before the event. The authority may impose technical conditions concerning the grant of the right, and it may decide on the extent of full compensation as provided in section 20(4), now § 212(4) of the Act on Electronic Communications Services (*see* § 213(1)ECSA). According to the preparatory works, compensation should be based on the prices paid for corresponding rights in

361. *See* Statement of the Constitutional Law Committee (PeVL 19/1998 vp).
362. Government bill (HE 112/2002 vp), 216.
363. Government bill (HE 112/2002 vp), 216.
364. Government bill (HE 112/2002 vp), 216.
365. Government bill (HE 112/2002 vp), 217.

competitive markets, and various factors are to be taken into account, such as the country of broadcast and the nature of the coverage (live or deferred).[366]

The provisions of section 20 and section 20a are now found respectively in section 212 and section 213 of the Act on Electronic Communications Services. According to the preparatory works, the new sections correspond to the previous provisions in the Act on Television and Radio Operations.[367] However, amendments were made, for instance, in the form of minor changes to wording and a reference to the codified AVMS Directive instead of the TVwF Directive.

Sections 344 and 345 of the Act on Electronic Communications Services provide provisions for appeal. Section 344(3) states that compliance with the decision of TRAFICOM concerning the conveyance of broadcasting rights pursuant to section 213 must be abided by despite an ongoing appeal. However, the appellate authority may later rule otherwise. It is also noted in the preparatory works that, despite an ongoing appeal, the decision in question should, in most cases, be enforceable, since televising an event might otherwise become impossible. The provisions correspond to section 40(3) of the Act on Television and Radio Operations.[368]

During 2020, the Ministry of Transport and Communications aims to assess the need to update the list of major events.[369]

§2. Short News Reporting

161. Article 3k of the AVMS Directive 2007/65/EC, which includes provisions on short news reporting, was implemented in Finland by amending the Copyright Act. The access of broadcasters to 'events of high interest to the public' transmitted on an exclusive basis was catered for by adding a new paragraph 5 to section 48 of the Act, which provides for the related right of broadcasting organizations (i.e., protection of broadcasting signals). The right to use short extracts of the signal is provided without prejudice to the rights of broadcasters. Furthermore, a reference to section 48(5) and a restriction to exclusive rights were added to section 25b of the Act.[370]

Prior to the provisions, section 48 of the Copyright Act precluded the use of the transmission signal for purposes other than those included in Chapter 2 on limitations to copyright and provisions concerning extended collective licence. The general right to quotation did not extend to presenting highlights of sports events as a part of news reporting. However, already before the implementation of the 'short reporting right' national television broadcasting organizations had agreed on arrangements for compensation for the use of each other's coverage in sport news. Moreover, some sports associations also provided for summaries on highlights to be

366. Government bill (HE 112/2002 vp), 217.
367. Government bill (HE 221/2013 vp), 171.
368. Government bill (HE 221/2013 vp), 235.
369. *See* https://valtioneuvosto.fi/hanke?tunnus=LVM028:00/2020 (26.7.2020).
370. Government bill (HE 87/2009 vp), 12, 26–28, and 10 which states that the regulation derives directly from the AVMS Directive. For more, *see* Alén 2010a: on proposing Changes to the Finnish Copyright Act due to the Implementation of the AVMS Directive. *See* Alén 2010b on implementing the AVMSD Resulted in Amending the Finnish Copyright Act.

sold to broadcasters. The use of material in sports news on (inter)national events of high interest had been agreed upon by channels and sports federations.[371] Coverage was also reciprocally exchanged between broadcasters.[372]

Paragraph 5 of section 48 reads so that notwithstanding the provisions in paragraphs 1–4 of section 48, a transmitting organization established in a country belonging to the EEA may use, for the purpose of news reports on an event of high interest to the public after the event has come to an end, short extracts for its general news programmes from a television transmission which has been transmitted on an exclusive basis by another transmitting organization. The extract may also be used after the news programme in an on-demand communication to the public. The source must be indicated unless impossible for reasons of practicality. Moreover, section 25b(2) states that a *work included in a television transmission* may be incorporated into a news report when using short extracts from the transmission in accordance with section 48(5). Section 25b is referred to in several provisions on related rights (i.e., §§ 45, 46, 46 a, 47, 49, and 49a) whereby it applies to that subject matter as well.[373] The so-called short reporting right in Article 15 AVMS Directive 2010/13/EU is thus guaranteed by establishing a full limitation to exclusive rights enshrined in the Copyright Act.[374]

162. The preparatory works to the amendments state that the national solution to provide a limitation to exclusive rights enables short extracts to be chosen freely. A full limitation also means that extracts are available on fair, reasonable, and non-discriminatory terms.[375] Some details are clarified in the preparatory works of the amendments. For example, the exact duration is not mentioned in the implementing provisions, but the underlying Government bill (HE 87/2009 vp) states that the maximum duration is ninety seconds. The duration acceptable and necessary in individual cases depends on the content and nature of the event in question as well as on informational needs. For example, reporting on the goals of, say, a football match is deemed different to reporting on an endurance event such as a marathon. Informational needs can mostly be met with extracts considerably shorter than ninety seconds.[376]

In the case of an event that consists of competitions in several different sports, each competition is usually regarded as an event of high importance; whereas for a competition in one sport covering several days, each day of competition is usually regarded as an event (e.g., cycling).[377] According to the preliminary works, two Committees had differing views on sports consisting of series or seasons. The Education and Culture Committee remarked on the extent to which such sports were neglected in the Government bill. The whole season or series was to be regarded as

---

371. Government bill (HE 87/2009 vp), 5–6.
372. Rauste 1997, 660.
373. Government bill (HE 87/2009 vp), 26–28.
374. For more on the news reporting right, *see* Alén-Savikko 2015b.
375. Government bill (HE 87/2009 vp), 26–27.
376. Government bill (HE 87/2009 vp), 27.
377. Government bill (HE 87/2009 vp), 27.

an event and the right to short reporting would apply on a daily basis.[378] The Transport and Communications Committee, in contrast, observed that in light of the submissions, the purpose of the directive and the regulation on short reporting was, unambiguously, to guarantee the right of the public to information – particularly in relation to sports consisting of series and seasons. Thus, each game, competition, or match was to be regarded as an event of high importance.[379] In Finland events of high interest have not been defined in detail (cf. listed major events above); in practice, they are defined following news criteria.[380]

163. The Government bill concerned states that, in principle, the voice of the commentator of the broadcaster whose signal is used may not be used, as this is unnecessary for the informational purposes of news reporting. Any original commentary on the event may, in contrast, be included.[381]

According to the preparatory works, the extracts may only be used in general news programmes, including sports news, but they may not be used in current affairs programmes or other programmes that are not news broadcasts. Moreover, they may be used only *after* the event in question, but they are not to be used after their newsworthiness is lost or in order to develop new business models. Such a limitation is justified, since the news is usually the end result of some competition. According to the proposal, an event typically loses its newsworthiness approximately two days after its end.[382]

The implementing provision contains a clause on the permitted use of short extracts after a news programme in on-demand communications to the public (§ 48(5) Copyright Act). However, the Government bill on the matter provides clarification by stating that an extract used in a linear transmission may be subsequently used for on-demand news transmission of the *same* transmitting organization.[383]

During implementation of the amendments, and after taking account of submissions from various specialists, the two Committees emphasized the imperative nature of the obligation to identify the source. With current technology, there should be basically no instances where this is impossible, except in the case of short technical problems.[384]

Moreover, the Constitutional Law Committee assessed the proposed legislation from the perspective of fundamental rights. In particular, it discussed the fact that no compensation was proposed for the use of short extracts. The proposal was regarded as a constitutional issue, as intellectual property is covered by section 15

378. Statement of the Education and Culture Committee (SiVL 9/2009 vp), 3.
379. Report of the Transport and Communications Committee (LiVM 2/2010 vp), 3–4.
380. For news criteria, *see* Tiilikka 2007, 95–96.
381. Government bill (HE 87/2009 vp), 27.
382. Government bill (HE 87/2009 vp), 27, 29; Statement of the Education and Culture Committee (SiVL 9/2009 vp), 3–4 and Report of the Transport and Communications Committee (LiVM 2/2010 vp), 3.
383. Government bill (HE 87/2009 vp), 27.
384. Statement of the Education and Culture Committee (SiVL 9/2009 vp), 4 and Report of the Transport and Communications Committee (LiVM 2/2010 vp), 3.

of the Constitution of Finland (731/1999) on the protection of property. The Committee's opinion was that the provision had only minor significance for the rightholders, since it concerned short extracts in news reporting. Furthermore, the source was to be identified. In contrast, the provision had major significance for the right of the public to information as a part of freedom of expression. The limitation was regarded as sufficiently proportionate and definite.[385]

164. More detailed arrangements are largely determined by established practices in the field of broadcasting. The importance of such practices in the practical definition of broadcasting extracts is also emphasized in the preparatory works.[386]

According to the above-mentioned section 48(5) of the Copyright Act, short extracts of 'events of high interest to the public' may be used by a transmitting organization established in a country belonging to the European Economic Area (EEA). However, the point of departure laid down in the AVMS Directive, that a broadcaster should first seek access from a broadcaster established in the same Member State with exclusive rights to the event of high interest, is also emphasized in the preparatory works of section 48(5) of the Copyright Act. Thus, Finnish transmitting organizations are likely to turn to each other for short reports.[387] It should be noted that *access* as such is not regulated in the Copyright Act; rather, the Copyright Act offers a limitation to protection offered by the Act and thereby enables *use* of short extracts.

385. Statement of the Constitutional Law Committee (PeVL 3/2010 vp), 4–5. *See also* Government bill (HE 87/2009 vp), 29–30.
386. Statement of the Education and Culture Committee (SiVL 9/2009 vp), 4 and Report of the Transport and Communications Committee (LiVM 2/2010 vp), 3.
387. Government bill (HE 87/2009 vp), 27.

Chapter 7. Access to Networks and Platforms

§1. INTRODUCTION

165. The 2003 Communications Market Act was enacted in order to meet the demands of relevant EU legislation, especially the Telecoms Package (including directives on access and universal service), and to support competition and development in the field.[388] The act had been amended following reforms at the EU level: for instance, the renewed 2009 telecommunications directives were implemented by amending the act.[389] The reform of the EECC is currently changing national legislation, including in the field of radio frequencies and infrastructure.[390]

Currently, Part III of the Act on Electronic Communications Services (917/2014) deals with imposing obligations on actors in the field of media and communications as well as universal service. Obligations may also be imposed in relation to non-discrimination and prices. The reform aimed to enable prior control pursuant to relevant EU Directives as opposed to *ex post* regulation of the market. The reform also emphasized a technology neutral basis for price control. The more recent reform of the EECC has led to proposed amendments, including those to facilitate 5G networks.

§2. MUST CARRY RULES

166. In Finland an obligation to transmit programmes and services is provided in section 227 of the Act on Electronic Communications Services (971/2014). Previously, section 134 of the Communications Market Act (393/2003) obliged telecommunication companies to transmit certain programmes and services to the public. According to section 227(1), a telecommunications operator providing a network service in a cable television network has the obligation to transmit the following free of charge:

1. public service television and radio programmes as referred to in section 7(1) of the Act on Yleisradio that can be received in the municipality of the network's location as well as freely receivable material supplied for a programme item and ancillary and supplementary services in terms of broadcasting in terrestrial mass communications networks;
2. television programming belonging to public interest television activity in the meaning of section 26 that can be received in the municipality of the network's location and broadcast by virtue of a national programming licence;
3. freely receivable material supplied for a programme item referred to in point (2) above, advertisements as well as ancillary and supplementary services included or related thereto.

388. Government bill (HE 112/2002 vp).
389. Government bill (HE 238/2010 vp).
390. Government bill (HE 98/2020 vp).

Points 2 and 3 of paragraph 1 were in force until the end of 2016 (§ 351).[391]

The programmes and services are to be provided to users free of charge, unmodified, and simultaneous to the original broadcast. A reasonable fee may be required for the maintenance of the network (§ 227(4–5)). Decoding may neither be added nor may it be removed.

167. The transmission obligation also applies to a telecommunications operator providing a network service over a cable television network if it uses unconventional cable television technology in the transmission provided that reception is possible with conventional equipment (§ 227(2)). IPTV service providers are thus covered. However, there is no 'must carry' obligation if the capacity is for the telecommunication operator's use in its television or radio operations or if it is necessary for this purpose in order to meet a reasonable future need (§ 227(3)).

The administrator owning or managing a joint antenna network within or between premises used for transmitting mass communications to users' terminals must ensure that programmes and services referred to in paragraph 1 are available to users unmodified and simultaneous to the original broadcast (§ 227(6)).

The programming covered by point 1 of section 227(1) includes Yleisradio's TV1, TV2, Fem, and Teema as well as HD versions of the first two while point 2 includes channels MTV3 and Nelonen. Prior to legislative amendments in 2011,[392] discussion focused on the issue of whether the 'must carry' obligation could also include non-public-service programming, as, contrary to the initial intent of the European Commission, the Communications Market Act enabled other programming to be subsumed under the obligation. By 2008 a notification from the Commission and the requirements of the 2002 Universal Service Directive had already resulted in a narrowing of the scope of the provision by excluding services subject to payment.[393] Subsequently, programming was further removed from the 'must-carry' obligation, leaving only certain programming of public interest within its ambit.[394]

The provisions in section 134 of the Communications Market Act[395] (393/2003) were amended in accordance with the renewal of the Universal Service Directive (as amended by 2009/136/EC). Only the following services were thereafter included in the scope: public service TV and radio programmes (point 1) and ancillary and supplementary services related thereto (point 2), as well as freely receivable television and radio programmes of public interest broadcast by virtue of a national programming licence and carrying the obligation for accompaniment with an audio-subtitling and subtitling service (point 3). In this regard, however, according to section 352(6) of the Act on Electronic Communications Services, the obligation pursuant to section 134(1) point 3 of the Communications Market Act remained in force until the entry into force of licences pursuant to section 26 of the Act on Electronic Communications Services. Thus, the programming to be carried included

391. For reintroducing compensation for 'must carry' in the Copyright Act, *see* Alén-Savikko 2015a.
392. Government bill (HE 13/2010 vp).
393. Government bill (HE 100/2007 vp).
394. For copyright, *see* Statement of the Education and Culture Committee (SiVL 9/2010 vp), 3.
395. This Act has now been replaced by the Act on Electronic Communications Services.

MTV Oy, programming MTV3 and Sanoma Entertainment Oy, programming Nelonen until mid-2017. Prior to changes in 2015, Fox was also included. Later the same year, both MTV3 and Alfa TV were granted public interest licences, while contractual arrangements exist in other regards.

168. In addition, the eventual amendments to the previous section 134 of the Communications Market Act came to emphasize technological neutrality. According to section 134(2), the obligation also applied to a telecommunications operator providing a network service using unconventional cable television technology in the transmission of programming through a cable television network, provided that reception of the programming were possible with conventional reception equipment. According to preparatory works, traditional equipment includes a TV, a set-top-box, and a radio receiver. Thus, the 'must-carry' obligation would not cover communications networks that are not *primarily* used for providing television and radio programmes or other material transmitted in identical form to all recipients. The programmes must be offered unaltered and simultaneously to the original transmission. However, the technical solution for the cable network is not decisive.[396] The explicit new paragraph was added in the course of the legislative process and was promoted in the Transport and Communications Committee report (LiVM 8/2010 vp).[397] The technology neutral stance adopted in the Government bill was welcomed but deemed too implicit. Old technology was also not to be unduly supported. It was necessary to highlight that the obligation did not extend to networks used primarily for purposes other than broadcasting or providing television and radio programmes or to other material transmitted in identical form to all recipients. The dispensability of the obligation vis-à-vis commercial programming was also discussed, and the obligation was to be a fixed term in that regard (until the end of 2016). It was estimated that there would probably be no need to renew the 'must carry' obligation, since technology and channels of distribution are constantly developing.[398] Moreover, the preparatory works highlighted the importance of defining 'programming of public interest' and ensuring the equal opportunity of citizens in all regions to enjoy pluralistic freedom of expression, which is the essential justification and goal of the 'must carry' obligation.[399]

§3. Obligations Related to Access and Interconnection

169. Finnish Transport and Communications Agency TRAFICOM must regularly define relevant communications markets, of which it prepares a market analysis pursuant to section 52 of the Act on Electronic Communications Services (§ 51). Section 52(1) states that market analysis of relevant wholesale and retail markets must be conducted on a regular basis in order to establish and maintain a state of

396. *See* Report of the Transport and Communications Committee (LiVM 8/2010 vp), 5–6.
397. Cf. Government bill (HE 13/2010 vp) and Government bill (HE 100/2007 vp), 15.
398. *See* Report of the Transport and Communications Committee (LiVM 8/2010 vp), 2, 4–5.
399. *See* Report of the Transport and Communications Committee (LiVM 8/2010 vp), 3–4; Statement of the Education and Culture Committee (SiVL 9/2010 vp), 3–4; Statement of the Constitutional Law Committee (PeVL 27/2010 vp), 3.

competition, and the more detailed provisions on time limits are also included in the provision. Section 52(2) deals with cross-border markets. In such cases, TRAFICOM must cooperate with the relevant authority in the other EEA state in conducting the analysis. Proposed changes relate to the process pursuant to the EECC.[400]

According to paragraph 3 of section 52, TRAFICOM must find that a company has significant market power if its analysis shows that the company (alone or with others) exerts such economic influence in a particular market which enables it to operate largely independent of competitors, consumers, or other users. The status may also be considered to cover related markets if the company is able to widen and strengthen its market power in those markets as well (§ 52(3)). TRAFICOM must amend its decision on significant market power if its analysis shows substantial changes in the competitive situation. A company's classification as an enterprise with significant market power must be changed if analysis indicates a lack of such power (§ 52(4)).

The Supreme Administrative Court of Finland has assessed FICORA's (now TRAFICOM) decision on significant market power and the imposition of pricing obligations from a procedural perspective. In its judgment (KHO 18.12.2009/3603), the Court found that companies which submitted their pricing to FICORA's scrutiny could file an appeal against a FICORA decision. The case concerned section 127 of the Communications Market Act, in force at the time, and section 6(1) of the Administrative Judicial Procedure Act (586/1996) in force at the time. The Court also took into account requirements stemming from the Framework Directive (2002/21/EC).

Similarly, the Supreme Administrative Court has also discussed FICORA's (now TRAFICOM) duty to amend its decision on significant market power on the basis of market analysis indicating changes in the competitive situation. The case (KHO 31.12.2008/3531) concerned section 17 of the Communications Market Act, in force at the time. According to a document titled 'market analysis' and letters sent to the companies concerned, FICORA had found no changes which would have justified amendments to its decision on significant market power. The Court found that FICORA had made a decision pursuant to section 5(1) of the Administrative Judicial Procedure Act (586/1996) which could be appealed.

170. Section 53 includes more detailed provisions on imposing obligations on an operator with significant market power in wholesale markets. Obligations pursuant to sections 56, 61, and 65 and Chapter 10 must be imposed if they are necessary in order to eliminate barriers to competition or to promote competition in the relevant market (§ 53(1)). The obligations must be proportional and the following factors are to be taken into account: the technical and economic appropriateness and the feasibility of access rights, requirements related to protection of privacy and information security, and industrial property rights and copyright. Moreover, the investments made and risks taken by the company in question, the long-term need to safeguard competition, and the provision of European services have to be taken

400. Government bill (HE 112/2002 vp), 31.

into account. TRAFICOM must also assess the impact of the obligations on the markets (§ 53(2)–(3)). Amendments have been proposed following the reform of the EECC.[401]

> Some 15 years ago, FICORA (now TRAFICOM) issued a decision concerning Digita Oy. In 2004, the company was deemed to have significant market power in the market for transmission services related to television and radio activity. The decision obliged it to assign capacity in the terrestrial mass communications network, publish service conditions, as well as use cost-oriented pricing and non-discriminatory conditions, among others (183/934/2004, 3.9.2004).
>
> A few years later, a new decision was made (1668/934/2008, 10.11.2008) concerning significant market power in the whole sale market for transmission services for television and radio. In this decision, obligations were imposed on Digita Oy concerning analogue nationwide radio transmission services. It was obliged to assign capacity in the terrestrial mass communications network, publish service conditions, as well as use non-discriminatory pricing and conditions. As a consequence, the obligation concerning cost-orientation was abolished.
>
> *See* a related case KHO 2012:7 in paragraph 171 below.

TRAFICOM must amend its decision on obligations if substantial changes occur in the factors or in the competitive situation (§ 53(4)).

171. Obligations to impose access rights (rights of use) are included in Chapter 8 of the Act on Electronic Communications Services. Section 56 regulates the imposition of various types of obligations on a company with significant market power: by a decision referred to in section 53, TRAFICOM may impose an obligation to permit others access to (right to use) a communications network or a part thereof or to network capacity. Access rights may also concern shared use, cables and masts as well as related services that enable provision of a communications network or services and operations related to roaming in a mobile network (§ 56). Proposed amendments include obligations related to other types of infrastructure.[402]

Obligations not based on significant market power are regulated in section 57. By decision, TRAFICOM may impose unbiased, fair, proportionate, and non-discriminatory obligations on a company pursuant to relevant provisions of the Act on Electronic Communications Services (§ 55). TRAFICOM must amend its decision if there are substantial changes in the circumstances affecting the imposition (§ 55(3)). Access rights concern subscriber connections, the electronic programme guides of digital television or radio, the programming interfaces of television and radio systems, as well as cables and antenna sites (§ 57).

Obligations related to locating and sharing property are regulated in section 58. Interconnection is regulated in Chapter 9. The obligation of companies to negotiate in matters related to interconnection is set out in section 60 of the Act on Electronic Communications Services.

---

401. Government bill (HE 112/2002 vp), 200–201.
402. Government bill (HE 112/2002 vp), 339–340.

Other possible obligations are regulated in Chapter 10 of the Act on Electronic Communications Services. These include technical obligations related to access rights (rights of use) as well as obligations concerning non-discrimination in pricing and terms, publishing information, such as supply conditions, and separation of operations in company accounts.

The reform aimed to shift the focus from *ex post* regulation to prior pricing control. TRAFICOM was thus granted more competence regarding pricing control. TRAFICOM may impose obligations for cost-oriented pricing where only the costs of the efficient provision of services are taken into account. Thereby, the inefficiencies of a dominant company cannot be included in pricing. The amendments were also drafted on a technology neutral basis.[403] Section 71 currently regulates the imposition of obligations related to pricing of access and interconnection on a company with significant market power, whereas section 72 applies in other cases. However, the preparatory works note that the purpose was to empower the regulatory authority to investigate potential abuse of past dominance. Thus, no provisions were proposed concerning FICORA's (now TRAFICOM) competence to examine the lawfulness of companies' former pricing levels.[404] Indeed, section 73(2) notes that TRAFICOM cannot assess the lawfulness of pricing retrospectively. The investigation of abuse of dominance in that regard is the responsibility of the competition authority.

> The Supreme Administrative Court of Finland has also discussed FICORA's (now TRAFICOM) competence in this regard. MTV Oy, Subtv Oy, Suomen Urheilutelevisio Oy, SW Television Oy/Nelonen, and Yleisradio Oy had requested that FICORA investigates the pricing of Digita Oy in the distribution of television and radio transmissions. FICORA did not investigate the pricing of nationwide radio transmission services before 10 November 2008, since the company had been released from any obligation from that date onwards. It also transferred the matter to the Competition Authority (FCA; now FCCA) to the extent that it concerned pricing used in the past. In its judgment (KHO 2012:7, 3.2.2012/132) the court concluded that it was not possible for FICORA to intervene in pricing retrospectively. Such an investigation was beyond the scope of its competence. FICORA's supervisory competence thus extends only to the pricing and contractual terms in force at the time and used by a company with significant market power.

By a decision referred to in section 53, TRAFICOM may impose obligations with regard to pricing, access or interconnection on a company with significant market power where market analysis indicates that no effective competition exists, thus allowing overly high pricing or the exertion of excessive pressure (§ 71(1)). A company may be obliged to use cost-oriented pricing, pricing based on a reduction of the retail price, or fair and reasonable pricing. When imposing an obligation regarding cost-oriented pricing, TRAFICOM may also set a maximum price for a product

403. Government bill (HE 221/2013 vp), 59; Report of the Transport and Communications Committee (LiVM 10/2014 vp).

404. Government bill (HE 221/2013 vp), 59.

or service. This may be done if there is a significant threat to the market. The maximum price may be set for a maximum of three-year period. The obligations must promote efficiency in the market, produce benefits for consumers, and encourage investment, while allowing a reasonable return on capital (§ 71(2)–(5)). Similar obligations may be imposed on a basis other than significant market power if deemed imperative for safeguarding access rights or interconnection (§ 72). Proposed changes include an extension to five-year period following the market analysis cycle.[405]

Section 73(1) states that the burden of proof concerning cost-oriented and non-discriminatory pricing rests with the company on whom TRAFICOM has imposed the obligation. However, in its assessments, TRAFICOM is not bound by the principles used by the company in cost-accounting (§ 73(3)).

§4. Universal Service Obligation

172. Universal service is regulated in Chapter 12 of the Act on Electronic Communications Services. Basically, universal service means the guarantee that every citizen has a telephone connection and internet access (§ 85). Additionally, previous provisions on universal service were amended and complemented with the enactment of the Information Society Code, now Act on Electronic Communications Services (917/2014): provision of directory inquiry services was included within the scope of universal service (section 89). Moreover, universal service operators are now required to publish their obligations and offer universal products and services (section 91).

The universal postal service is regulated in the Postal Act (*postilaki* 415/2011).[406] Some changes have been proposed following the EECC.[407]

According to section 85(2) of the Act on Electronic Communications Services, TRAFICOM must appoint one or more companies as a universal service operator, provided it is necessary for the provision of universal service in certain geographic area. The company with the best possible prerequisites is to be appointed. The procedure must be efficient, unbiased, open, and non-discriminatory. TRAFICOM must amend its decision if there are significant changes in the factors on which the decision is based (§ 85(3)). An obligation concerning telephone services is provided in section 86, whereas internet service obligations are included in section 87. Section 88 includes provisions on obligations and rights related to the provision of a telephone and internet connection.

173. A broadband connection of 1 Mb/s is part of the universal service in Finland. The obligation is technology neutral and can be met by either a fixed or mobile

405. Government bill (HE 112/2002 vp), 215.

406. Unofficial translation by the Ministry of Transport and Communications: https://www.finlex.fi/en/laki/kaannokset/2011/en20110415_20170698.pdf (29.8.2019).

407. Government bill (HE 112/2002 vp), 226–227.

connection. In 2008 the Government launched the so-called broadband project, aiming to provide all Finns (over 99% of the population) with a fast fibre-optic or cable network.

Section 87 includes provisions on universal service with regard to internet services. The company appointed by TRAFICOM as the universal service provider of internet connection services pursuant to section 85 is obliged to offer a subscription (connection to communications network) at the user's or subscriber's permanent place of residence or location. The subscription must be offered regardless of the geographic location and at a reasonable price, and it must be delivered in due time (§ 87(1)). TRAFICOM may issue detailed orders on the technical execution or features (§ 87(4)). In any case, the connection must allow appropriate and functional access. Provisions on the minimum speed of internet access are laid down in a decree by the Ministry of Transport and Communications (§ 87(3)). Section 1(1) of the current Decree (439/2015) states that the minimum speed for incoming traffic is 2 Mbit/s. However, it is sufficient for the average speed to reach 1.5 Mbit/s during a twenty-four-hour period and 1 Mbit/s during any given four-hour period (§ 1(2)). Moreover, the provisions note that revision of paragraph 1 will be conducted in 2017 in light of achieving the goal set for 2021, that is 10 Mbit/s (§ 1(3)).

Section 89 of the Act on Electronic Communications Services regulates the provision of directory inquiry services. TRAFICOM assigns the universal service operator for numbering and directory inquiry services pursuant to section 85. This operator may be an actor other than a telecommunications operator.

A universal service obligation concerning network services is included in section 90. Obligation thus exists in order to establish USO service providers' access to network.

§5. Conditional Access

174. Chapter 32 of the Act on Electronic Communications Services regulates obligations related to use of decoder systems. Section 270 includes provisions on obligations imposed on companies that use decoder systems, such as the so-called principle of one decoder card. In other areas, pay-television companies are subject to the provisions of the Consumer Protection Act.

First, section 270 obliges the company to ensure that the system does not hinder distribution or reception of other programmes or ancillary services in the terrestrial digital network. Necessary technical services are to be provided to other companies on a cost-oriented and non-discriminatory basis (§ 270(1)–(2)). Section 270(1) states that a company using a decoder system is obliged to ensure that the system does not hinder the distribution or reception of radio and television programming or the ancillary and supplementary services of another company in the terrestrial digital network. To this end, the company is also obliged to provide necessary technical services to other companies using cost-oriented, non-discriminatory pricing (§ 270(2)). If the costs of technical services cannot be agreed upon in negotiation and mediation referred to in section 314(2) is not successful, TRAFICOM may decide on the level of compensation (§ 270(7)).

175. Second, according to section 270(6), a company using a decoder system for provision of linear pay-television services in the terrestrial digital network must ensure the availability of television programming in the meaning of Chapter 4 of the Act in a manner which allows the reception of different fee-based television services with one decoder card or some other technical solution. This requires that a pre-announced programme schedule is followed. The provision does not cover on-demand services. However, the aim is clearly to cover all the players in the value chain in a consumer-friendly manner.[408]

> The original provision in Section 136 of the Communications Market Act explicitly concerned *telecommunications* companies – not companies solely offering pay-television services. However, a widening of the scope to include other companies was considered justified. This also covered the situation where parts of the activity were outsourced.[409]
>
> However, despite the provisions, consumers in Finland were still unable to enjoy one-card viewing of pay-television channels over antenna networks.[410] FICORA (now TRAFICOM) discussed the principle of one decoder card in the digital terrestrial television network in Case 1459/9220/2011, 7.5.2012, and it urged DNA Oy and DigiTV Plus Oy to ensure that consumers did not have to change cards during viewing. The decision was appealed against, but the appeal was subsequently cancelled. In 2013, DigiTV Plus was acquired by DNA.

According to the Government bill leading up to the Information Society Code, now the Act on Electronic Communications Services, the provisions of the previous section 136 required amendment and modernization due to developments in the field of pay-television, where cooperation between companies had been insufficient to guarantee a user-friendly environment. Moreover, encryption was increasingly moving from cards to programming and set-top-boxes provided by operators using internet applications. The regulation thus aimed to cover any future technological solutions for encryption.[411] Cooperation is still possible and remains the primary means of realizing the 'one card principle', but in case no agreement is reached concerning the costs between companies pursuant to section 270(1), TRAFICOM is to mediate and finally to decide on the matter (§ 270(7)).[412]

The protection for conditional access systems was previously provided in the Act on the Prohibition of Certain Decoding Systems (1117/2001). Currently, sections 2–3 of the Act are included in section 269(2) of the Act on Electronic Communications Services. Supervisory and penalty provisions are included in the Act while criminal offences are in Chapter 38 of the Criminal Code.

408. Government bill (HE 221/2013 vp), 63.
409. Government bill (HE 48/2007 vp), 8.
410. Government bill (HE 221/2013 vp), 55.
411. Government bill (HE 221/2013 vp), 55, 195.
412. Government bill (HE 221/2013 vp), 63.

§6. Network Neutrality

176. National provisions concerning network neutrality were, for the first time, included in section 110 of the Act on Electronic Communications Services. In 2016, Government bill (HE 67/2016 vp) was introduced to tackle section 110, among others. The provisions of section 110 were deemed to overlap and partly contradict with EU law, that is, the Roaming and Open Internet Regulation (EU) 2015/2120.[413] Consequently, by Act 456/2016, previous national provisions were replaced by a new section 110 which refers to the Regulation; the latter includes provisions on open internet access (Article 3). TRAFICOM will be competent to issue necessary and more detailed orders pursuant to the Regulation (Article 5) with regard to technical characteristics and minimum quality, as well as documentation, among others (§ 110(2)). However, the Transport and Communications Committee noted in its report (LiVM 12/2016 vp) that the high level safeguarded by the previous provisions should not be lowered when applying the Regulation.[414] Following the reform of the EECC, new provisions on switching the service provider have been proposed.[415]

Previously, the provisions expressly prohibited internet access service from restricting traffic in regard to particular web addresses or types of traffic. The ability of the subscriber or user to use their internet access and choose services was to be safeguarded. However, exceptions were provided in four cases:

1. where imperative for the provision of features of the service (e.g., quality, speed) defined in clear and comprehensive manner in the service agreement;
2. on the basis of decisions by authorities or court rulings;
3. where necessary for information security or remedying interruptions pursuant to sections 243, 272, and 273, or in a manner provided in law comparable to these; or
4. where necessary to meet requirements related to quality pursuant to sections 243–244 (e.g., security, durability, interoperability).

According to the preparatory works, the list was exhaustive. It was also considered to correspond to the situation and established practice at the time of drafting.[416] The decisions or court orders referred to in point (2) above could derive mainly from other legislation, such as copyright law. However, they might have involved section 273 or 331 of the Act on Electronic Communications Services on remedying hindrances or decisions on network neutrality by TRAFICOM pursuant to section 110(5)) of the Act.[417] The restrictions referred to in points (1)–(4) above were to be executed in a non-discriminatory manner and in a way which did not

413. *See* Government bill (HE 67/2016 vp). Contradiction was detected also with regard to s. 108 subs. 2 on communication service agreement. Other provisions of the Code were not deemed contradictory even if they would overlap with EU law. The bill also refers to general consumer law, that is Directives 2005/29/EC and 2011/83/EU, which are transposed into national law (*ibid.*).
414. Report of the Transport and Communications Committee (LiVM 12/2016 vp), 2-3.
415. Government bill (HE 112/2002 vp), 241.
416. Government bill (HE 221/2013 vp), 144.
417. Government bill (HE 221/2013 vp), 144.

limit intended use or the ability of the subscriber or user to use the desired applications or services. Furthermore, the restrictions were not to unduly slow down the connection (access service) (§ 110(2), points 1–3).

The service provider was to ensure that the subscriber and user were informed of the possible effects of the restrictions on the use of the service, for instance, by way of marketing (§ 110(3)). This provision on the obligation to inform customers was added during the legislative process. It was considered beneficial to consumers that different types of subscriber connections continued to exist. Restrictions related to speed or concerning certain applications and services as well as the prioritization of HD video were not considered problematic where the consumer wanted such a connection. However, the terms and information were to be clear and comprehensive.[418]

The previous provisions also included the possibility for TRAFICOM to order more detailed regulations, notably concerning restrictions on network neutrality (§ 110(4)). It could also oblige the service provider to execute measures in order to combat the disadvantages referred to in paragraph 2 or to refrain from activities that caused such disadvantages (§ 110(5)).

During initial drafting, the Constitutional Law Committee deemed the national provisions on network neutrality as essential for freedom of expression and, indirectly, for other fundamental rights. It also pointed to the constitutional requirements concerning the restrictions and exceptions.[419]

§7. CONFIDENTIALITY AND PRIVACY

177. Part VI of the Act on Electronic Communications Services currently deals with questions of confidentiality and privacy. Chapters 17–20 include provisions that are of particular relevance from the perspective of users and subscribers. General provisions on processing messages and identification data are included in Chapter 17,[420] while special provisions on processing by corporate or association subscribers and data retention (i.e., data storage for the purposes of the authorities) are included in Chapters 18–19, respectively. Provisions concerning location data are included in Chapter 20, with the user's right to cancel consent, forbid processing, and access data in section 162.

Alongside codification of existing provisions, the Act also came to include the new concept of a 'communications provider'. This means 'a telecommunications operator, corporate subscriber, or other party that conveys electronic communications for other than personal or comparable private purposes' (§ 3, point 36). The exclusion of private purposes was deemed necessary in order to limit the scope so as not to include such things as centralized home networks. In other cases it was considered appropriate to extend the provisions on confidentiality and protection of

418. Report of the Transport and Communications Committee (LiVM 10/2014 vp).

419. *See* Statement of the Constitutional Law Committee (PeVL 18/2014 vp).

420. Government bill (HE 67/2016 vp) brought temporary (five-year-long) amendments to section 136 of the Code on confidentiality of messages and traffic data so as to facilitate processing of data by statistical means. The conditions include anonymization. The definition of traffic data in section 3 was also temporarily amended.

privacy to cover all who act as intermediaries in electronic communications. The regulation was drafted on an actor neutral basis, taking into account technological development.[421]

Provisions on obligations to store data for the purposes of various authorities were previously included in the Act on the Protection of Privacy in Electronic Communications (516/2004). With the Act on Electronic Communications Services, the provisions were included in Chapter 19 of the Act and the scope of the companies under the obligation to retain data was limited. The obligation currently applies only to those specified in the decision of the Ministry of the Interior (§ 157).[422] Changes have been proposed to retention obligations, including a de minimis rule for those obliged.[423]

178. After the April 2014 CJEU ruling in Joined Cases (C-293/12 and C-594/12), the Data Retention Directive (2006/24/EC) could no longer be referred to as the basis of regulation, nor could interpretation of national legislation refer to the directive as a source of content and meaning. In general, both existing and proposed national legislation were to be assessed in the light of both national provisions on fundamental rights, especially section 10 on privacy and confidentiality, and the articles of the Charter of fundamental rights on privacy and data protection (Articles 7–8) that were discussed in the judgment by the CJEU.[424] The Transport and Communications Committee noted that the proposed Chapter 19 was stricter than the directive and many of the concerns referred to by the CJEU in its ruling had already been taken into account at national level when implementing the directive. The bill was however revised along the lines of the Constitutional Law Committee's statement.[425]

Thus, the proposed provisions of Chapter 19 of the Information Society Code, now Act on Electronic Communications Services, were somewhat amended during the legislative process so as to define in more detail the data to be retained, to reduce the scope of retention, and to introduce differentiated time limits for retention for each type of data, among others. Section 157(1) of the Act came to state that a service provider obliged to submit a notification on telecommunications operations is to ensure that data, as provided in following paragraphs 2–3, is retained in accordance with paragraph 4. References to Directive 2006/24/EC were removed, the scope of retainable data was narrowed, and the general retention period of twelve months was replaced by the following more detailed periods in paragraph 4: twelve months for data related to mobile network phone services and SMS services, nine months for data related to internet phone services, and six months for internet connection services. For instance, fixed network telephone services, email services and multimedia services were removed from the scope (*see* paragraphs 2–3). In addition, the Parliament required the establishment of a working group for the assessment of data retention, the demands of public officials and privacy. The group was

421. Government bill (HE 221/2013 vp), 53; *see also* the Report of the Transport and Communications Committee (LiVM 10/2014 vp).
422. Government bill (HE 221/2013 vp), 53, 155.
423. Government bill (HE 112/2002 vp), 248.
424. Statement of the Constitutional Law Committee (PeVL 18/2014 vp), 4–5.
425. Report of the Transport and Communications Committee (LiVM 10/2014 vp).

to evaluate the need for legislative amendments. Moreover, a report concerning confidentiality was to be submitted to the Transport and Communications Committee by September 2017.

In 2009, legislative amendments (so-called *Lex Nokia*) came into force which entailed new rights for corporate subscribers concerning the processing of identification data in cases of misuse (e.g., leaks of trade secrets).[426] The provisions were previously included in the Act on the Protection of Privacy in Electronic Communications (516/2004) which was replaced by the Information Society Code, now Act on Electronic Communications Services. Corresponding provisions are included in Chapter 18 of the Act.

426. Government bill (HE 48/2008 vp).

Chapter 8. Standards and Interoperability

179. Communications networks and communications services are subject to criteria for their quality. These provisions concerning interoperability, among others, are included in Chapter 29 of the Act. As regards planning, construction and maintenance section 243 notes that public communications networks and communications services as well as the communications networks and services connected thereto are to have high standard technical quality (point 1). They must also be durable and reliable (e.g., points 2, 5, and 14). Moreover, they must function together and meet the needs of connectivity as well as compatibility with television receivers which fulfil the requirements laid down in the Act (points 10, 12). The same criteria apply to supplementary operations and services of significant nature (§ 243(4)). These are defined in section 3 of the Act so that supplementary operations refer, for instance, to masts and other physical constructions or elements enabling or supporting the provision of communications network or service (point 9) while supplementary services include, among others, electronic programme guides and identification or location services (point 8).

TRAFICOM may issue regulations concerning the aforementioned quality criteria, interoperability, and security (§ 244). The regulations may concern, *inter alia*, interoperability, technical characteristics of cable networks and antenna systems, as well as applicable standards (points 8–9, 13). Various regulations to these ends have been issued by TRAFICOM during the years: notably, sections 243–244 of the Act coordinate a few previously existing provisions, including section 129 of the Communications Market Act.

According to section 246(1), users cannot be prevented from connecting to public communications network terminal equipment or receivers which fulfil the requirements laid down in the Act. However, the duty of care applies to maintenance, as instructed by the telecommunications operator (§ 246(3)).

Regarding the obligations concerning decoder systems, section 270 of the Act on Electronic Communications Services was discussed above.

Part IV. Cross-Ownership Regulation

§1. Competition Law

180. In the media sector, general rules of competition, abuse of dominance, incumbency, and concerted practices apply. There is no specific legislation for the media in this regard, although circumstances specifically related to the media may be taken into account in the application and interpretation of general provisions. The Finnish Competition and Consumer Authority (FCCA from 1 January 2013; formerly the Finnish Competition Authority; FCA) intervenes in violations of the Competition Act (*kilpailulaki* 948/2011).[427] The previous act was called the Act on Competition Restrictions (480/1992); it was amended multiple times while in force. It must be noted that part of the praxis discussed here dates back to this act. Some provisions of the new Competition Act more or less correspond to the previous ones while other provisions are clarified, modernized, or amended. Indeed, the new act in particular aimed for increased compatibility with EU law (e.g., the concept of an undertaking, provisions on concentrations), and core reforms concerned sanctions, damages, the procedure, and control of concentrations.[428] The Damages Directive (2014/104/EU) was transposed into national law by means of a dedicated act on such damages (1077/2016), as well as by introducing amendments to the Competition Act (e.g., consistency of terminology).[429]

There are situations where general competition law is insufficient. Specific provisions exist concerning incumbency and market definitions for purposes of defining and imposing obligations on telecommunications operators with significant market power. These were previously included in Chapter 3 of the Communications Market Act (393/2003). In 2014, the provisions were incorporated into the Information Society Code, now Act on Electronic Communications Services. Part III of the Act deals with imposing obligations and universal service. According to the preparatory works, the aim is to promote the functioning of the market and competition as well as to enable entry into the market.[430]

Chapter 2 of the Competition Act includes provisions on prohibited restraints on competition. These include horizontal restrictions, such as fixing prices and limiting or sharing markets, (§ 5) as well as abuse of dominance (§ 7). As regards the former,

427. *See* unofficial translation by the FCA and the Ministry of Employment and the Economy; amendments up to 948/2011 included: https://www.finlex.fi/fi/laki/kaannokset/2011/en20110948.pdf (29.8.2019).
428. *See* Government bill (HE 88/2010 vp).
429. Government bill (HE 83/2016 vp).
430. Report of the Transport and Communications Committee (LiVM 10/2014 vp).

agreements and concerted practices fulfilling certain cumulative requirements, including indispensability and benefit to consumers, are however exempted (§ 6).[431]

The Market Court has jurisdiction in competition matters. According to section 12 of the Competition Act (948/2011), it may impose a penalty payment at the behest of the FCCA. According to section 42(1), a competition infringement issue shall be brought before the Market Court by a proposal referred to in section 12(3), 25(1), or 30(2), an appeal referred to in section 44(1), or an application referred to in section 26(2), 36(3) or 45(2). The Market Court may, upon receipt of a proposal from the FCCA, prohibit or order an acquisition to be dissolved, or attach conditions on its implementation if it may significantly impede effective competition in the Finnish markets or a substantial part thereof (§ 25(1)). Damages are regulated in section 20 of the Competition Act.

In case of restrictions capable of affecting trade between EU Member States, Articles 101 and 102 TFEU apply as well (§ 3).[432]

§2. Media Ownership and Concentrations

181. There is no special legislation for media ownership and media concentration in Finland. Nevertheless, the specificities in the field of media and communications may be taken into account in applying general laws and provisions in media-related cases. However, the auction process for network licences contains requirements related to free and fair competition. For example, section 13(2) of the Act on Electronic Communications Services includes a ban on multiple participation in the case of a corporate group: only one enterprise from the group is allowed to participate in the auction. Moreover, cooperation is prohibited between the participants in the auction. This means agreements on bids, exchange of information about the bids, and any other activity likely to affect the process and result of the auction (§ 13(3), points 1–3).

In addition, section 18(1) of the Act on Electronic Communications Services regulates the transfer of a network licence: only transfer within the same corporate group is allowed, and the Government must be notified of the transfer. If control over the licence holder changes, the Government is to be notified, after which it has two months to decide whether to cancel the licence (§ 18(2)). In cases of acquisition pursuant to Regulation No. 139/2004, the Government decision must be delivered within two months of the approval of the acquisition by the Commission (§ 18(5)). A network licence granted in an auction pursuant to section 11 may also be transferred at request if there is no risk of hinders to competition nor a risk to national security (§ 18(6)). Following the reform of the EECC, changes have been proposed regarding the transfer of license.[433]

431. These ss 5–7 correspond to the previous ones (ss 4–6); *see* Government bill (HE 88/2010 vp).
432. This provision was somewhat reformulated and updated; *see* Government bill (HE 88/2010 vp).
433. Government bill (HE 112/2002 vp).

182. Control of concentrations (acquisitions, mergers) in general is regulated in Chapter 4 of the Competition Act.[434] The FCCA is to be notified where the turnover limits prescribed by law are exceeded and the case falls within the scope of the provisions (§§ 22–24). The FCCA may decide on further investigations or give approval to the acquisition. It may also attach conditions to the implementation of a merger. Indeed, the FCCA must negotiate and primarily resort to conditioning the concentration if the detrimental effects can thereby be combated and if they are accepted by the notifier (§ 25(2)). Finally, the FCCA may propose that the Market Court attach conditions on, prohibit, or dissolve a concentration which could significantly impede effective competition in the Finnish markets or a substantial part thereof, in particular by creating or strengthening a dominant position (§§ 25(1), 26). The acquisition must not be implemented prior to a final decision if not prescribed otherwise (§ 27).[435] The decisions may involve actors from the field of media and communications.

In Case 223/KKV14.00.10/2013, 29.8.2013, the FCCA approved an acquisition involving DNA Oy and Digi TV Plus Oy, whereby the former acquired exclusive control of the latter. DNA Oy provided services in the field of telecommunication and data processing to both consumers and corporate customers. It offered mobile phone, broadband, and television services to consumers and communication services for corporations. Moreover, it offered equipment related to mobile phone and pay-television activities. DNA Oy also offered wholesale products for other operators. Digi TV Plus offered pay-television services through the antenna network to both consumers and corporate customers. Further investigation showed that no intervention was required, as the acquisition was seen to have no harmful effects on competition which would have required intervention. On the contrary, positive effects were deemed possible with regard to pay-television services through antenna networks.[436]

In another case concerning an acquisition (579/81/2008, 27.11.2008), the FCA found that a prospective media grouping involving TV4 AB and C More Group AB was likely to lead to decreased competition in the market for acquisition of rights; nevertheless, it approved the acquisition. The impediments or harmful effects of the concentration were deemed avoidable by attaching a set of conditions to the implementation of the acquisition. The FCA stated that without such arrangements, the consolidation could have a significant effect on consumer choices by packaging the most attractive content separately and by limiting the opportunities of operators to package other content along with the new entity's products. The FCA's decision was appealed against, but the Market Court rejected the appeal. Moreover, the Supreme

---

434. These provisions were reformed and clarified along the lines of EU law (esp. the EC Merger Regulation (no) 139/2004; e.g., the criteria related to dominant position was relaxed. *See* Government bill (HE 88/2010 vp), 68–72. The Government bill (HE 88/2010 vp, 70) notes that previous praxis concerning market dominance may be utilized in interpreting the new s. 25 even if the provision does not *exclusively* build on that concept anymore.

435. The decisions of the FCCA (formerly FCA) are available in Finnish at http://www.kkv.fi/ratkaisut-ja-julkaisut/. Proposals to the Market Court at http://www.kkv.fi/ratkaisut-ja-julkaisut/kilpailuasiat/esitykset-markkinaoikeudelle/ (29.8.2019).

436. Cf. the previous FCCA decision concerning the need for further investigation (223/KKV14.00.10/2013, 24.6.2013).

Administrative Court rejected an appeal concerning immediate enforcement of the conditions (e.g., concerning volume discounts for operators).[437] In 2015, the FCCA accepted a request to abolish conditions set for the acquisition since it no longer considered them necessary in light of the changes in the Finnish pay-television market.[438]

§3. Market Dominance and Cartels

183. As noted, prohibited restraints on competition include horizontal restrictions (§ 5) and abuse of dominance (§ 7). The FCCA decides on measures to be taken against prohibited restraints on competition pursuant to the Competition Act (948/2011) (Chapter 3). It is prohibited to apply or implement restraints on competition unless otherwise prescribed by the Market Court (§ 8). The FCCA may require termination of the unlawful conduct or delivery on similar terms to similar undertakings (§ 9). It may also require that commitments submitted by parties in an alleged infringement are binding on them (§ 10), and it may propose to the Market Court the imposition of a penalty payment (§ 12).[439] Some cases concerning alleged dominant positions have involved actors in the field of media and communications.

In Case 351/14.00.00/2012, 11.12.2013, Canal Digital Finland Oy accused Elisa Oyj of abusing its dominant position in the transmission of pay-television signals. The situation involved those Canal Digital corporate customers (e.g., restaurants) relying on Elisa's cable network for pay-television content because, for instance, the location of their premises rendered antenna or other means of reception impossible. However, the FCCA dismissed the case, since it only involved a limited number of parties and was not of national relevance.

Digita Oy has also been subject to proceedings due to alleged abuse of dominance alongside being accused of infringing the Communications Market Act (in force at the time) as well as FICORA's (now TRAFICOM) guidelines. Case 533/14.00.00/2010, 8.4.2013 concerned unfair and discriminatory pricing as well as the bundling of services. Prior to this Digita Oy had been investigated by FICORA for possible breaches of licence terms regarding its alleged refusal to assign distribution capacity. The case was partially transferred to the FCCA, where it was dismissed. The decision on partial transfer of the matter from FICORA to the Competition Authority (FCA; now FCCA) was appealed against to the Supreme Administrative Court, which subsequently dismissed the appeal (KHO 1899/2/08, 18.12.2009). With regard to competition law, media companies then accused Digita

---

437. *See* decisions of the Market Court (MAO:525/09 and temporary ban MAO Dnro 580/08/KR, 22.1.2009) and the Supreme Administrative Court (536/2/09, no 1201, 18.5.2009).

438. FCCA decision (559/KKV14.00.10/2014, 5.2.2015).

439. These provisions (§§ 8–12) basically correspond to the previous ones (§§ 7, 13, 18); however, clarifications and amendments were made, i.a., following EU law and ECJ case law. *See* Government bill (HE 88/2010 vp), 57.

of abuse of dominance. The FCCA found no ground to proceed with investigation.[440] For its part, FICORA's decision concerning Digita's pricing was appealed, but upheld by the Supreme Administrative Court.[441]

Decision 559/14.00.00/2009, 4.12.2012 concerned the alleged abuse of dominance by MTV Oy in the sales of television advertising. Sanoma Entertainment Oy, Nelonen Media accused MTV Oy of using abusive arrangements in its customer agreements. These included target volumes and significant reductions in prices, or offering other benefits, in return for maintaining or increasing the target volumes. The FCCA noted that such arrangements were liable to have restrictive effects on competition and should be used by dominant companies only with caution. However, there was no evidence that the arrangements in question had an adverse effect on competition in the market for television advertising. The FCA (now FCCA) found no need for further action.

§4. Further Issues

184. In principle, the general provisions of competition law apply across the field of media and communications in Finland.[442]

As regards acquisitions, multiple platforms, and groups of companies in the field of media and communications the following interesting cases may be mentioned from the time of the previous Act on Competition Restrictions. They concern mergers approved without conditions by the FCA.

185. Decision 360/14.00.10/2010, 29.6.2010 involved, among others, Sanoma Oyj and DNA Oy. The latter acquired from the former the so-called Welho business activity and the former received shares of the latter. Consequently, Sanoma together with a few other companies gained control over DNA. The activities of DNA covered general telecommunications, mobile phones, broadband, and television services in the areas of its own cable network coverage. Sanoma for its part constituted a large corporation in the field of communication ranging from print media to television channels and other activities. 'Welho' operated in the field of cable television and broadband.

For example, the threat of detrimental effects to the advertising market and the delivery of electronic content is mentioned in the decision. However, no detrimental effects on competition were detected and the concentration did not imply incentive to vertical exclusion. None of the relevant markets (incl. broadband services, television services, advertising, and mobile services) analysed in the case witnessed dominance hindering competition in the Finnish market or a significant part thereof.

---

440. FCCA decision (352/V1.6.61/2008, 11.12.2015).

441. *See* FICORA decision 249/9313/200, 16.3.2010 and Supreme Administrative Court's judgment KHO 1386/3/10, 7.5.2012.

442. Cf. Legislative powers of the Åland Parliament include postal service and the right to conduct broadcast and cable transmission activities (Act on the Autonomy of Åland, s. 18, subs. 1 (20)) while the State has legislative powers in the field of promoting competition and consumer welfare (s. 27, subs. 1 (10)).

Decision 256/81/2007, 3.4.2007 concerned the acquisition by Bonnier & Bonnier AB of control over Nordic Broadcasting Oy. The former constituted a major corporation in the field of communication ranging from publishing to music production and movie theatres. The latter was a Finnish holding company, established by Bonnier and Proventus, owning all shares of MTV Oy. No detrimental effects to competition were detected.

§5. State Aid

186. Finnish state subsidies, both indirect and direct aid, to the media have traditionally been relatively high compared to average levels in Europe. The situation has, however, changed considerably. For instance, with the legislative amendments late 2011, newspapers faced the abolition of a specifically tailored exemption on value added taxation, but they gained a reduction in the VAT rate in return.[443] The amending Act 1202/2011 took effect on 1 January 2012.

Moreover, in the past, newspapers' reduced delivery charges were a significant form of general support, since direct delivery has been the dominant method of distributing newspapers to readers in Finland, rather than single sales through newsagents or street vendors. Not including the exception of the reduced VAT rate, both direct and indirect subsidies to the press have been all but removed, with the period 2008–2012 seeing the most changes. Nevertheless, newspapers in Swedish and Sámi still receive subsidies.[444]

As discussed above, the State has offered support for rural areas in pursuance of a nationwide broadband network and availability of a high-speed broadband connection.

The act (1202/2011) amending value added taxation for newspapers and periodicals entailed, in some cases, a leap from no value added taxation to a reduced tax rate of 9% as compared to the standard rate of 23%. The background for these changes is found in the decisions made in the context of the 2012 state budget.[445] Previously, section 55 of the Value Added Tax Act (*arvonlisäverolaki* 1501/1993)[446] stated that tax was not payable on the sale of newspapers and periodicals in the form of a subscription of at least a month's duration. The supply of one month's copies (generally sold by subscription) free of charge was also exempt. According to section 131(1) point 1 of the Value Added Tax Act, entrepreneurs were also entitled to a tax refund in the acquisition of goods or services related to an activity exempted by section 55. Moreover, the import of newspapers and periodicals referred to in section 55 was also exempt (§ 94, point 6).

The rates of VAT were subsequently readjusted and set at 10% and 24% respectively (as of 1 January 2013).[447]

---

443. Lehtisaari et al. 2012, 7; Nieminen – Nordenstreng – Harjuniemi 2013, 189.
444. Nieminen – Nordenstreng – Harjuniemi 2013, 185–186, 188–189; Lehtisaari 2015, 142–143.
445. *See* Government bill (HE 52/2011 vp). *See also* Nieminen – Nordenstreng – Harjuniemi 2013, 189.
446. *See* unofficial translation by the Ministry of Finance; amendments up to 1071/2002 are included: https://www.finlex.fi/fi/laki/kaannokset/1993/en19931501_20021071.pdf (29.8.2019).
447. For more, *see* https://vm.fi/en/value-added-tax (29.8.2019).

The Act on Value Added Tax does not define the concept of 'newspapers and periodicals'. In this regard, the definition included in section 2 of the FEA can be referred to.[448]

In a ruling of the Supreme Administrative Court (KHO 31.12.2013/4119), the contract between two companies (A and B) regarding the publishing of a paper was not deemed to render Company B a subscriber from the perspective of value added tax. Company B purchased the manufacture of the paper it published and the contents of which it determined from Company A which operated in the field of publishing. It was not a question of at least a month's subscription by a customer from the publisher in return for payment and to a specific address.

It should be noted that sales of single issues of newspapers and periodicals were already subject to the standard rate of value added tax. The legislative amendments introduced no changes in this regard. Furthermore, the exemption in section 56 for sale of an edition to a corporation promoting public good and operating outside the commercial publishing sphere was retained (e.g., publications for members).

> Similar to the above case (KHO 31.12.2013/4119) where the relation of Company A to non-profit associations with regard to various activities related to the manufacture of membership-based publications was not covered by the exemption. Finland has been exempted in the EU framework only with regard to the sale of press activity.

It must also be noted that the reduced rate only applied to subscriptions of printed copies. Electronic versions or online newspapers and periodicals were not covered. Indeed, the Supreme Administrative Court ruled (KHO 2007:65), with references to EU law at the time, that an online paper was to be regarded as a separate product which fell under the scope of services (cf. goods). Even when sold in connection to the printed paper it did not benefit from the tax rate of the printed paper (then 0%). Due to more recent EU-level developments (Directive (EU) 2018/1713), Member States are, however, able to apply the lower tax to electronic publications. In Finland, the Act on Value Added Tax was amended so that a lower rate (10%) covers electronic versions of papers since 1 July 2019.[449]

187. Furthermore, the implementation of the requirements of the directive on postal services (2008/6/EC) by the Postal Act (415/2011) led to legislative amendments in the name of opening markets and affected newspaper delivery, especially in rural areas.[450] Despite being open in principle, the Finnish market was characterized by a relative lack of competition, partly due to previous legislation. Accommodating postal operations to changes in the market had also led to increasing challenges. Consequently, the Act on Postal Services (313/2001) was replaced by the Postal Act which applies to all postal services (§ 1). Importantly, however, the

---

448. *See also* https://www.vero.fi/syventavat-vero-ohjeet/ohje-hakusivu/48354/kirjojen-ja-lehtien-arvon lisäverotuksesta/ (29.8.2019).
449. *See* Government bill (HE 303/2018 vp).
450. Lehtisaari et al. 2012, 7; Nieminen – Nordenstreng – Harjuniemi 2013, 189.

scope of the Postal Act does not cover services concerning newspapers and periodicals (§ 1(3), point 1), as regulation of such delivery has been regarded as contrary to free speech, especially concerning the constitutionally protected freedom of the press.[451] Despite the exclusion, the regulation arguably includes elements that have implications for their nationwide delivery. Postal operations concerning items of correspondence required a licence, granted by the Government (§§ 3–4). Currently, section 3 has been repealed and section 4 contains only the responsibility for notification to TRAFICOM, not a licence.[452]

In 2014, company X was granted a delivery licence for the Päijät-Häme region. The previous licence granted in 2012 had been appealed against and replaced by the new licence. The 2012 licence had contained terms concerning non-discrimination, frequency of delivery, establishment of an office, and other obligations. The company deemed these terms unlawful and comparable to universal service obligations. In its judgment (KHO 2014:153, 22.10.2014) the Supreme Administrative Court found some of the some licence terms unlawful and the matter was returned to the Government.

Some other companies have also been granted a licence for regional operations while Posti (ex Itella) operates nationwide.

188. Universal postal services are regulated in Chapters 3–6 of the Postal Act. These services must be available throughout the country and provided on equal terms. According to section 23, TRAFICOM imposes a universal service obligation on the basis of market analysis. Posti Oyj, formerly Itella Oyj, is the Finnish corporation currently operating under universal service obligations. The legislative amendments leading to the Postal Act meant subjecting any compensation to the corporation under the USO to EU rules regarding state aid.[453]

In contrast to the abolition of subsidies for newspapers, the so-called public broadcasting tax was developed and introduced in the same period. Moreover, provisions on *ex ante* testing were enacted. Yleisradio's services can nonetheless be submitted for assessment in procedures defined by legislation on competition and state aid.[454]

In 2017, a Government Decree to support the news and current affairs of public interest channels was passed. The aim is to incentivise news production and promote pluralism. According to the Decree, the Ministry of Transport and Communications grants aid upon application to public interest channels (section 3; *see* section 26 ECSA). The Decree refers to different types of aid, such as services of general economic interest aid, production support in the form of general aid pursuant to Section 5(2) of the Act on Discretionary Government Transfers (688/2001 (ADGT), and start-up or development support in the form of special aid pursuant to Article 5(3)(4) of ADGT (section 5). Editorial material in national languages (Finnish/Swedish) produced or commissioned by the beneficiary are within the

451. *See* Government bill (HE 216/2010 vp), 74.
452. *See* more at https://www.maaseuduntulevaisuus.fi/politiikka/postin-toimiluvista-luovutaan-ilmoitus-viestintävirastolle-riittää-1.147137 (29.8.2019).
453. *See* Government bill (HE 216/2010 vp), 119, 141.
454. *See* Statement of the Constitutional Law Committee (PeVL 14/2012 vp), 3–4; *see also* Tarhonen 2014.

scope of the support. The beneficiary is vested with a fixed-term service obligation, while annual reporting is mandatory. There are minimum requirements for the amount and frequency of news and current affairs programmes, while net costs of service provision may be supported between 25% and 50% depending on the nature of the activity. Annual aid may amount to EUR 2 million for one beneficiary.[455] Both MTV3 and Alfa TV applied, but the Ministry granted the support only to MTV3. The Decree was in force until the end of 2019.

455. *See* Alén-Savikko 2017.

Part V. Supervision: Media Regulator

§1. Organization

189. Before the Finnish Communications Regulatory Authority (FICORA) (*Viestintävirasto*) was the media regulatory authority in Finland. The scope of FICORA's authority covered operators in the field of telecommunication, television, radio, and postal communication, as well as other providers of communications and various aspects of electronic communication.[456] As of 1 January 2019, the Finnish Transport Safety Agency (Trafi), the Finnish Communications Regulatory Authority (FICORA) and certain functions of the Finnish Transport Agency merged to form the Finnish Transport and Communications Agency (TRAFICOM).[457] The Act on the Finnish Transport and Communications Agency (935/2018; TRAFICOM Act) entered into force on 1 January 2019.

190. TRAFICOM is a state authority that acts in field of operation of the Ministry of Transport and Communications. Led by a Director-General (section 4 TRAFICOM Act), TRAFICOM has a net budgeted income within the State budget, and it also collects fees.[458] Application fees for various licences are included in Chapter 36 of the Act on Electronic Communications Services (*see* § 351 on entry into force). Yleisradio, in contrast, is currently financed by through taxation.

TRAFICOM (previously FICORA) activities are a continuation of the work of the Telecommunications Administration Centre (TAC). The Centre was established in 1988 as a development stemming from the need to separate administration from business activities. The new name, corresponding more closely to the converged media landscape, was adopted in late 2001.[459]

In 2014, much of the previously dispersed regulations and provisions concerning FICORA's tasks and functions were incorporated into the Information Society Code, now Act on Electronic Communications Services (917/2014). However, general provisions were still included in the Act on Communications Administration (625/2001).[460] This law has now been repealed.

---

456. More in Markkanen – Nieminen 2013, 30–32.
457. *See* https://www.traficom.fi/en/traficom/about-traficom (29.8.2019).
458. For more on FICORA (TRAFICOM), *see* Markkanen – Nieminen 2013, 31.
459. *See* https://www.viestintavirasto.fi/en/FICORA/presentationandduties/history.html (updated 21.11.2014) (29.8.2019); More in Markkanen – Nieminen 2013, 32, 35–36.
460. Unofficial translation by the Ministry of Transport and Communications; amendments up to 397/2003 included: http://www.finlex.fi/en/laki/kaannokset/2001/en20010625.pdf (29.8.2019).

§2. TASKS

191. Section 2 of the Act on Communications Administration provided for the relevant legislation with regard to FICORA's duties.

According to Section 2 of the TRAFICOM Act, the agency has multiple tasks in the field of transport and communications, including those related to licences regarding electronic media and spectrum administration. The National Cyber Security Center Finland (NCSC-FI; *Kyberturvallisuuskeskus*), as part of TRAFICOM, is responsible for supporting, supervising, and guiding the maintenance of security and privacy in electronic communications (section 3 TRAFICOM Act).

The Information Society Code, now Act on Electronic Communications Services, brought changes to FICORA's (now TRAFICOM) role regarding domain names. However, the Domain Name Act remained in force until 4 September 2016. After that, the regulator still maintained the registry for domain names, but a domain name service provider, which is responsible for the practicalities, will always act as an intermediary. The move was from a mixed model towards a service provider model so that TRAFICOM is not directly contacted by aspiring domain name holders. This new regulation is included in Chapter 21 of the Act on Electronic Communications Services, and the provisions concerning intermediaries came into force on 5 September 2016 (§ 351(4)). The purpose was also to render the regulation more allowing towards foreign operators, legal and natural persons, and thereby more compatible with EU law.[461]

According to section 303 of the Act on Electronic Communications Services, TRAFICOM's duty is to supervise compliance with the Act and resultant provisions and decisions unless otherwise stipulated. However, its competence is restricted in regard to agreements between operators and subscribers or a telecommunications operator's right to recourse, protection of health and safety, information society services, not including obligations to inform, as well as installation of cables, stations, and masts (§ 303(2)–(5)).

192. Additional special duties are listed in section 304 of the Act on Electronic Communications Services: TRAFICOM must promote the functionality and security of telecommunications as well as its freedom from interference. TRAFICOM must participate in contingency planning, supervise and develop technical contingency measures, administer radio frequencies, telecommunications, and numbering and identifiers for communication networks and services, as well as coordinate industry standards. In addition, TRAFICOM collects and/or publishes information on the availability, quality and prices of network and communications services as well as violations and threats to information security. It investigates the reasons both for the latter and also for interference and disturbance in communications. TRAFICOM informs the European Commission in cooperation concerning information

461. *See*, *e.g.*, Report of the Transport and Communications Committee (LiVM 10/2014 vp). Ch. 21 applies to domain names with region codes 'fi' (Finland) and 'ax' (Åland) as well as to administration thereof. The provisions on TRAFICOM's domain name register also apply to the register of domain names with the region code 'ax' (Åland) (§ 163). Administration of these domain names has been transferred to the Government of Åland by Presidential Decree (*see* TPa 188/2006).

security and supervision liable to have effects on the functioning of the Internal Market. With the amendments brought about by Government bill (HE 67/2016 vp) and Act 456/2016, the provisions also include TRAFICOM's duty to perform the task of a responsible authority regarding Public Regulated Service (PRS) pursuant to the Galileo programme.[462] Following the reforms of the AVMS Directive and the EECC, TRAFICOM would also have proposed duties related to accessibility, among others.[463]

TRAFICOM must foster co-regulation or self-regulation in the field where these forms of regulation can be used to fulfil the requirements and achieve the objectives of the Act on Electronic Communications Services (§ 303(6)). In sum, TRAFICOM offers advice, drafts recommendations, and offers information on good practice in the field of media and communications. It also negotiates and mediates disagreements and discrepancies within the scope of its competence, inspects various matters, and notifies actors of misconduct. Marketing activities or the content of communication are not within TRAFICOM's supervisory competence.

Furthermore, TRAFICOM delivers decisions in matters assigned to it. These decisions may be appealed against to the administrative courts, the Supreme Administrative Court, or the Market Court depending on the issue in question and following the procedure prescribed by law (§§ 343–345 ECSA).

The merger of separate organisations into TRAFICOM did not imply any fundamental changes to the operations of the organizations.[464]

193. Other authorities in the field of audiovisual media and communications include the Government, the Ministry of Transport and Communications, the Finnish Competition and Consumer Authority (FCCA) and the Consumer Ombudsman. The Data Protection Ombudsman also has supervisorial duties pursuant to the Act on Electronic Communications Services (§ 305; i.a., Chapter 18, Chapter 20).

According to section 302 of the Act on Electronic Communications Services, the general guidance and development of activities within the scope of the Act are vested in the Ministry of Transport and Communications. The Government must ensure that regulatory activities and matters concerning state ownership and control are separated (§ 302(2)).

Section 306 states that the Consumer Ombudsman supervises compliance with section 214(4) with regard to marketing targeted at children. Pursuant to the Consumer Protection Act, the Ombudsman also supervises the lawfulness of contractual terms, marketing, and conduct in customer relations from the perspective of consumer protection. However, the Consumer Ombudsman cannot target ideological or political advertising.

---

462. *See* Government bill (HE 67/2016 vp); PRS Decision No 1104/2011/EU. The National Cyber Security Center Finland (NCSC-FI; *Kyberturvallisuuskeskus*) performs duties related to PRS. For more, *see* TRAFICOM 'Galileo Public Regulated Service': https://legacy.viestintavirasto.fi/en/cybersecurity/prs.html (29.8.2019).
463. Government bill (HE 112/2002 vp).
464. For more information, *see* https://valtioneuvosto.fi/en/article/-/asset_publisher/viestintavirasto-ja-trafi-yhdistyvat-liikenne-ja-viestintavirastoksi-liikennevirastosta-tulee-vaylavirasto (29.8.2019).

In addition, certain other authorities, notably the police, the Border Guard, and customs, have duties pursuant to section 307 of the Act on Electronic Communications Services.

Cooperation between authorities is regulated in section 308, whereby the Ministry of Transport and Communications, TRAFICOM, Data Protection Ombudsman, competition authorities and consumer authorities must collaborate in fulfilling their duties. TRAFICOM must also cooperate with its European colleagues (§ 308(2)). Proposed changes include adding the National Audiovisual Institute, KAVI, to this list due to its role with regard to video-sharing platform services.[465] Moreover, it must consult and cooperate with the Ministry of Transport and Communications in matters concerning delegated regulatory power. It must consult with the Ministry of Finances on matters concerning the general development of public administration as well as matters concerning the structure, direction, and development of state administration and electronic services, information security, and information administration (§ 303(7)).

§3. Sanctioning Powers

194. Chapter 42 of the Act on Electronic Communications Services includes provisions on supervisory decisions and coercive measures, including provisions on interim measures and penalty payments as well as the imposition of conditional fines, threats of termination and completion and ordering closure and suspension. According to section 330, TRAFICOM may notify the person in violation of the Act on Electronic Communications Services or provisions, orders, decisions, or licence terms issued by virtue of it. TRAFICOM may also order rectification in due time. As regards the provisions supervised by the Consumer Ombudsman (*see* § 306), Chapter 2 of the Consumer Protection Act applies (§ 330(2) ECSA).

465. Government bill (HE 112/2002 vp), 274.

Selected Bibliography

Alén-Savikko 2017
Alén-Savikko, Anette: Decree on financial support for news and current affairs television content. IRIS 2017-10:1/14: http://merlin.obs.coe.int/iris/2017/10/article14.en.html (27.10.2019).
Alén-Savikko 2016
Alén-Savikko, Anette: Finland: Report Assessing the Media Market. EMR Newsletter 2016-1.
Alén-Savikko 2015a
Alén-Savikko, Anette: Reintroduction of Remuneration for 'Must Carry' Retransmission. IRIS 2015-7:/13: http://merlin.obs.coe.int/iris/2015/7/article13.en.html (29.8.2019).
Alén-Savikko 2015b
Alén-Savikko, Anette: Tekijänoikeus ja urheilun liikkuva kuva. In Korpisaari, Päivi (ed.): Viestintäoikeus nyt: Viestintäoikeuden vuosikirja 2014. Forum Iuris – Helsingin yliopiston oikeustieteellisen tiedekunnan julkaisuja, 84–127, 2015.
Alén-Savikko 2014
Alén-Savikko, Anette: Law and Community in the New Media Landscape: Critical Perspectives on Audiovisual Sport Coverage in the European Union. Helsinki: University of Helsinki, 2014 (Dissertation).
Alén 2010a
Alén, Anette: Proposed Changes to the Finnish Copyright Act due to the Implementation of the AVMS Directive. IRIS 2010-1:Extra: http://merlin.obs.coe.int/iris/2010/1/article122.en.html (29.8.2019).
Alén 2010b
Alén, Anette: Implementing the AVMSD Resulted in Amending the Finnish Copyright Act. IRIS 2010-6:1/26. http://merlin.obs.coe.int/iris/2010/6/article26.en.html (29.8.2019).
Bruun 2001
Bruun, Niklas. Intellectual Property Law in Finland. The Hague/London/Boston: Kluwer Law International, Helsinki: Kauppakaari, 2001.
Bruun 1999
Bruun, Niklas: International Encyclopaedia of Copyright Law. Finland: Kluwer Law International, 1999.
Hallberg et al. 2011

Selected Bibliography

Hallberg, Pekka – Karapuu, Heikki – Ojanen, Tuomas – Scheinin, Martin – Tuori, Kaarlo – Viljanen, Veli-Pekka: Perusoikeudet. Helsinki: Werner Söderström lakitieto WSLT, 29–59, 2011.

Hellman 2012

Hellman, Heikki: Koko illan ilo?: kolmostelevisio ja television kaupallistuminen Suomessa 2012. Tampere: Suomalaisen kirjallisuuden seura, 2012.

Hellman 1999

Hellman, Heikki: From Companions to Competitors. The Changing Broadcasting Market and Television Programming in Finland. Tampere: University of Tampere, 1999.

Hellman 1988

Hellman, Heikki: Uustelevision aika? Yleisradiotoiminnan edellytykset television rakennemuutoksessa. Helsinki: Hanki ja Jää, 1988.

Hoikka 2009

Hoikka, Mikko: Sananvapaus Euroopan unionin oikeudessa. Helsinki: Suomalainen Lakimiesyhdistys, 2009.

Khaldarova – Laaksonen – Matikainen 2012

Khaldarova, Irina – Laaksonen, Salla-Maaria – Matikainen, Janne: The Use of Social Media in the Finnish Parliament Elections 2011. Media and Communication Studies Research Reports 3/2012, CRC, Helsinki: University of Helsinki, 2012. Available at http://www.helsinki.fi/crc/Julkaisut/SoMe_Elections.pdf (29.8.2019).

Korpisaari, Comment on case KKO 2018:51

Korpisaari, Päivi: Comment on case KKO 2018:51. In Timonen, Pekka (ed.): KKO:n ratkaisut kommentein 2018 II, 2019.

Korpisaari 2019

Korpisaari, Päivi: Henkilötietojen ja yksityiselämän suoja vuonna 2018 – katsaus sääntelyyn ja ratkaisukäytäntöön. In Korpisaari, Päivi (ed.): Data, viestintä ja sääntely: Viestintäoikeuden vuosikirja 2018. Forum Iuris – Helsingin yliopiston oikeustieteellisen tiedekunnan julkaisuja, 27 – 54, 2019.

Kulla – Koillinen 2014

Kulla, Heikki – Koillinen, Mikael: Julkisuus ja henkilötietojen suoja viranomaistoiminnassa. Turku: Turun yliopiston oikeustieteellinen tiedekunta, 2014.

Lehtisaari 2015

Lehtisaari, Katja: Mediatalouden ja viestintäpolitiikan risteyskohtia. In Karppinen, Kari et al.: Kenen media? Johdatus viestintäpolitiikan tutkimukseen. Tampere: Vastapaino, 130–146, 2015.

Lehtisaari et al. 2012

Lehtisaari, Katja -- Karppinen, Kari -- Harjuniemi, Timo -- Grönlund, Mikko -- Lindén, Carl-Gustav – Nieminen, Hannu – Viljakainen, Anna: Media Convergence and Business Models: Responses of Finnish Daily Newspapers. Communication Research Centre CRC, Department of Social Research, University of Helsinki, 2012.

Manninen 1995a

Manninen, Sami: Perusoikeusuudistus ja uusi sananvapaussäännös. Oikeus 1995, 361–371.

Manninen 1995b

Manninen, Sami: Sananvapaudesta ja mainonnasta. Lakimies 1995, 571–606.
Markkanen – Nieminen 2013
Markkanen, Anna-Laura – Nieminen, Hannu: Finland. In Sousa, H. et al. (eds). Media Regulators in Europe: A Cross-Country Comparative Analysis. Braga, CECS, University of Minho, 28–38, 2013: http://www.lasics.uminho.pt/ojs/index.php/cecs_ebooks/article/view/1533/1436 (29.8.2019).
Matikkala 2005
Matikkala, Jussi: Tahallisuudesta rikosoikeudessa. Helsinki: Suomalainen Lakimiesyhdistys, 2005.
Mäenpää 2016
Mäenpää, Olli: Julkisuusperiaate. Juva: WSOYpro, 2016.
Neuvonen 2014
Neuvonen, Riku: Yksityisyyden suoja Suomessa. Lakimiesliiton kustannus: Helsinki, 2014.
Neuvonen 2012
Neuvonen, Riku: Sananvapauden sääntely Suomessa. Helsinki: Lakimiesliiton kustannus, 2012.
Neuvonen 2010
Neuvonen, Riku: Kuvaohjelmien sääntely Suomessa – nykytila ja haasteet. Lakimies 1/2010, 40–60.
Nieminen 2013:
Nieminen, Hannu: European Broadband Regulation: The 'Broadband for All 2015' Strategy in Finland. In Löblich, Maria – Pfaff-Rüdiger, Senta (eds.): Communication and Media Policy in the Era of the Internet: Theories and Processes. Baden-Baden: Nomos Verlagsgesellschaft, 119–131, 2013.
Nieminen – Nordenstreng – Harjuniemi 2013
Nieminen, Hannu – Nordenstreng, Kaarle – Harjuniemi Timo: Finland: The Rise and Fall of a Democratic Subsidy Scheme. In Murschetz, Paul (ed.): State Aid for Newspapers: Theories, Cases, Actions. Springer-Verlag, 179–194, 2013.
Niiranen – Sotamaa – Tiilikka 2013
Niiranen, Valtteri – Sotamaa, Petteri – Tiilikka, Päivi: Sananvapauslaki: Tulkinta ja käytäntö. Helsinki: Sanoma Pro Oy, 2013.
Ojanen – Tiilikka – Vairimaa 2012
Ojanen, Tuomas – Tiilikka, Päivi – Vairimaa, Inka: Selvitys ohjelmistolupajärjestelmän perustuslainmukaisuudesta sananvapauden ja elinkeinovapauden näkökulmasta. Helsinki, University of Helsinki, Institute of International Economic Law, 2012.
Ollila 2009
Ollila, Riitta: Sananvapaus ja sopimattoman markkinoinnin sääntely. Defensor Legis 2009, 276–291.
Ollila 2001
Ollila, Riitta: Freedom of Speech and Protection of Privacy in Convergence of Electronic Communications. Rovaniemi: University of Lapland, 2001.
Paukku 2005
Paukku, Eero: Sananvapaus televisio- ja radiotoiminnan sääntelyssä. Helsinki: Helsingin yliopisto, 2005.
Pihlajarinne 2011

Pihlajarinne, Taina: Keskustelupalstojen ylläpitäjän vastuu: EU-sääntelystä kansalliseen oikeuteen – sananvapausrikokset ja tekijänoikeusrikos. Lakimies 6/2011, 1192–1214.
Pihlajarinne 2012
Pihlajarinne, Taina: Internetvälittäjä ja tekijänoikeuden loukkaus. Lakimiesliiton kustannus, Helsinki, 2012.
Rauste 1997
Rauste, Olli: Urheiluoikeus. Helsinki: Lakimiesliiton kustannus, 1997.
Rautiainen 2012
Rautiainen, Pauli: Kuvataiteilijan oikeudellinen asema: ammattimaista taiteellista toimintaa rajoittava ja edistävä oikeussääntely. Tampere: Tampere University Press, 2012.
Saraviita 2012
Saraviita, Ilkka: Finland. International Encyclopedia of Constitutional Law. In Alen, André and Haljan, David (eds.): IEL Constitutional Law. Netherlands: Kluwer Law International, 2012: https://kluwerlawonline.com/EncyclopediaChapter/IEL+Constitutional+Law/CONS20190017.
Saressalo – Tulin 2008
Saressalo Lassi-Tulin, Matti: Kertomus kaapelitelevisiosta – Suomen Kaapelitelevisioliitto 1973–2007. Helsinki: Ficom ry, 2008.
Savola 2015
Savola, Pekka: Internet Connectivity Providers as Involuntary Copyright Enforcers: Blocking Websites in Particular. Helsinki: University of Helsinki, 2015.
Ståhlberg 1913
Ståhlberg, Kaarlo J: Painovapaus Suomessa. Helsinki: Kustannusosakeyhtiö Otava, 1913.
Sumiala-Seppänen 1999
Sumiala-Seppänen, Johanna: A Longstanding Experiment. The History of the Finnish Broadcasting Model. Department of Communication, Jyväskylä: University of Jyväskylä, 1999: http://www.jyu.fi/viesti/verkkotuotanto/broadcasting/index.html (29.8.2019).
Tapani 2013:
Tapani, Jussi: Esirikoksen yksilöitävyys ja olosuhdetahallisuus. Defensor Legis 5/2013, 787–798.
Tapani 2009
Tapani, Jussi: Sattumaa vai ei – korkein oikeus, kieltoerehdys ja tahallisuuden kohde. Lakimies 2009/3, 470–481.
Tapani 2006
Tapani, Jussi: Mistä puhumme, kun puhumme olosuhdetahallisuudesta? 2006 Edilex 28.8.2006.
Tarhonen 2014:
Tarhonen, Laura (2014): Julkisen palvelun yleisradiotoiminta Suomessa – palveluiden ja toimintojen ennakkoarvioinnilla kohti tulevaisuuden haasteita. In Tiilikka, Päivi (ed.): Sananvapaus puntarissa. Viestintäoikeuden vuosikirja 2013. Helsinki: Helsingin yliopisto, Oikeustieteellisen tiedekunnan julkaisuja, Forum Iuris, 87–137.
Tiilikka 2013

Tiilikka Päivi: Access to Information as a Human Right in the Case Law of the European Court of Human Rights. Journal of Media Law 5 no. 1 (2013): 79–103.
Tiilikka 2012a
Tiilikka, Päivi: Act concerning the Funding of Public Service Broadcasting. IRIS – Legal Observations of the European Audiovisual Observatory 2012-7:1/2: http://merlin.obs.coe.int/iris/2012/7/article20.en.html (29.8.2019).
Tiiilikka 2012b
Tiilikka, Päivi: Päätoimittajan vastuu yleisön tuottamasta verkkosisällöstä. Lakimies 1/2012, 53–78.
Tiilikka 2008
Tiilikka, Päivi: Journalistin sananvapaus. Helsinki: WSOYpro, 2008.
Tiilikka 2007
Tiilikka, Päivi: Sananvapaus ja yksilön suoja. Lehtiartikkelin aiheuttaman kärsimyksen korvaamisesta. Helsinki: WSOYpro, 2007.
Tolvanen: Comment on case 2019:112
Tolvanen, Matti: Comment on case KKO 2019:112. In Timonen, Pekka (ed.): KKO:n ratkaisut kommentein 2019 II, 2020.
Tommila – Salokangas 1998
Tommila, Päiviö – Salokangas, Raimo: Sanomia kaikille. Suomen lehdistön historia. Helsinki: Oy Edita Ab, 1998.
Utriainen 2019
Utriainen, Terttu: Finland. International Encyclopaedia of Criminal Law. In Verbruggen, Frank – Franssen, Vanessa (eds.): Alphen a/d Rijn: Kluwer Law International, 2019.
Valcke – Lievens 2010
Valcke, Peggy – Lievens, Eva: Belgium. In Blanpain, Roger – Hendrickx (eds.) International Encyclopaedia of Media Law. International Encyclopaedia of Laws. Alphen a/d Rijn: Kluwer Law International., 2010.
Viitanen: Comment on case 2019:67
Viitanen, Markku: Comment on case KKO 2019:67. In Timonen, Pekka (ed.): KKO:n ratkaisut kommentein 2019 II, 2020.
Viljanen 2001
Viljanen, Veli-Pekka: Perusoikeuksien rajoitusedellytykset. Helsinki: WSOY lakitieto, 2001.

Government Bills

Mostly available in Finnish at https://www.eduskunta.fi/FI/search/Sivut/vaskiresults.aspx (29.8.2019).
Government bill on amending Chapter 27 of the Criminal Code, Sections 18 and 39 of the Act on the Freedom of the Press and Sections 1 and 2 of the Act on the Publicity of Judicature (Hallituksen esitys eduskunnalle laeiksi rikoslain 27 luvun, painovapauslain 18 ja 39 §:n sekä oikeudenkäytön julkisuudesta annetun lain 1 ja 2 §:n muuttamisesta) (HE 84/1974 vp).
Government bill on amending the fundamental rights provisions of the constitutions. (Hallituksen esitys eduskunnalle perustuslakien perusoikeussäännösten muuttamisesta (HE 309/1993 vp).

Government bill on Act on the Openness of Government Activities (Hallituksen esitys eduskunnalle laiksi viranomaisten toiminnan julkisuudesta ja siihen liittyviksi laeiksi) (HE 30/1998 vp).
Government bill for legislation on television and radio operations (Hallituksen esitys eduskunnalle televisio- ja radiotoimintaa koskevaksi lainsäädännöksi) (HE 34/1998 vp).
Government bill on renewing the penal provisions concerning offences against privacy, public peace and personal reputation (Hallituksen esitys Eduskunnalle yksityisyyden, rauhan ja kunnian loukkaamista koskevien rangaistussäännösten uudistamiseksi) (HE 184/1999 vp).
Government bill on renewing the general principles of criminal law (Hallituksen esitys Eduskunnalle rikosoikeuden yleisiä oppeja koskevan lainsäädännön uudistamiseksi) (HE 44/2002 vp).
Government bill for the Act on the Exercise of Freedom of Expression in Mass Media and certain laws relating to this (Hallituksen esitys eduskunnalle laiksi sananvapauden käyttämisestä joukkoviestinnässä ja eräiksi siihen liittyviksi laeiksi) (HE 54/2002 vp).
Government bill for amending legislation concerning the Communications Market (Hallituksen esitys eduskunnalle viestintämarkkinoita koskevan lainsäädännön muuttamisesta (HE 112/2002 vp).
Government bill on amending the Communications Market Act and Sections 2 and 5 of the Act on the Protection of Privacy in Electronic Communications (Hallituksen esitys eduskunnalle laeiksi viestintämarkkinalain sekä sähköisen viestinnän tietosuojalain 2 ja 5 §:n muuttamisesta) (HE 48/2007 vp).
Government bill on amendments to the Communications Market Act (Hallituksen esitys eduskunnalle laiksi viestintämarkkinalain muuttamisesta) (HE 100/2007 vp).
Government bill on amending the Act on Protection of Privacy in Electronic Communications and Certain Related Acts (Hallituksen esitys eduskunnalle sähköisen viestinnän tietosuojalain ja eräiden siihen liittyvien lakien muuttamisesta) (HE 48/2008 vp).
Government bill on Acts amending the Act on Auctioning Certain Radio Frequencies and Sections 4 and 12 of the Communications Market Act (Hallituksen esitys eduskunnalle laeiksi eräiden radiotaajuuksien huutokaupoista sekä viestintämarkkinalain 4 ja 12 §:n muuttamisesta) (HE 37/2009 vp).
Government bill on amendments and temporary amendments to the Finnish Act on Television and Radio Operations as well as amendments to sections 25 b and 48 on the Copyright Act (Hallituksen esitys eduskunnalle laeiksi television- ja radiotoiminnasta annetun lain muuttamisesta ja väliaikaisesta muuttamisesta sekä tekijänoikeuslain 25 b ja 48 §:n muuttamisesta) (HE 87/2009 vp).
Government bill on amendments to the Provision on Entry into Force of the Act amending Section 134 of the Communications Market Act, Section 134 of the Communications Market Act and the Act on Television and Radio Operations (Hallituksen esitys eduskunnalle laeiksi viestintämarkkinalain 134 §:n muuttamista annetun lain voimaantulosäännöksen, viestintämarkkinalain 134 §:n ja televisio- ja radiotoiminnasta annetun lain muuttamiseksi) (HE 13/2010 vp).

Government bill for Competition Act (Hallituksen esitys eduskunnalle kilpailulaiksi) (HE 88/2010 vp).
Government bill on renewing the legislation on audiovisual programmes (Hallituksen esitys eduskunnalle kuvaohjelmalainsäädännös uudistamiseksi) (HE 190/2010 vp).
Government bill on the Postal Act and the adoption of the Universal Postal Convention and implementation of its provisions concerning legislative matters (Hallituksen esitys eduskunnalle postilaiksi sekä Maailman postiliiton yleissopimuksen hyväksymiseksi ja laiksi sen lainsäädännön alaan kuuluvien määräysten voimaansaattamisesta) (HE 216/2010 vp).
Government bill on reforming legislation on criminal investigations and coercive measures (Hallituksen esitys Eduskunnalle esitutkinta- ja pakkokeinolainsäädännön uudistamiseksi) (HE 222/2010 vp).
Government bill on Acts amending the Communications Market Act, Act on Radio Frequencies and Telecommunications Equipment, Act on the Protection of Privacy in Electronic Communications and Act on Certain Proceedings before the Market Court (Hallituksen esitys eduskunnalle laeiksi viestintämarkkinalain, radiotaajuuksista ja telelaitteista annetun lain, sähköisen viestinnän tietosuojalain ja eräiden markkinaoikeudellisten asioiden käsittelystä annetun lain muuttamisesta) (HE 238/2010 vp).
Government bill on the approval of the Protocol on Hate Crimes to the Council of Europe Convention on Cybercrime and on legislation bringing into force its provisions and act amending Section 15 of the Act on provision of information society services (Hallituksen esitys Eduskunnalle Euroopan neuvoston tietoverkkorikollisuutta koskevan yleissopimuksen lisäpöytäkirjan, joka koskee tietojärjestelmien välityksellä tehtyjen luonteeltaan rasististen ja muukalaisvihamielisten tekojen kriminalisointia, hyväksymisestä ja laiksi sen lainsäädännön alaan kuuluvien määräysten voimaansaattamisesta sekä laeiksi rikoslain ja tietoyhteiskunnan palvelujen tarjoamisesta annetun lain 15 §:n muuttamisesta) (HE 317/2010 vp).
Government bill on amending the Value Added Tax Act (Hallituksen esitys eduskunnalle arvonlisäverolain muuttamisesta) (HE 52/2011 vp).
Government bill on amendments to the Act on Yleisradio Oy and the Act on the State Television and Radio Fund (Hallituksen esitys eduskunnalle laeiksi Yleisradio Oy:stä annetun lain sekä valtion televisio- ja radiorahastosta annetun lain muuttamisesta) (HE 29/2012 vp).
Government bill on Acts amending the Act on Auctioning Certain Radio Frequencies and for temporary amendments to the Communications Market Act (Hallituksen esitys eduskunnalle laeiksi eräiden radiotaajuuksien huutokaupoista annetun lain muuttamisesta sekä viestintämarkkinalain väliaikaisesta muuttamisesta) (HE 72/2012 vp).
Government bill on amending the Criminal Code, Section 7 of Chapter 10 of the Coercive Measures Act and Section 9 of Chapter 5 of the Police Act (Hallituksen esitys eduskunnalle laeiksi rikoslain, pakkokeinolain 10 luvun 7 §:n ja poliisilain 5 luvun 9 §:n muuttamisesta) (HE 19/2013 vp).

Selected Bibliography

Government bill on amending the Act on the National Audiovisual Archive and certain related acts (Hallituksen esitys eduskunnalle laiksi Kansallisesta audiovisuaalisesta arkistosta annetun lain muuttamisesta sekä eräiksi siihen liittyviksi laeiksi) (HE 48/2013 vp).

Government bill on amending Sections 33 and 40 of the Alcohol Act (Hallituksen esitys eduskunnalle alkoholilain 33 ja 40 §:n muuttamisesta) (HE 70/2013 vp).

Government bill for the Act on Electronic Communications Services and Acts amending Section 161 of the Land Use and Building Act and Section 8b of Chapter 38 of the Criminal Code (Hallituksen esitys eduskunnalle tietoyhteiskuntakaareksi sekä laeiksi maankäyttö- ja rakennuslain 161 §:n ja rikoslain 38 luvun 8 b §:n muuttamisesta) (HE 221/2013 vp).

Government bill on the reform of Chapter 17 of the Code of Judicial Procedure and related legislation on presentation of evidence in general courts (Hallituksen esitys eduskunnalle oikeudenkäymiskaaren 17 luvun ja siihen liittyvän todistelua yleisissä tuomioistuimissa koskevan lainsäädännön uudistamiseksi) (HE 46/2014 vp).

Government bill on Acts amending the Act on the Sámi Parliament and Section 11 of Chapter 40 of the Criminal Code (Hallituksen esitys eduskunnalle laeiksi saamelaiskäräjistä annetun lain ja rikoslain 40 luvun 11 §:n muuttamisesta) (HE 167/2014 vp).

Government bill for act amending the Administrative Judicial Procedure Act and certain related acts (Hallituksen esitys eduskunnalle laiksi hallintolainkäyttölain muuttamisesta ja eräiksi siihen liittyviksi laeiksi) (HE 245/2014 vp).

Government bill for Tobacco Act and certain related acts (Hallituksen esitys eduskunnalle tupakkalaiksi ja eräiksi siihen liittyviksi laeiksi) (HE 15/2016 vp).

Government bill on amending and temporary amendments to the Act on Electronic Communications Services as well as amending the act on notified bodies for certain product groups (Hallituksen esitys eduskunnalle laeiksi tietoyhteiskuntakaaren muuttamisesta ja väliaikaisesta muuttamisesta sekä eräitä tuoteryhmiä koskevista ilmoitetuista laitoksista annetun lain muuttamisesta) (HE 67/2016 vp).

Government bill for Act on Damages for Infringements of Competition Law and act amending the Competition Act (Hallituksen esitys eduskunnalle laeiksi kilpailuoikeudellisista vahingonkorvauksista ja kilpailulain muuttamisesta) (HE 83/2016 vp).

Government bill on amending section 85a of the Value Added Tax Act (Hallituksen esitys eduskunnalle laiksi arvonlisäverolain 85 a §:n muuttamisesta) (HE 303/2018 vp).

Government bill on amending the Act on Electronic Communications Services and certain related acts (Hallituksen esitys eduskunnalle laiksi sähköisen viestinnän palveluista annetun lain muuttamisesta ja eräiksi siihen liittyviksi laeiksi) (HE 98/2020 vp). The progress of the process can be tracked at https://valtioneuvosto.fi/hanke?tunnus=LVM004:00/2019 (26.7.2020).

Committee Statements and Reports

Mostly available in Finnish at https://www.eduskunta.fi/FI/search/Sivut/vaskiresults.aspx (29.8.2019).

Reports of the Constitutional Law Committee

Report of the Constitutional Law Committee on the Government bill on amending the legislation concerning fundamental rights (Perustuslakivaliokunnan mietintö hallituksen esityksestä perustuslakien perusoikeussäännösten muuttamisesta) (PeVM 25/1994 vp).

Report of the Constitutional Law Committee on the Government bill on the Exercise of Freedom of Expression in Mass Media and certain laws relating to this (Perustuslakivaliokunnan mietintö hallituksen esityksestä laiksi sananvapauden käyttämisestä joukkoviestinnässä ja eräiksi siihen liittyviksi laeiksi) (PeVM 14/2002).

Report of the Constitutional Law Committee on the Prosecutor General's request for permission to prosecute an MP (Perustuslakivaliokunnan mietintö: Valtakunnansyyttaöjaön syyttaömislupaa koskeva pyyntoö asettaa kansanedustaja syytteeseen) (PeVM 21/2020 vp—M 5/2019 vp).

Reports of the Legal Affairs Committee

Report of the Legal Affairs Committee on the Government bill for legislation on preliminary investigation and coercive measures in criminal matters (Lakivaliokunnan mietintö hallituksen esityksestä eduskunnalle esitutkintaa ja pakkokeinoja rikosasioissa koskevaksi lainsäädännöksi) (LaVM 9/1986 vp).

Report of the Legal Affairs Committee on the Government bill on amending the Criminal Code, Section 7 of Chapter 10 of the Coercive Measures Act and Section 9 of Chapter 5 of the Police Act (Lakivaliokunnan mietintö hallituksen esityksestä eduskunnalle laeiksi rikoslain, pakkokeinolain 10 luvun 7 §:n ja poliisilain 5 luvun 9 §:n muuttamisesta) (LaVM 11/2013 vp).

Statements of the Constitutional Law Committee

Statement of the Constitutional Law Committee on the Government bill for amending the Alcohol Act and the Act of Medium Strength Beer (Perustuslakivaliokunnan lausunto hallituksen esityksestä laeiksi alkoholilain sekä keskioluesta annetun lain muuttamisesta) (PeVL 3/1976 vp).

Statement of the Constitutional Law Committee on the Government bill on Tobacco Act and member of the Parliament Saimo's bill 577/1975 and member of the Parliament Salmenkivi and others' bill 578/1975 (Perustuslakivaliokunnan lausunto hallituksen esityksestä laiksi toimenpiteistä tupakoinnin vähentämiseksi (HE 156/1975 II vp) sekä kansanedustajien Saimon lakialoitteesta n:o 577/1975 II vp ja kansanedustaja Salmenkiven ym. aloitteesta n:o 578/1975 II vp) (PeVL 4/1976 vp).

Statement of the Constitutional Law Committee on the Government bill on legislation concerning cable broadcasting and member of the Parliament Laurila and others' bill 76/1985 on Act on cable broadcasting and member of the Parliament Alppi and others' bill 85/1985 on Act on cable broadcasting (Perustuslakivaliokunnan lausunto hallituksen esityksestä kaapelilähetystoimintaa koskevaksi lainsäädännöksi ja kansanedustaja Laurilan ym. lakialoitteesta n:o 76/1985 vp laiksi kaapelilähetystoiminnasta sekä kansanedustaja Alpin ym. lakialoitteesta n:o 85/1985 vp laiksi kaapelilähetystoiminnasta) (PeVL 2/1986 vp).

Statement of the Constitutional Law Committee on the Government bill for legislation concerning television and radio activity (Perustuslakivaliokunnan lausunto hallituksen esityksestä televisio-ja radiotoimintaa koskevaksi lainsäädännöksi) (PeVL 19/1998 vp).

Statement of the Constitutional Law Committee on the Government bill on renewing the penal provisions concerning offences against privacy, public peace and personal reputation (Perustuslakivaliokunnan lausunto hallituksen esityksestä yksityisyyden, rauhan ja kunnian loukkaamista koskevien rangaistussäännösten uudistamiseksi) (PeVL 36/1998 vp).

Statement of the Constitutional Law Committee on the Government bill on Lotteries Act and certain laws relating to this (Perustuslakivaliokunnan lausunto hallituksen esityksestä arpajaislaiksi ja eräiksi siihen liittyviksi laeiksi) (PeVL 23/2000 vp).

Statement of the Constitutional Law Committee on the Government bill on Act on Provision of Information Society Services and certain laws relating to this (Perustuslakivaliokunnan lausunto hallituksen esityksestä laiksi tietoyhteiskunnan palvelujen tarjoamisesta ja eräiksi siihen liittyviksi laeiksi) (PeVL 60/2001 vp).

Statement of the Constitutional Law Committee on the Government bill for amending legislation concerning the Communications Market (Perustuslakivaliokunnan lausunto hallituksen esityksestä viestintämarkkinoita koskevan lainsäädännön muuttamisesta) (PeVL 8/2002 vp).

Statement of the Constitutional Law Committee on the Government bill for amending the Medicines Act and certain laws relating to this (Perustuslakivaliokunnan lausunto hallituksen esityksestä laeiksi lääkelain ja eräiden muiden lakien muuttamisesta) (PeVL 19/2002 vp).

Statement of the Constitutional Law Committee on the Government bill for amending legislation concerning the Communications Market (Perustuslakivaliokunnan lausunto hallituksen esityksestä viestintämarkkinoita koskevan lainsäädännön muuttamisesta) (PeVL 61/2002 vp).

Statement of the Constitutional Law Committee on the Government bill on the Act on Protection of Privacy in Electronic Communications and Certain Related Acts (Perustuslakivaliokunnan lausunto hallituksen esityksestä sähköisen viestinnän tietosuojalaiksi ja eräiksi siihen liittyviksi laeiksi) (PeVL 9/2004).

Statement of the Constitutional Law Committee on the Government bill on Food Act and amending the Health Protection Act (Perustuslakivaliokunnan lausunto hallituksen esityksestä elintarvikelaiksi sekä laiksi terveydensuojelulain muuttamisesta) (PeVL 37/2005 vp).

Statement of the Constitutional Law Committee on the Government bill for amending the Alcohol Act (Perustuslakivaliokunnan lausunto hallituksen esityksestä laiksi alkoholilain muuttamisesta) (PeVL 54/2006 vp).

Statement of the Constitutional Law Committee on the Government bill on amendments and temporary amendments to the Finnish Act on Television and Radio Operations as well as amendments to sections 25 b and 48 on the Copyright Act (Perustuslakivaliokunnan lausunto hallituksen esityksestä laeiksi televisio- ja radiotoiminnasta annetun lain muuttamisesta ja väliaikaisesta muuttamisesta sekä tekijänoikeuslain 25 b ja 48 §:n muuttamisesta) (PeVL 3/2010 vp).

Statement of the Constitutional Law Committee on the Government bill on amendments to the Provision on Entry into Force of the Act amending Section 134 of the Communications Market Act, Section 134 of the Communications Market Act and the Act on Television and Radio Operations (Sivistysvaliokunnan lausunto laeiksi viestintämarkkinalain 134 §:n muuttamisesta annetun lain voimaantulosäännöksen muuttamisesta, viestintämarkkinalain 134 §:n ja televisio- ja radiotoiminnasta annetun lain muuttamiseksi) (PeVL 27/2010 vp).

Statement of the Constitutional Law Committee on the Government bill on amendments to the Act on Yleisradio Oy and the Act on the State Television and Radio Fund (Hallituksen esitys eduskunnalle laeiksi Yleisradio Oy:stä annetun lain sekä valtion televisio- ja radiorahastosta annetun lain muuttamisesta) (PeVL 14/2012 vp).

Statement of the Constitutional Law Committee on the Government bill on amending the Criminal Code, Section 7 of Chapter 10 of the Coercive Measures Act and Section 9 of Chapter 5 of the Police Act (Perustuslakivaliokunnan lausunto hallituksen esityksestä eduskunnalle laeiksi rikoslain, pakkokeinolain 10 luvun 7 §:n ja poliisilain 5 luvun 9 §:n muuttamisesta) (PeVL 16/2013 vp).

Statement of the Constitutional Law Committee on the Government bill for the Act on Electronic Communications Services and Acts amending Section 161 of the Land Use and Building Act and Section 8b of Chapter 38 of the Criminal Code (Perustuslakivaliokunnan lausunto hallituksen esityksestä eduskunnalle tietoyhteiskuntakaareksi sekä laeiksi maankäyttö- ja rakennuslain 161 §:n ja rikoslain 38 luvun 8 b §:n muuttamisesta) (PeVL 18/2014).

Statement of the Education and Culture Committee

Statement of the Education and Culture Committee on the Government bill on amendments and temporary amendments to the Finnish Act on Television and Radio Operations as well as amendments to sections 25 b and 48 on the Copyright Act (Sivistysvaliokunnan lausunto hallituksen esityksestä laeiksi televisio- ja radiotoiminnasta annetun lain muuttamisesta ja väliaikaisesta muuttamisesta sekä tekijänoikeuslain 25 b ja 48 §:n muuttamisesta) (SiVL 9/2009).

Statement of the Education and Culture Committee on the Government bill on amendments to the Provision on Entry into Force of the Act amending Section 134 of the Communications Market Act, Section 134 of the Communications Market Act and the Act on Television and Radio Operations (Sivistysvaliokunnan lausunto laeiksi viestintämarkkinalain 134 §:n muuttamisesta annetun lain voimaantulosäännöksen muuttamisesta, viestintämarkkinalain 134 §:n ja televisio- ja radiotoiminnasta annetun lain muuttamiseksi) (SiVL 9/2010 vp).

Reports of the Transport and Communications Committee

Report of the Transport and Communications Committee on the Government bill on amendments and temporary amendments to the Finnish Act on Television and Radio Operations as well as amendments to sections 25 b and 48 on the Copyright Act (Liikenne- ja viestintävaliokunnan mietintö hallituksen esityksestä laeiksi televisio- ja radiotoiminnasta annetun lain muuttamisesta ja väliaikaisesta muuttamisesta sekä tekijänoikeuslain 25 b ja 48 §:n muuttamisesta) (LiVM 2/2010 vp).

Selected Bibliography

Report of the Transport and Communications Committee on the Government bill on amendments to the Provision on Entry into Force of the Act amending Section 134 of the Communications Market Act, Section 134 of the Communications Market Act and the Act on Television and Radio Operations (Liikenne- ja viestintävaliokunnan mietintö hallituksen esityksestä laeiksi viestintämarkkinalain 134 §:n muuttamisesta annetun lain voimaantulosäännöksen muuttamisesta, viestintämarkkinalain 134 §:n ja televisio- ja radiotoiminnasta annetun lain muuttamiseksi) (LiVM 8/2010 vp).

Report of the Transport and Communications Committee on the Government bill for the Act on Electronic Communications Services and Acts amending Section 161 of the Land Use and Building Act and Section 8b of Chapter 38 of the Criminal Code (Liikenne- ja viestintävaliokunnan mietintö hallituksen esityksestä eduskunnalle tietoyhteiskuntakaareksi sekä laeiksi maankäyttö- ja rakennuslain 161 §:n ja rikoslain 38 luvun 8 b §:n muuttamisesta) (LiVM 10/2014).

Report of the Transport and Communications Committee on the Government bill on amending and temporary amendments to the Act on Electronic Communications Services as well as amending the act on notified bodies for certain product groups (Liikenne- ja viestintävaliokunnan mietintö hallituksen esityksestä eduskunnalle laeiksi tietoyhteiskuntakaaren muuttamisesta ja väliaikaisesta muuttamisesta sekä eräitä tuoteryhmiä koskevista ilmoitetuista laitoksista annetun lain muuttamisesta) (LiVM 12/2016 vp).

Other Official Reports and Publications by Officials

Liikenne- ja viestintäministeriö: Digitaaliseen televisioon siirtyminen. Seurantaryhmän loppuraportti. Liikenne- ja viestintäministeriön julkaisuja 12/2008 (Switchover to all-digital television. Final report of the follow-up working group. Publications of the Ministry of Transport and Communcations 12/2008): https://julkaisut.valtioneuvosto.fi/bitstream/handle/10024/77794/1_LVM12_2008.pdf (29.8.2019).

Liikenne- ja viestintäministeriö: IPTV:n lähitulevaisuus – työryhmän väliraportti. (The Near Future of IPTV – Interim Report of the Working Party. Ministry of Transport and Communications) 2010: http://julkaisut.valtioneuvosto.fi/bitstream/handle/10024/78176/IPTV-tyoryhman_valiraportti.pdf?sequence=1&isAllowed=y (29.8.2019).

Liikenne- ja viestintäministeriö: Maanpäällisen televisiotoiminnan seuraava teknologiasiirtymä. Työryhmän väliraportti. Liikenne- ja viestintäministeriön julkaisuja 33/2013 (The next technological transition in terrestrial television broadcasting. Interim report. Publications of the Ministry of Transport and Communications 33/2013): http://julkaisut.valtioneuvosto.fi/bitstream/handle/10024/77945/Julkaisuja_33-2013.pdf (29.8.2019).

Liikenne- ja viestintäministeriö: Media- ja viestintäpolitiikan nykytila ja mittaaminen. Liikenne- ja viestintäministeriön julkaisuja 4/2018 (The state of media- and communications policy and how to measure it Final report. Publications of the Ministry of Transport and Communications 4/2018): http://julkaisut.valtioneuvosto.fi/bitstream/handle/10024/160714/04_18_Media-%20ja-viestintapolitiikan-nykytila.pdf?sequence=1&isAllowed=y (6.7.2020).

Liikenne- ja viestintäministeriö: Media- ja viestintäpolitiikan seurantaraportti 2019. Liikenne- ja viestintäministeriön julkaisuja 2020:4 (Media and Communication Policy Monitoring report 2019. Publications of the Ministry of Transport and Communications 2020:4): https://julkaisut.valtioneuvosto.fi/bitstream/handle/10024/162144/LVM_2020_04.pdf?sequence=1&isAllowed=y (6.10.2020).

Liikenne- ja viestintäministeriö: Muistio VN/9067/2020 (Memorandum VN/9067/2020. Ministry of Transport and Communications) 3.12.2020 (unpublished).

Liikenne- ja viestintäministeriö: Pätevät pärjäävät – Kotimaisia mediamarkkinoita arvioivan työryhmän raportti. Liikenne- ja viestintäministeriö, raportit ja selvitykset 2/2015 (The competent will thrive. Report by the working group assessing the Finnish media market. Ministry of Transport and Communications, Reports 2/2015): http://julkaisut.valtioneuvosto.fi/bitstream/handle/10024/78283/Raportit_ja_selvitykset_2-2015.pdf?sequence=1&isAllowed=y (29.8.2019).

Liikenne- ja viestintäministeriö: Radion tulevaisuus. Liikenne- ja viestintäministeriön julkaisuja 8/2014 (The Future of Radio. Publications of the Ministry of Transport and Communications 8/2014): http://julkaisut.valtioneuvosto.fi/bitstream/handle/10024/77910/Julkaisuja_8-2014.pdf?sequence=1&isAllowed=y (29.8.2019).

Liikenne- ja viestintäministeriö: Valtioneuvoston asetus valtionavustuksesta journalistisen sisällön edistämiseen. Liikenne- ja viestintäministeriön muistio VN/9067/2020 (Government decree regarding government aid for promoting journalistic contents. Memorandum VN/9067/2020 of the Ministry of Transport and Communications) 15.6.2020: https://api.hankeikkuna.fi/asiakirjat/28728680-1fc0-44dc-a366-2b4d3e6f6ac9/403f7144-b676-4890-bebc-8d23a6b97288/LIITE_20200618071017.pdf (20.8.2020).

Liikenne- ja viestintäministeriö: Yleisradio Oy:n julkisen palvelun tehtävät ja siihen liittyvät muut uudistukset. Parlamentaarisen työryhmän muistio (Yleisradio Oy's public service remit and other related reforms. Report of the parliamentary working group): http://www.lvm.fi/lvm-site62-mahti-portlet/download?did=207240 (29.8.2020).

Liikenne- ja viestintäministeriö: Yleisradion hallinnon ja ohjauksen kehitys 1926–2017. Kehityskaari eduskunnan alaiseksi yhtiöksi. Liikenne- ja viestintäministeriön julkaisuja 17/2017 (Development of the administration and control of Yleisradio 1926–2017. Development trajectory into a company subordinate to the Parliament. Publications of the Ministry of Transport and Communications 17/2017): http://julkaisut.valtioneuvosto.fi/handle/10024/160414 (13.8.2020).

Ministry for Foreign Affairs: Åland in the European Union. Europe Information. Publications of the Ministry for Foreign Affairs: https://julkaisut.um.fi/media/attachments/3cd4e/ET-100004-EN.pdf (28.8.2019).

Ministry of Transport and Communications: Turning Finland into the world leader in communication networks - Digital Infrastructure Strategy 2025. Publications of the Ministry of Transport and Communications 2019:7: https://julkaisut.valtioneuvosto.fi/bitstream/handle/10024/161434/LVM_7_19_Digital_Infrastructure_WEB.pdf?sequence=1 (13.12.2020).

Selected Bibliography

Oikeusministeriö: Sananvapausrikokset, vainoaminen ja viestintärauhan rikkominen. Oikeusministeriön mietintöjä ja lausuntoja 24/2012 (Freedom of Expression crimes, persecution and breach of communications peace. Publications of the Ministry of Justice 24/2012): http://julkaisut.valtioneuvosto.fi/bitstream/handle/10024/76361/omml_24_sananvapausrikokset_tyoryhma_148s.pdf (29.8.2019).

Opetusministeriö: Monikanavajakelua selvittävän työryhmän raportti. Opetusministeriön työryhmämuistioita ja selvityksiä 2008:18 (Report of the Working Group on Multichannel Distribution. Working group memorandums and reports of the Ministry of Education 2008:18): https://julkaisut.valtioneuvosto.fi/bitstream/handle/10024/79380/tr18.pdf?sequence=1 (3.9.2019).

Opetusministeriö: Monikanavajakelun jatkoselvitys. Opetusministeriön työryhmämuistioita ja selvityksiä 2009:20 (Further Report on multichannel distribution. Working group memorandums and reports of the Ministry of Education 2009:20): http://julkaisut.valtioneuvosto.fi/bitstream/handle/10024/78894/tr20.pdf?sequence=1&isAllowed=y (29.8.2019).

Opetus- ja kulttuuriministeriö: Määrärahojen jako OKM/2018/58. Vähemmistökielisen sanomalehdistön tuki vuonna 2018. Päätös (Allocation of appropriations OKM/2018/58. Support for minority language newspapers in 2018. Decision of the Ministry of Education and Culture): https://minedu.fi/paatos?decisionId=0900908f805d34d3 (3.9.2019).

Perusoikeuskomitea: Perusoikeuskomitean mietintö 1992:3 (Report 1992:3 of the Constitutional Rights Committee).

Sisäasiainministeriö: Esitutkinta- ja pakkokeinotoimikunnan mietintö 2009:2 (Ministry of the Interior: Report 2009:2 of the Criminal Investigation and Coercive Measures Committee): http://julkaisut.valtioneuvosto.fi/bitstream/handle/10024/160866/342009.pdf (29.8.2019).

Swedish parliament: Fritt ord 250 år. Tryckfrihet och offentlighet i Sverige och Finland – ett levande arv från 1766 (Press Freedom 250 Years. Freedom of the Press and Public Access to Official Documents in Sweden and Finland – a living heritage from 1766): https://www.riksdagen.se/globalassets/15.-bestall-och-ladda-ned/andra-sprak/tf-250-ar-eng-2018.pdf (26.7.2020).

TRAFICOM: Mainonnan kestoa ja sijoittelua koskeva ohje (Instructions. Advertising duration and placement) 31.1.2004, updated 22.3.2011: https://www.traficom.fi/sites/default/files/media/regulation/Mainonnan-kestoa-ja-sijoittelua-koskeva-ohje.pdf (29.8.2019).

Valtioneuvosto: Journalismin koronatuet. Hanke (Support for journalism due to the coronavirus situation. Government project): https://valtioneuvosto.fi/hanke?tunnus=LVM040:00/2020 (13.8.2020).

Valtioneuvosto: Sähköisen median viestintäpoliittinen ohjelma, Valtioneuvoston selonteko eduskunnalle 2012 (Communications Policy Programme for Electronic Media, Government Report to the Parliament of Finland 2012): https://www.eduskunta.fi/FI/vaski/selonteko/Documents/vns_4+2012.pdf (28.10.2019).

Valtioneuvosto: Yhteiskunnallisesti merkittävien tapahtumien listan päivitystarpeiden arviointi. Hanke (Assessment of the need to update the list of socially significant events. Government project): https://valtioneuvosto.fi/hanke?tunnus=LVM028:00/2020 (26.7.2020).

Viestintävirasto: Muistio 1800/69/20 verkkoneutraliteetin (net neutrality) sääntelytilanteesta, Suomi ja EU (FICORA's memo 1800/69/20 on the regulatory situation of net neutrality, Finland and EU) 4.10.2012: http://pilvi.viestintavirasto.fi/attachments/NetNeutralityMuistioLoka2012.pdf (29.8.2019).
Viestintävirasto: Viestintäviraston kannanotto jaetun kuvaruudun käytöstä mainonnassa, 1162/9220/2010 (FICORA's statement 1162/9220/2010 on the use of split screens in advertising) 21.12.2010: http://vivi-test.abako.fi/attachments/Viestinta viraston_kannanotto_jaetun_kuvaruudunkaytosta..pdf (26.7.2020).

Selected Bibliography

Table of Cases

European Court of Human Rights

Available at http://hudoc.echr.coe.int/sites/eng/Pages/search.aspx#.
Jersild v. Denmark (23.9.1994).
Goodwin v. United Kingdom (GC, 27.3.1996).
Z v. Finland (25.2.1997).
Amann v. Switzerland (16.2.2000).
P4 Radio Hele Norge v. Norway (6.5.2003).
von Hannover v. Germany (21.6.2004).
Sidabras and Sziautas v. Lithuania (27.7.2004).
Karhuvaara and Kustannusosakeyhtiö Iltalehti v. Finland (16.11.2004).
Selistö v. Finland (16.11.2004).
Erbakan v. Turkey (6.7.2006).
Balsytė-Liedeikienė v. Lithuania (4.11.2008).
Eerikäinen and others v. Finland (10.2.2009).
Feret v. Belgium (16.7.2009).
Financial Times Ltd ym. v. United Kingdom (15.12.2009).
Flinkkilä and others v. Finland (6.4.2010).
Jokitaipale and others v. Finland (6.4.2010).
Ruokanen v. Finland (6.4.2010).
Soila v. Finland (6.4.2010).
Tuomela and others v. Finland (6.4.2010).
Niskasaari and others v. Finland (6.7.2010).
Sanoma Uitgevers B.V. v. the Netherlands (GC 14.9.2010).
Saaristo and others v. Finland (12.10.2010).
Reinboth and others v. Finland (25.1.2011).
Lahtonen v. Finland (17.1.2012).
von Hannover 2 v. Germany (7.2.2012).
Ojala and Etukeno Oy v. Finland (14.1.2014; no violation)
Ruusunen v. Finland (14.1.2014; no violation)
Pentikäinen v. Finland (4.2.2014).
Pentikäinen v. Finland (GC, 20.10.2015).
Satakunnan Markkinapörssi Oy and Satamedia Oy v. Finland (GC 7.6.2017; no violation).

European Commission

Table of Cases

Commission Decision 2007/481/EC C of 25 June 2007 on the compatibility with Community law of measures taken by Finland pursuant to Article 3a(1) of Council Directive 89/552/EEC on the coordination of certain provisions laid down by law, regulation or administrative action in Member States concerning the pursuit of television broadcasting activities, OJ L 180, 10.7.2007, pp. 38–41. Available at http://eur-lex.europa.eu/legal-content/EN/TXT/?uri=uriserv:OJ.L_.2007.180.01.0038.01.ENG.
European Commission C(2010) 3062 final, Brussels 6.5.2010: http://ec.europa.eu/competition/state_aid/cases/235159/235159_1106591_26_1.pdf (29.8.2019).
European Commission C(2012) 6182 final, Brussels 7.9.2012: http://ec.europa.eu/competition/state_aid/cases/243482/243482_1396581_81_2.pdf (29.8.2019).

Court of Justice of the European Union

Available at http://curia.europa.eu (29.8.2019).
Digital Rights Ireland Ltd v. Minister for Communications, Marine and Natural Resources, Minister for Justice, Equality and Law Reform, Commissioner of the Garda Síochána, Ireland and Attorney General, andKärntner Landesregierung, Michael Seitlinger and Christof Tschohl and others, Joined Cases C-293/12 and C-594/12, ECLI:EU:C:2014:238.
Sanoma Media Finland Oy – Nelonen Media v Viestintävirasto, C-314/14, ECLI-:EU:C:2016:89.

Supreme Court of Finland

Available in Finnish at http://www.finlex.fi/fi/oikeus/kko/.
KKO 2000:54.
KKO 2001:72.
KKO 2003:96.
KKO 2004:30.
KKO 2005:136.
KKO 2006:10.
KKO 2006:62.
KKO 2007:56.
KKO 2009:3.
KKO 2010:88.
KKO 2011:71.
KKO 2011:72.
KKO 2011:101.
KKO 2012:58.
KKO 2013:69.
KKO 2018:51
KKO 2018:81
KKO 2018:112
KKO 2019:112

Supreme Administrative Court of Finland

Available in Finnish at http://www.finlex.fi/fi/oikeus/kho/ (29.8.2019).
KHO 2002:90.

KHO 2003:77.
KHO 2004:25.
KHO 2005:26.
KHO 2007:65.
KHO 2007:83.
KHO 2008:52.
KHO 536/2/09, 18.5.2009
KHO 2010:31.
KHO 2011:27.
KHO 2012:3.
KHO 2012:7.
KHO 2012:124.
KHO 1386/3/10, 7.5.2012.
KHO 2013:90.
KHO 31.12.2013/4119.
KHO 2014:87.
KHO 2018:25
KHO 2018:154
KHO 2018:164

Market Court

MAO Dnro 580/08/KR, 22.1.2009 (Temporary ban)
MAO:525/09
MAO:68/19

Finnish Communications Regulatory Authority (FICORA (now TRAFICOM))

See TRAFICOM's website at https://www.traficom.fi/en/traficom/about-traficom.
183/934/2004 (3.9.2004).
1668/934/2008 (10.11.2008).
249/9313/200 (16.3.2010).
1952/9224/2010 (17.6.2011).
1650/9220/2011 (9.3.2012).
603/932/2014 (30.6.2014).
917/932/2014 (5.12.2014).
918/932/2014 (5.12.2014).

Finnish Competition and Consumer Authority (FCCA) (ex FCA)

Mostly available in Finnish at http://www.kkv.fi/ratkaisut-ja-julkaisut/ratkaisut/haku/.
256/81/2007 (3.4.2007).
579/81/2008 (27.11.2008).
360/14.00.10/2010 (29.6.2010).
559/14.00.00/2009 (4.12.2012).
533/14.00.00/2010 (8.4.2013).
223/KKV14.00.10/2013 (24.6.2013).
351/14.00.00/2012 (11.12.2013).
559/KKV14.00.10/2014 (5.2.2015).

352/V1.6.61/2008 (11.12.2015).

Parliamentary Ombudsman of Finland

Available in Finnish at http://www.eduskunta.fi/thwfakta/eoatied/eoaratk/eoar3000.shtml.
3149/4/10 (21.12.2011).
5342/2013 (7.1.2015).

Praxis of the Council for Mass Media

Available in Finnish at http://www.jsn.fi/paatokset/?year=2015.
4152/L/09.
4459/YLE/10.
4495/TV/11.
4527/TV/11.
4592B-G/YLE+SL+TV/11, 21.9.2011
4720/TV/11.
4767/TV/11.
4863/YLE/12.
4910/R/12.
4979/R/12.
4983/YLE/12.
4988/SL/12.
5014/SL/12.
5069/SL/12.
5107/AL/13.
5140/AL/13.
5312/SL/13.
5327/R/13.
5345/SL/13.
5357/R/13.
5360/R/13.
5411/TV/14.
5459/R/14.
5472/SL/14.
5551/SL/14.
5569/YLE/14.
5570/SL/14.
5571/SL/14.
5574/SL/14.
5577/SL/14.
5580/R/14.
5588/SL/14.
5610/AL/14.
5615/AL/14.
5618/SL/14.
5623/SL/14.
5648/SL/14.

5640/SL/14.
5641/YLE/14.
5654/SL/14.
5606/SL/14.
5660/TV/14.
5694/SL/14.
5499/SL/14
5722/SL/15.
5723/SL/15.
5729/AL/15.
6016/SL/15
6025/SL/15
6028/SL/15
5987/SL15
6071/SL/16
6398/YLE/16
6401/YLE/16
6512/PL/17
6650/YLE/17
6689/SL/17
6686/YLE/17
6599/MTV/17
6738/SL/17
6874/SL/18
6899/YLE/18
7012/SL/18
7027/MTV/18
6969/AL/18
6872&SL/18
6831//PL/18
7072/SL/19

Online Sources

4Front and Gaia Consulting/Business Finland: 'Median innovaatiotuen arviointi. Loppuraportti' Raportti 6/2018 (Evaluation of media innovation support. Final report. Report 6/2018) https://www.businessfinland.fi/globalassets/julkaisut/median_innovaatiotuen_arviointi.pdf (31.10.2019).

Administrative courts: 'Publicity of court proceedings' 12.4.2017: http://oikeus.fi/tuomioistuimet/hallintooikeudet/en/index/julkisuus.html (29.8.2019).

Borenius Attorneys at Law: 'Kilpailuvaikutusten ennakkoarviointi' (Report on the assessment of effects to competition), 29.4.2014.

CMM: Basic Agreement of the Council for Mass Media: http://www.jsn.fi/en/Council_for_Mass_Media/basic-agreement-of-the-council-for-mass-media/ (6.7.2020).

CMM: 'Council for Mass Media in Finland': http://www.jsn.fi/en/Council_for_Mass_Media/the-council-for-mass-media-in-finland/ (29.8.2019).

Table of Cases

CMM: 'Guidelines for Journalists': http://www.jsn.fi/en/guidelines_for_journalists/ (29.8.2019).

Consumer Disputes Board: 'About the Consumer Disputes Board': http://www.kuluttajariita.fi/en/index.html (29.8.2019).

Digita Oy: http://www.digita.fi/in_english (29.8.2019).

District courts: 'Basic information on court proceedings' 25.7.2019: http://oikeus.fi/tuomioistuimet/karajaoikeudet/en/index/openness/basicinformationoncourtproceedings.html (29.8.2019).

District courts: 'Oral hearing' 25.7.2019: https://oikeus.fi/tuomioistuimet/karajaoikeudet/en/index/openness/oralhearing.html (8.10.2020).

European Centre for Press and Media Freedom: 'Study on Investigative Journalism': https://ec.europa.eu/digital-agenda/en/media-freedom-pilot-projects) (28.8.2019).

European Court of Human Rights: Violations by Article and by State: https://www.echr.coe.int/Documents/Stats_violation_1959_2018_ENG.pdf (30.10.2019).

FCCA decisions (formerly FCA) are available in Finnish at http://www.kkv.fi/ratkaisut-ja-julkaisut/. Proposals to the Market Court at http://www.kkv.fi/ratkaisut-ja-julkaisut/kilpailuasiat/esitykset-markkinaoikeudelle/ (29.8.2019).

FiCom ry: 'Maksu-tv' (Pay-TV), https://www.ficom.fi/ict-ala/tilastot/maksu-tv last updated 17.3.2020 (8.10.2020).

FiCom ry: 'Televisiot lähetyskanavittain ja katselutavoittain' (Televisions by broadcast channel and viewing mode) last updated 4.5.2020: https://www.ficom.fi/ict-ala/tilastot/televisiot-lähetyskanavittain-ja-katselutavoittain (28.9.2019).

FICORA: Letter No. 145/9220/2012, 29.3.2012.

FICORA: Ohjelmiston eurooppalaisuus ja riippumattomuus vuonna 2017 (Europeanness and independence of the programmes in 2017): https://www.traficom.fi/sites/default/files/media/file/Tv-ohjelmien_eurooppalaisuus_ja_riippumattomuus_.pdf (29.8.2019).

FICORA: 'Presentation and Duties': https://www.viestintavirasto.fi/en/FICORA/presentationandduties/history.html updated 21.11.2014 (29.8.2019).

FICORA: 'Tehokkuutta toimilupien myöntämiseen' (Efficiency in licensing) Newsletter 23.4.2015: http://pilvi.viestintavirasto.fi/viestintavirasto/signaali/signaali12015/tehokkuuttatoimilupienmyontamiseen.html (29.8.2019).

Finnish Government: http://valtioneuvosto.fi/en/government (29.8.2019).

Finnish Supreme Court: http://korkeinoikeus.fi/en/index.html (28.8.2019).

Finnish Tax Administrator: 'Public broadcasting tax': https://www.vero.fi/en/About-us/newsroom/visual_aids_for_presentations_and_for_t/public_broadcasting_tax/ (29.8.2019).

Finnpanel: 'Katseluosuudet ja tavoitettavuudet' (Share and Reach): https://www.finnpanel.fi/tulokset/tv/vuosi/sharev/viimeisin/ (28.9.2019).

Helsingin Sanomat: 'Neljäs kansanedustajaa koskeva esitutkinta alkaa: Sebastian Tynkkystä epäillään kiihottamisesta kansanryhmää vastaan' (A piece of news relating to MP Sebastian Tynkkynen and his investigation for ethnic agitation) 27.8.2019: https://www.hs.fi/kotimaa/art-2000006218410.html (30.10.2019).

JSN: 'Julkisen sanan neuvoston toimintakertomus 2018' (CMM's yearly report in 2018): http://www.jsn.fi/ContentFiles/6/Sisaltosivut/JSN_toimintakertomus2018[5].pdf (29.8.2019).

JSN: 'Julkisen sanan neuvoston toimintakertomus 2019' (CMM's yearly report in 2019): http://www.jsn.fi/ContentFiles/6/Sisaltosivut/Vuosiljulkaisu%202019.pdf (25.9.2020).

JSN: 'Kannanotto sananvapauden merkityksestä sekä journalistin ohjeiden ja lainsäädännön suhteesta 2018' (Statement on the Importance of Freedom of Expression and the Relationship Between the Journalist's Guidelines and Legislation in 2018) 6736/L/17 22.8.2018: http://www.jsn.fi/lausumat/kannanotto-sananvapauden-merkityksesta-seka-journalistin-ohjeiden-ja-lainsaadannon-suhteesta-2018/ (30.10.2019).

JSN: 'Lausuma lain ja eettisten ohjeiden suhdetta koskevassa asiassa 2002' (CMM's Statement on the relationship between law and ethical guidelines) 3206/L/02 19.12.2002: http://www.jsn.fi/lausumat/lausuma-lain-ja-eettisten-ohjeiden-suhdetta-koskevassa-asiassa-2002/ (30.10.2019).

JSN: 'Lausuma medialle mainonnan merkitsemisestä 2015' (CMM's Statement to the media on the labeling of advertising in 2015) 20.5.2015: http://www.jsn.fi/lausumat/lausuma-medialle-mainonnan-merkitsemisesta-2015/ (29.8.2019).

Kauppakamari (Boards): http://kauppakamari.fi/en/boards/council-of-ethics-in-advertising/ and http://kauppakamari.fi/en/boards/board-of-business-practice/ (29.8.2019).

KAVI: 'Ikärajat' (Age limits): https://kavi.fi/ikarajat/ (8.10.2020).

KAVI: 'Media Education': https://kavi.fi/en/media-education/ (29.8.2019).

KAVI: 'Televisio-ohjelmien lähetysajat ja ikärajat' (Transmission times and age limits in television programs): https://kavi.fi/ikarajat/annapalautetta/annapalautetta-mediasta/ (13.12.2020).

Kuntaliitto: 'Kaupunkien ja kuntien lukumäärät ja väestötiedot' (Association of Finnish Municipalities: Number of Cities and Municipalities and Demographics) 3.4.2019: https://www.kuntaliitto.fi/tilastot-ja-julkaisut/kaupunkien-ja-kuntien-lukumaarat-ja-vaestotiedot (1.9.2019).

Kuntaliitto: 'Kuntanumerot ja kuntapohjaiset aluejaot' (Association of Finnish Municipalities: Municipality numbers and municipalities' regional divisions) 19.12.2019: https://www.kuntaliitto.fi/asiantuntijapalvelut/kuntanumerot-ja-kuntapohjaiset-aluejaot (29.8.2019).

Maanmittauslaitos: Maanmittaus 2013. Maanmittauslaitoksen vuositilastoja (National Land Survey of Finland: Land survey 2013. Annual statistics of National Land Survey of Finland): https://www.maanmittauslaitos.fi/sites/maanmittauslaitos.fi/files/old/mml_vuositilasto_2013.pdf (29.8.2019).

Maaseudun tulevaisuus (Newspaper): 'Postin toimiluvista luovutaan, ilmoitus viestintävirastolle riittää' (Posti's licenses are waived, notification to FICORA is sufficient) 4.6.2016: https://www.maaseuduntulevaisuus.fi/politiikka/postin-toimiluvista-luovutaan-ilmoitus-viestintävirastolle-riittää-1.147137 (29.8.2019).

Ministry of Finance: 'Value Added Tax': https://vm.fi/en/value-added-tax (29.8.2019).

Ministry of Justice: 'Proposal reforming the Act on the Sámi Parliament is not taken forward' 25.9.2018: https://oikeusministerio.fi/-/saamelaiskarajalain-uudistamisesityksella-ei-edellytyksia-edeta?languageId=en_US (1.9.2019).

Ministry of Social Affarirs and Health: 'Comprehensive reform of Alcohol Act': https://stm.fi/en/comprehensive-reform-of-alcohol-act (29.8.2019).

Ministry of Transport and Communications: 'COVID-19 support to help the media' Press release 1.10.2020: https://www.lvm.fi/-/covid-19-support-to-help-the-media-1233741 (3.12.2020).
Ministry of Transport and Communications: 'Finnish Communications Regulatory Authority and Transport Safety Agency merge into Transport and Communications Agency – Transport Agency becomes Transport Infrastructure Agency' Press release 22.11.2018: https://valtioneuvosto.fi/en/article/-/asset_publisher/viestintavirasto-ja-trafi-yhdistyvat-liikenne-ja-viestintavirastoksi-liikennevirastosta-tulee-vaylavirasto (29.8.2019).
Ministry of Transport and Communications: 'Minister Kiuru: Media support for new digital services' Press release 8.10.2014: http://www.lvm.fi/pressreleases/4421900/minister-kiuru-media-support-for-new-digital-services (29.8.2019).
Ministry of Transport and Communications: 'Request for opinions on the 700 MHz auction' Press release 22.6.2016: http://www.lvm.fi/en/-/request-for-opinions-on-the-700-mhz-auction (29.8.2019).
Ministry of Transport and Communications: 'Telecom companies and the state to accelerate construction of high-speed broadband connections with new commitment' Press release 12.11.2020: https://vnk.fi/en/-/10184/telecom-companies-and-the-state-to-accelerate-construction-of-high-speed-broadband-connections-with-new-commitment (13.12.2020).
Ministry of Transport and Communications: 'Working group: Parliamentary consensus on the duties and funding of Yle' News Article 20.6.2016: http://www.lvm.fi/en/-/working-group-parliamentary-consensus-on-the-duties-and-funding-of-y-1 (29.8.2019).
MTV / Kurio, the Social Media Age(ncy) / Laurea ammattikoulu: White paper 001/0015 'Suomalaisten sosiaalisen median käyttö 2015' (a research about Finns' social media usage in 2015): https://im.mtv.fi/blob/4941078/6c812d65a85598db50814610bd1da47b/suomalaisten-sosiaalisen-median-kaytto-2015-mtv-white-paper-data.pdf (23.7.2019).
MTV Uutiset: 'MTV:n rikostoimittaja kiteyttää Helsingin Sanomien kohujutun ongelman ytimen: "Punaleimapornoa" (Finnish media company MTV's crime reporter's sums up the core problem of Helsingin Sanomat's splash) 17.12.2017: https://www.mtvuutiset.fi/artikkeli/mtv-n-rikostoimittaja-kiteyttaa-helsingin-sanomien-kohujutun-ongelman-ytimen-punaleimapornoa/6700272#gs.dd6tty (30.10.2019).
Mörä, Tuomo – Tiilikka, Päivi: Reporter's Privilege in the Era of the Internet: http://hq.ssrn.com/submissions/MyPapers.cfm?partid=1820352 (29.8.2019).
Oikeusministeriö: Lainkirjoittajan opas, kansallisten säädösten kirjoittamista koskevat ohjeet (Ministry of Justice: Legislator's Guide, Guidelines for Writing National Legislation): http://lainkirjoittaja.finlex.fi/4-perusoikeudet/4-1/ (29.8.2019).
Om Vox Publica: 'Skatt Istedenfor TV-lisens. Erfaringer fra Finland' (Tax Instead of the TV license. Experiences from Finland), https://voxpublica.no/2016/06/skatt-istedenfor-tv-lisens-erfaringer-fra-finland/ (29.8.2019).
Parliament of Finland: 'Eduskunta – Riksdagen. The Parliament of Finland': https://www.eduskunta.fi/EN/Pages/default.aspx (29.8.2019).

Parliamentary Ombudsman: 'What does the Parliamentary Ombudsman do?' https://www.oikeusasiamies.fi/en_GB/web/selkosuomi/what-does-the-parliamentary-ombudsman-do- (28.10.2019).

President of the Republic of Finland: https://www.presidentti.fi/en/ (6.10.2020).

RadioMedia: 'Radiovuosi 2018' (Radio year 2018) https://www.radiomedia.fi/radiomainonta/tutkimustietoa-radiosta/radion-kuuntelu/radiovuosi-2018 (28.9.2019).

Reporters Without Borders: 'Finland': https://rsf.org/en/finland (3.9.2019).

Sámediggi: 'The Sámi in Finland': https://www.samediggi.fi/sami-info/?lang=en (29.8.2019).

Sámediggi: 'The Sámi Parliament – The representative self-government body of the Sámi': https://www.samediggi.fi/task/?lang=en (29.8.2019).

Statistics Finland: 'True Finns the biggest winner in elections. Coalition Party the largest party in the Parliamentary elections 2011': http://tilastokeskus.fi/til/evaa/2011/evaa_2011_2011-04-18_tie_001_en.html (29.8.2019).

Suomen Journalistiliitto: 'SJL:n työmarkkinatutkimus 2018' (Labour Market Survey of the Union of Journalists in Finland 2018), made by Kantar TNS Oy/Sakari Nurmela: https://journalistiliitto.fi/wp-content/uploads/2018/10/220401648_sjl_ty%C3%B6markkinatutkimus_2018_yhteenveto.pdf (7.10.2020).

Tilastokeskus: 'Joukkoviestinnän markkinatrendit ennallaan vuonna 2018' (Statistics Finland: Mass media market trends remain unchanged in 2018): https://www.stat.fi/til/jvie/2018/jvie_2018_2019-11-22_tie_001_fi.html (13.8.2020).

Tilastokeskus: 'Suomalaisten internetin käyttö 2018 – viestintää, asiointia, tiedonhakua ja medioiden seuraamista' (Statistics Finland: How Finns use the Internet in 2018 – communication, transactions, information retrieval and media monitoring): https://www.stat.fi/til/sutivi/2018/sutivi_2018_2018-12-04_tie_001_en.html (28.8.2019).

Tilastokeskus: 'Ulkomaalaiset Suomessa' (Statistics Finland: Foreigners in Finland): http://www.stat.fi/tup/tietoaika/ta_03_05_ulkomaalaiset_suomessa.html, *see also* https://www.tilastokeskus.fi/tup/maahanmuutto/maahanmuuttajat-vaestossa/ulkomaan-kansalaiset.html (29.8.2019).

Tilastokeskus: 'Ulkomaan kansalaiset' (Statistics Finland: foreign nationals): https://www.tilastokeskus.fi/tup/maahanmuutto/maahanmuuttajat-vaestossa/ulkomaan-kansalaiset.html (1.9.2019).

Tilastokeskus: 'Väestö kielen mukaan' (Statistics Finland: population by language): http://www.tilastokeskus.fi/til/vaerak/2018/vaerak_2018_2019-03-29_tau_001_fi.html (1.9.2019).

Tilastokeskus: 'Väestön ennakkotilasto' (Statistics Finland: preliminary population statistics): http://www.tilastokeskus.fi/til/vamuu/2019/07/ (29.8.2019).

Tilastokeskus: 'Väestötilastot' (Statistics Finland: population statistics): http://www.tilastokeskus.fi/tup/suoluk/suoluk_vaesto.html (29.8.2019). Toimiluvat (Licenses): http://www.lvm.fi/lvm-toimiluvat (29.8.2019).

TRAFICOM: 'Galileo Public Regulated Service (PRS)' Last updated 16.11.2017: https://legacy.viestintavirasto.fi/en/cybersecurity/prs.html (29.8.2019).

TRAFICOM: 'Laajakaista 2015 -hanke' (The "broadband project" 2015) http://pilvi.viestintavirasto.fi/ohjausjavalvonta/laajakaista2015/hankkeeneteneminen.html (29.8.2019).

TRAFICOM: 'Suomen antennitelevision teknologiasiirtymä viivästyy' (Delays in the technological transition for Finnish terrestrial television) 26.10.2018: https://legacy.viestintavirasto.fi/viestintavirasto/ajankohtaista/2018/suomenantennitelevisionteknologiasiirtymaviivastyy.html (3.9.2019).

Union of Journalists in Finland: 'About the Union of Journalists in Finland' https://journalistiliitto.fi/en/about/about-ujf/ (30.10.2019).

Verohallinto: 'Kirjojen ja lehtien arvonlisäverotuksesta' (Guidelines of the Finnish Tax Administration on value added tax for newspapers and periodicals) 24.6.2019: https://www.vero.fi/syventavat-vero-ohjeet/ohje-hakusivu/48354/kirjojen-ja-lehtien-arvonlisäverotuksesta/ (29.8.2019).

World Press Freedom Index 2014: https://rsf.org/en/world-press-freedom-index-2014 (29.8.2019).

World Press Freedom Index 2015: https://rsf.org/en/ranking/2015 (29.8.2019).

World Press Freedom Index 2019: https://rsf.org/en/ranking (29.8.2019).

Yle: Raportti Yleisradion teräväpiirtotelevisiolähetysten yhteiskunnallisia vaikutuksia koskevasta ennakkoarvioinnista (Report on the preliminary assessment of the social impact of Broadcasting's high-definition television broadcasts): http://avoinyle.fi/www/fi/liitetiedostot/Raportti_Yleisradion_teravapiirtotelevisiolahetysten_yhteiskunnallisia_vaikutuksia_koskevasta_arvioinnista_Nieminen.pdf (29.8.2019).

Yle: Sosiaalisen median toimintalinjaukset (Social media policies): http://yle.fi/aihe/artikkeli/2015/01/11/sosiaalisen-median-toimintalinjaukset (29.8.2019).

Yle: 'Toimintaperiaatteet' (Yle's operating principles): http://yle.fi/yleisradio/toimintaperiaatteet/merkittavien-palvelujen-ennakkoarviointi (29.8.2019).

Yle: 'Ylen ohjelmatoiminnan ja sisältöjen eettiset ohjeet' (Yle's code of conduct in programming and content): http://yle.fi/yleisradio/toimintaperiaatteet/ots-ohjeet (old ones) and https://yle.fi/aihe/artikkeli/2017/11/20/ylen-ohjelmatoiminnan-ja-sisaltojen-eettiset-ohjeet (new ones) (29.8.2019).

Yle in Russian: http://yle.fi/uutiset/novosti/ (29.8.2019).

Yle in Sámi: http://yle.fi/uutiset/sapmi/ (29.8.2019).

Yle Uutiset: 'Eduskunta ei antanut lupaa syyttää perussuomalaisten Mäenpäätä – Halla-ahon mukaan asian käsittely "häpeällinen farssi", näin kansanedustajat äänestivät' (A piece of news that relates to the parliament not voting in favour of the prosecution of MP Juha Mäenpää) 26.6.2020: https://yle.fi/uutiset/3-11418220 (13.8.2020).

Yle Uutiset: 'Kansanedustaja Sebastian Tynkkysen tuomio kiihottamisesta kansanryhmää vastaan pysyi hovissa – aikoo valittaa Euroopan ihmisoikeustuomioistuimeen' (A piece of news that relates to the judgment of Court of Appeal, according to which MP Sebastian Tynkkynen was found guilty of ethnic agitation) 2.7.2020: https://yle.fi/uutiset/3-11429491 (13.8.2020).

Yle Uutiset: 'Puolueille myönnettiin puolueavustuksia liki 30 miljoonaa euroa' (Nearly EUR 30 million of subsidies was granted to parties) 26.1.2016 https://yle.fi/uutiset/3-8626255 (13.8.2020).

Yle Uutiset: 'Päivi Räsänen: Valtakunnansyyttäjä määräsi esitutkinnan puheista, joita ei tv-ohjelmassa sanottu – "Tutkintapyynnössä esitetään muistinvaraisia sitaatteja" (A piece of news that relates to MP Päivi Räsänen and how she is suspected of ethnic agitation) 14.7.2020: https://yle.fi/uutiset/3-11446839 (13.8.2020).

Yle Uutiset: 'Whatsappia käytetään eniten, Instagramia suosivat naiset' (Whatsapp is used the most, Instagram is preferred by women) 7.4.2018: https://yle.fi/uutiset/3-10148277 (25.10.2019).

Yle Uutiset: 'Yle hakee valituslupaa markkinaoikeuden päätökseen HD-jakelukilpailutuksesta' (A piece of news that related to that Yle is applying for leave to appeal against the Market Court's decision on the competitive HD distribution tender) 21.3.2019: https://yle.fi/aihe/artikkeli/2019/03/21/yle-hakee-valituslupaa-markkinaoikeuden-paatokseen-hd-jakelukilpailutuksesta (25.10.2019).

Yle Uutiset: 'Ylen hallintoneuvoston ennakkoarvioinnin tulos: Yle saa vuokrata studiokapasiteettiaan ulkopuolisille' (Result of Yle's Supervisory Board's preliminary assessment: Yle may lease its studio capacity to third parties) 29.4.2014, last updated 18.7.2016: http://yle.fi/aihe/artikkeli/2014/04/29/ylen-hallintoneuvoston-ennakkoarvioinnin-tulos-yle-saa-vuokrata (29.8.2019).

Åland.ax: 'Fakta om Åland – Statistik ock fakta' (Facts about the Åland Islands) last updated 2.1.2016: http://www.aland.ax/fakta/statistik/ (29.8.2019).

Åland.ax: 'Åland, the Nordic Council and EU' 25.11.2014: http://www.aland.ax/en/facts-about-aland/aland-the-nordic-council-and-the-eu/ (29.8.2019).

Index

The numbers here refer to the paragraph numbers.

Index

www.ingramcontent.com/pod-product-compliance
Ingram Content Group UK Ltd.
Pitfield, Milton Keynes, MK11 3LW, UK
UKHW020143290926
15471UKWH00004B/660

9 789403 531304